The Working Mother's Guide to CHILD DEVELOPMENT

F. Philip Rice teaches at the University of Maine and is a marriage and divorce counselor. He is the author of 12 books, including *The Adolescent: Development, Relationships and Culture*, 2nd Edition; *Marriage and Parenthood; Stepparenting;* and *Sexual Problems in Marriage.*

The Working Mother's Guide to CHILD DEVELOPMENT

Dr. F. Philip Rice

Prentice-Hall, Inc., *Englewood Cliffs, New Jersey* 07632

Library of Congress Cataloging in Publication Data

Rice, F   Philip.
  The working mother's guide to child development.

  (Spectrum Book)
  Bibliography: p.
  Includes index.
  1. Children of working mothers—United States.
2. Child development.   3. Children—Management.
I. Title.
HQ777.6.R5   649'.1   79-20326
ISBN 0-13-967810-7
ISBN 0-13-967802-6 pbk.

To Debbie Rice and Kathy Sola

© 1979 by Prentice-Hall, Inc.,
Englewood Cliffs, New Jersey 07632

A SPECTRUM BOOK

All rights reserved.
No part of this book may be reproduced
in any form or by any means
without permission in writing from the publisher

10 9 8 7 6 5 4 3 2 1

Printed in the United States of America

PRENTICE-HALL INTERNATIONAL, INC., *London*
PRENTICE-HALL OF AUSTRALIA PTY. LIMITED, *Sydney*
PRENTICE-HALL OF CANADA, LTD., *Toronto*
PRENTICE-HALL OF INDIA PRIVATE LIMITED, *New Delhi*
PRENTICE-HALL OF JAPAN, INC., *Tokyo*
PRENTICE-HALL OF SOUTHEAST ASIA PTE. LTD., *Singapore*
WHITEHALL BOOKS LIMITED, *Wellington, New Zealand*

Contents

Preface   viii

Part I   CHILD DEVELOPMENT

1 Some Important Principles
  of Child Development   3

2 The Development
  of Attachments   24

3 Separation Anxiety
  and Strangers   39

4 The Development
  of Love and Security   55

5 How Does Working
    Affect Children? 72

6 Mental Development
    and School 87

7 Socialization,
    Moral Development,
    and Moral Behavior 106

8 Some Questions
    of Discipline 121

9 Sex Education 142

10 Sex-Role Development 156

11 Friends and Peer
    Relationships 168

12 Adolescents
    and Working Mothers 184

Part II   CHILD CARE

13 Baby Sitters
    and Substitute Care 195

14 Family Day-care Homes,
    Group Day-care Homes,
    Infant-care Centers,
    and Day-care Centers 211

15 Child Care
    in Other Countries 225

Part III   THE FAMILY

16 Working
    and Pregnancy 235

17 Husbands and Fathers   250

18 Two-Career Families   261

19 Work Schedules and Home Management   273

20 Your Marriage   286

21 Mothers Alone: Divorced and Widowed   297

References   311

Index   325

Preface

Over half of all women with children 6 to 17 years old and with a husband present are employed. Over a third of those with children under 6 years old and with a husband present are working outside the home. These numbers and percentages continue to increase each year so that working mothers now comprise a significant proportion of persons in the labor force.

One of the most important concerns of these mothers is their children. Most wonder: How will working outside the home affect my children? How old should they be before I can leave them to go to work? Will they be harmed if I return to work soon after they are born? What effects does working have on school-age children or on my teen-agers?

Most of these mothers have to work, either for personal or financial reasons, yet many are torn by guilt and conflict over their loyalties to themselves, their families, and their jobs.

Many would feel much better about themselves and their situations if they had more exact understanding of many of the questions about child development that they encounter as conscientious mothers. They are concerned about how they can help their children do well in school, about questions of discipline, and about their children's social and moral training. Changing concepts of sex roles and sexual behavior raise perplexing questions about sex education.

These mothers are also involved with trying to find substitute child care while they work. What should they look for in baby sitters? What effect does leaving a small baby with a sitter have on the mother's relationship with her child and on the child? What about infant day care? Group home care? How can you select a good day-care center? What about working during pregnancy in relation to its effect on the development of the child? What are some of the particular problems of mothers of adolescents?

Then, too, mothers are concerned about their husbands, about the effect of their jobs on their marriages, and about how to meet everyone's needs when they themselves are involved in careers, in marriage, and in mothering. How can a woman manage a job, a house, a husband, and her children? What about the millions of women—some single, some divorced or widowed—who are raising their children by themselves? What principles of child development apply especially to them, and how can they manage alone?

How can our society help the working mother? What needs to be done so that she feels support instead of condemnation in performing the most difficult job on earth—the job of being a mother?

This book is written to give guidance and help to all persons who share these concerns. It uses the scientific knowledge of many hundreds of research studies concerning children, but it presents the information in such a way that it can be understood by all.

The Working Mother's Guide to
CHILD DEVELOPMENT

PART I

CHILD DEVELOPMENT

1

Some Important Principles of Child Development

If I had started this book twenty-five years ago, I would have found it much easier to write. Ten years of college and graduate school had given me as complete an education in psychology, marriage and family relationships, and child development as I could obtain. I was all set to go out into the world to tell people how to have happy marriages and how to raise healthy, mature children. Now, after spending thousands and thousands of hours in family life classes, parent education groups, and in personal counseling, and after raising two fine children, I really feel that anyone who tries to sum up the most important principles of child development in one chapter is a damned fool. There is so much to know and so much to learn! And every family and every child is different. As soon as parents begin to feel they have one problem licked, another one comes along to puzzle them. Valuable lessons learned in raising one child may be completely useless in raising the next one. Yet I've also found that one way I can be most helpful as a family life educator is to try to reduce important principles of child development to basic fundamentals that parent can clutch onto and use in solving the practical, everyday problems they encounter during the long years of bringing up their children. At the risk of oversimplification, this is what I've tried to do in this chapter—to summarize what I feel are the six most important principles for parents to remember in child rearing.

PRINCIPLE NUMBER ONE

The Role of Parents

The first principle sounds unbelievably simple, but it is hard to follow. It deals with the role of parents. It is this: *The role of parents is to meet the needs of children so they can grow* (Chess, 1972). What this says is that the job of parents is to find out what their children's needs are and to fulfill those needs. Then their children will grow in the way they were intended. This principle implies that children were made to grow, that within them are the "seeds of growth," so that parents don't have to teach children how to grow. Children just do grow if their growth needs have been supplied.

Physical Growth

In this way, a child's physical growth is analagous to the development of all other living creatures. Every plant, for example, needs basic nutrients plus sun, water, and protection from the elements for it to develop. If basic requirements are provided it, the plant will grow strong and healthy. If not, it will be stunted and more subject to disease and injury. The most careful botanist knows that most plants have similar requirements, but he also knows that individual plants have somewhat different needs which have to be supplied. But above all, the botanist understands that the plant already has within it the tendency to grow and that once its nature and needs are understood, its physical potential can be developed to the fullest.

The task of human parents is to learn as much as possible about the physical needs of children: what kind of food to offer and how much; appropriate activities and exercise at each age level; the proper amount of rest and fresh air; how to protect their children from injury, accident, and disease; and how to dress them to protect them from the elements. Parents have much to learn about basic physical requirements at each age level, and then they have to care enough about their children to care for them properly.

Significant studies have been made in understanding the relationship between adequate nutrition and physical and mental growth. One of the impressive facts is that people grow a lot taller today than they used to. The height between decks on the average ship during the Revolutionary War was only 5 feet 8 inches. The average Miss America today is as tall as was the average American doughboy during World War I. The significant differences in height between then and now are due to better nutrition. But there are exceptions. I know one family where all the children were stunted and had bowed legs, even though both parents were quite tall. One of the daughters commented: "We all had rickets when we were children." Rickets is caused by a deficiency of Vitamin D and of calcium. Nutritional deficiencies can also cause severe mental retardation (Grotberg, 1971, p. 342). It must be emphasized that the tendency to grow is so strong that only by extreme physical deprivation can parents prevent physical development and that even then, some development takes place.

Emotional Needs

Similarly, the parental task is to fulfill emotional needs so children can grow to become emotionally secure and stable persons. These needs include love, affection, physical contact, sucking, response, recognition, acceptance, belonging, approval, security, independence, achievement, and new experiences. These needs are sometimes divided into belongingness and love needs, status or esteem needs, safety needs, and self-actualization needs (Garrison, Kingston, Bernard, 1967, p. 67). If these needs are supplied, children develop into secure, loving, trusting, stable, and autonomous persons. But if their emotional needs are withheld, the children become fearful, hostile, insecure, distrustful, unstable, and overly dependent or independent persons (Rice, 1979a, p. 559).

Social Needs

Children also have social needs. They are born gregarious persons. They want to be with others, generally like other people, and ordinarily try to please them and be accepted by them. But their natural tendencies are unsophisticated. Children want friends, but they don't know how to socialize. They want others to like them, but they don't know how to please. Their need is for companionship and for socialization, to build on their normal desire to belong and to relate by teaching them group mores, morals, customs, manners, and habits so they can fit into the group. The parental task is to provide their children with the necessary opportunities for socialization so that they can become part of society and know how to live and work harmoniously with others.

Intellectual Needs

The capacity for intellectual growth is also inborn. Children are born naturally curious. They want to learn about everything. They desire a variety of new experiences through which this learning can take place. The parental role is to fulfill these intellectual needs by providing sensory stimulation and a variety of learning experiences involving observation, reading, conversation, and a maximum amount of contacts with others and with the natural world. As long as the environment in which children are placed is a stimulating one, as long as the curiosity of children is encouraged, their cognitive development proceeds at an unbelievably fast rate. But once their surroundings become sterile, unchanging, and uninteresting or their human contacts and experience become limited, growth stops or slows down because of intellectual deprivation (Rice, 1979a, p. 559).

One of the most interesting exhibits at the World's Fair in Montreal was the display of three cages of chimpanzees. Each cage held a family group. One family had been in their cage for several months, the second family had been in their cage for several weeks, and the third family had been recently introduced into the cage. Members of the family that had been in their cage the longest sat practically motionless; they were very lethargic and took little interest in what was going on around them. The family members that had been in their cage for several weeks were more alert and lively, busily engaged in picking fleas off one another and moving about the cage. The most recently introduced family members were liveliest of all. They were swinging from a tree branch, exploring every corner of the cage, and were much interested in the visitors who came to see them.

This exhibit illustrates very well the role that sensory stimulation and new experiences play in the intellectual development of children. The parental task is to provide an intellectually stimulating environment in which children can learn. Children who are deprived never develop their full intellectual capacities.

Moral Needs

Children also have the capacity for moral growth. They are born trusting persons, and they only become disbelievers and mistrusting when they learn they can't depend upon people around them. They are also born with a capacity for the development of a sensitive conscience and with an ability to distinguish different moral values, once these are taught. But their ability is only a potential one; it has to be developed. The parental role here is to fulfill their children's moral needs for trust and ethical values.

The Nature of Children

This concept of child-rearing emphasizes that what parents need to do is to learn how to cooperate with and develop innate tendencies with which children are already endowed. Thus, parents don't have to make children learn or to pound knowledge into them, contrary to their desires. They don't have to drive evil out of them before they can instill what is right and good. Rather, they only have to nourish the love and goodness within them, for that is the way children were meant to be. Some parents behave as though their children were their worst enemies, and as though they have to break their wills and spirits before they can raise decent human beings. Nothing could be farther from the truth. Parents don't have to work contrary to a child's nature. They need to learn to understand that nature and to fulfill it.

Deprivation

Sometimes, of course, children's needs aren't met, either because parents can't or won't fulfill them. The children aren't given proper physical requirements. They aren't loved; they aren't socialized; they are deprived intellectually and spiritually. When this happens, growth stops or slows down, so the children remain physically, emotionally, socially, intellectually, or morally retarded. *Growth takes place by fulfilling needs; retardation occurs because of deprivation.*

PRINCIPLE NUMBER TWO

Changing Philosophies

The second important principle of child development emphasizes the fact that views of how best to raise children change from one generation to the next and that *children can still survive and even thrive under various philosophies.* The changes in child-rearing philosophies are quite evident in "how to" books for parents. The government's bulletin on *Infant Care* is a good example (U.S. Dept of Health, Education, and Welfare, 1977). Since it was first published in 1914, it has gone through twelve editions and has been completely rewritten six times. Between 1914 and 1921, the dangers of thumb-sucking and masturbation were emphasized: Parents were advised to bind their children to the bed, hand and foot, so they would not suck their thumbs, touch their genitals, or rub their thighs together. Between 1929 and 1938, autoerotic impulses were not considered dangerous, but lack of proper bowel training or improper feeding habits were. The emphasis was on a rigid schedule, strictly according to the clock. Bowel training must be pursued with great determination. Weaning and the introduction of solid foods must be accomplished with firmness, never yeilding to the baby's protests for one instant for fear the infant will dominate the parents. Between 1942 and 1945, all of this changed. The child was devoid of sexual or dominating impulses. Mildness was advocated in all areas. Thumb-sucking and masturbation were not to be interfered with. Weaning and toilet training were put off until later and were accomplished more gently.

At the present time, *Infant Care* has a fairly permissive attitude toward thumb-sucking, weaning, discipline, and bowel and bladder training, even though some of the popular periodicals are now shifting toward greater restrictiveness, especially in relation to discipline (Gordon, 1968). *Infant Care* (1977) suggests:

Most babies get their thumbs and fingers in their mouths and suck on them. Many seem to find it especially enjoyable and do it often. It causes no harm and can be ignored [p. 62].

The word "discipline" means teaching. It does not mean punishment as many people think. . . . The key to learning and discipline is not punishment but reward . . . punishment doesn't work well in the first years of life. The baby usually can't figure out just what behavior is being punished [pp. 33, 34].

Feed the baby when he seems hungry. . . . Most new babies will fall into a pattern of 6 or 7 feedings about 3 to 5 hours apart. If your baby is more irregular than this, you can get him on a more regular schedule by waking him a little early or letting him be hungry a little longer. It is easier and better to get a regular schedule by working from the baby's own schedule than by just deciding he will be fed at certain times whether he is hungry or not [p. 6].

Weaning and masturbation are not mentioned in this edition. It is evident that child-rearing philosophies change from one generation to the next, so that parents often have to sort out conflicting advice.

Husband-Wife Differences

Husbands and wives often differ with one another on their basic philosophies of child rearing, a situation that creates marital conflict and confusion for the child. Each parent tends to feel that the way he or she was reared is the "right way" and that other methods will not achieve as good a result. Parents can relax somewhat, however, if they realize that there is not always only one "right way" and one "wrong way" to raise children. There are various ways, and children may benefit from the best features of different philosophies.

PRINCIPLE NUMBER THREE

Quality of Relationship

The third principle of child development emphasizes that *the quality of the relationship which parents establish with their children is the most important factor in rearing them to maturity* (Bromwich, 1976). It doesn't really matter, for example, how long a mother breast-feeds her child, or the age at which a child is toilet trained, or whether or not a mother is strict about bedtime routines. What is most important, according to the best information available, is the amount and quality of affection which parents give their children. Parents who like their offspring and are easy-going, warm, and loving are those who do the best job in raising children to maturity (McClelland et al., 1978).

This means that the length of time the mother and children are together is not as important as the quality of their relationship (Fleisher, 1977). Full-time care by the mother does not necessarily ensure optimal care (Murray, 1975, p. 788). Optimal care must be measured in terms of the mother's attitudes and feelings, her warmth, responsiveness, and sensitivity to her child, rather than in terms of the hours of contact (Lancaster, 1975, p. 1323).

Different Outcomes

Different types of parent-child relationships do create different results in children. I know one mother who was very strict about making her children clean their rooms, perform their chores, and do their homework. She expected instant obedience and compliance with her requests, which the children generally observed. She was authoritarian and demanding but emotionally cold. She seldom showed her children outward signs of affection, and she rarely talked to them in a friendly, informal way. Most of her contacts were orders to do things. Consequently, her children grew up well behaved and obedient but were lacking a sense of humor, a warmth of personality, and a friendly attitude and feeling toward other persons. They never felt close to their mother, and they couldn't wait to get away from home. They seldom showed initiative, creativity, and originality in their work; rather, they were cooperative team workers and did as their bosses directed. They had difficulty making close friends and in establishing personal, intimate relationships in marriage.

I know another mother who was just the opposite of this first one. She was fairly lax in her discipline and in teaching her children to mind or to do chores, but she was friendly and outgoing and talked with her children a great deal. In fact, when her daughters became teen-agers, they could tell her intimate things about their dates or boy friends that few adolescents discuss with their parents. The children maintained close family ties after they were married.

It is obvious that different types of parent-child relationships develop different personalities in children. It depends on what parents are seeking. We do know that children who are reared quite strictly; who have been restricted in their tendency to be noisy, aggressive, or demand attention; and who are reared without love; tend to become rigid, loveless persons.

When parents are concerned with using their power to maintain an adult-centered home, the child is not as likely to become a caring, understanding adult (McClelland et al., 1978, p. 45). However, if parents are kind but firm in their approach to discipline, and if there is a great deal of warmth and love in the parent-child relationship, children are likely to grow up as responsible, cooperative persons, and to be caring and loving in their human relationships. The important thing is that the type of discipline alone is not as important as the degree of warmth and love in the parent-child relationship. McClelland writes: "We found that when parents—particularly mothers—really loved their children, the sons and daughters were likely to achieve the highest levels of social and moral maturity" (McClelland et al., 1978, p. 45).

Principle Number Four

Individual Differences

The fourth important principle of child development states that *because children are different, parents react to each one differently, so it is impossible to bring all of them up the same way* (Cohen & Beckwith, 1977) Child development books used to emphasize the effect of mothers on children. Now, the emphasis includes the effect of children on mothers, which, in turn, influences how the mothers treat their children.

Some children are much harder to love than others. Just recently, a new granddaughter was born into our family. I'm sure I'm prejudiced, but she is one of the most beautiful babies I have ever seen. She has a beautiful, round head (she was delivered by Caesarean section); pink, blemish-free skin; beautiful, bright dark eyes; a sensitive, bow-shaped mouth; and a perfectly shaped body. She is bright, alert, and smiling all of the time and in every way is a real doll. Who wouldn't love her?

In contrast, I know a three-year-old boy who is really hard even to like. He has big ears, thick lips, a wide nose, and a hostile, fresh manner. His language is atrocious. He is loud, overaggressive, and noisy in the wrong places and at the wrong times. He isn't cute or appealing in either appearance or behavior. He is a hard, hard child to love. Even his mother has trouble liking him.

Parents who say they try to treat all of their children the same are not being realistic. In fact, because each child is different, mothers can't and shouldn't try to treat them all the same. It's impossible to do so, and it is not good for the children.

Isn't it unfair to show one child more love than you show another one?

If one child complains that another receives more love, then it's unfair and unwise and needs to be remedied. But some children need far more love and attention than others, at least during limited periods of time. It's unfair and perhaps damaging to them if these children don't receive what they need at the time they need it most. Mothers have to convince their children that they love them all, but love may need to be expressed in one way to one child and in another to another one. One child may need firmness, another permissiveness and encouragement, in order to develop their potentialities. The best parents learn to be flexible.

Age and Sex Factors

It has also been shown that the mother's behavior toward any one child changes as the child gets older. One investigator found that the amount of time a mother holds her baby decreased by 30 percent between the time the baby was three weeks and three months of age (Schaffer, 1977, p. 53). This same researcher found that at three months of age mothers were more likely to cuddle girls when they cried than they were to cuddle boys (Schaffer, 1977, p. 54). Certainly, these differences were likely to result in some boy-girl differences in behavior as the children grew older.

Environmental Influences

Environmental conditions also change at different periods of a child's life. Unexpected unemployment, poverty, physical or mental illness, an increase in marital problems or a change of marital status, or changes in housing or the neighborhood residence may stimulate stress and anxiety in a mother, which impairs her treatment of her children. Thus, many factors influence mothering, which, in turn, affects children.

Individual Sensitivity

What all of this means is that the most effective mothers need to become sensitive to the varying needs of their individual children and to try to relate objectively and helpfully to each one, not according to what each deserves but according to what each needs. Does a child have to be beautiful or well behaved in order to be loved? Some children are extremely active from the time they are infants. They're never still; they're into something all the time. Obviously, a mother has to plan her home, her schedule, and her activities differently to take into account this child's high energy level than she does if she has a child who is lazy and lethargic. Unfortunately, what so often happens is that nervous, overactive children, who most need a calming, reassuring, patient mother, make their mothers nervous, upset, and impatient. It certainly is a lot easier to be a calm mother with a calm child than with an excitable child. But a lethargic child may be just the one who needs more maternal activity and stimulation. Children who become emotionally demanding because of need may end up putting too great a strain on their mothers and being rejected more than children who are already more secure.

Knowing Oneself

Mothers also have to learn to know their own strengths and weaknesses and to determine which are influencing their children. Mothers who know that they are impatient and can take only so much from their children will be wise to enlist more outside care than mothers who can handle the task without upset. Mothers who know that they are too lenient and overindulgent should welcome the aid of husbands who can be sterner and stricter in guidance. A mother who is not feeling well may not be good for her children, so that she would be wise to encourage others to take over more responsibility during this period.

Can I learn to love my daughter? I really resent her, primarily because she was the reason I had to get married before I was ready.

Most such mothers can learn to love, but most need counseling help. The mother who resents her daughter because she resulted in a forced marriage has some unresolved conflicts she has to work through. She usually needs the help of a competent counselor, preferably a psychologist, psychotherapist, or psychiatrist, to do this. It's hard to understand one's negative feelings and to be objective enough about them to be able to change them oneself.

PRINCIPLE NUMBER FIVE

Other Family Influences

The fifth important principle of child development states that *many other persons and influences besides the mother*

Some Important Principles of Child Development • 17

affect the total development of children. The most obvious other influences are other family members: the father, brothers and sisters, or relatives in the home. I know of one family where the mother is a very competent and loving mother. She cares for her children and about them. But much of her positive influence is offset by her tyrannical husband, who is a very unstable, emotional person, given to fits of rage. He drinks too much, disciplines cruelly and inconsistently, and gives his wife little help in the children's day-by-day care. He is a very insecure person who constantly criticizes and depreciates his children, especially his son, whom he hates because his mother loves him and tries to protect him. Fortunately, the father has a travel job and is not home very much, but when he is home, the household is in a constant turmoil. The children are very emotional, easily upset, and quite nervous, and as a result, they have many insecurities.

Older brothers and sisters can also have significant influences on younger children, especially if they are made responsible for much of their care, as is the case in many households. Some older children are very good with younger brothers and sisters; others are a very disturbing, negative influence. If parents suspect that their younger children are not being properly cared for, they need to give more guidance to those in charge or get substitute sitters.

Many working mothers leave younger children, even infants, in the care of older siblings. If some of these mothers knew how the younger children were being treated, they would not be so willing to make such arrangements. For years, a next door neighbor to us in the town where I grew up left her young son in the care of his sister—who was ten years older than he. The boy used to cry almost constantly for hours while his mother was gone, primarily because the sister teased him unmercifully, probably because he was an only son and she was quite jealous of him. This boy grew up really hating girls, especially any who reminded him of his sister.

Relatives can also have a positive, helpful influence or a very negative influence. I know of one grandmother who really hates her grandson and adores her grandaughter. Whenever she visits, she brings candy and other gifts to her grandaughter and none to her grandson. Obviously, the boy is quite hurt by her constant rejection of him. She constantly criticizes him and praises his sister. If this goes on long enough, she will have a significant effect on her grandson's self-concept, unless the parents step in and try to correct the situation. Actually, the mother knows what is happening, but she doesn't try to prevent it: She really doesn't like her son too much either, because he reminds her of her husband. She's always telling him: "You're just like your father." And she means this in a negative way.

Working mothers do have a problem if they employ the volunteer services of unqualified parents or in-laws to care for their children while they themselves are at work. Mothers usually prefer to have the child's grandmother baby-sit, but it may not be the best arrangement unless the grandparents can really meet the needs of children. If not, it's worth the sacrifice to get someone more competent.

Influences Outside the Family

As children get older, they are more and more influenced by their peers and by other persons outside the family. The less attention the mother is able to give her children, the more influence peers will exert. Mothers who tend to let children grow up by themselves, not devoting enough time and attention to them when they are home, are asking for trouble. One child psychologist suggests that it is only adults who are able to teach values such as cooperation, unselfishness, consideration for others, and responsibility (Bronfenbrenner, 1975, p. 49).

Peer values often emphasize aggressive, antisocial behavior. Thus, by default, through their own noninteraction with their children, neglecting parents expose their children to harmful influences.

Because of the possible negative effects of peers, mothers have to be concerned about the type of neighborhood they live in, the character of the other children their child plays with, and the types of groups with which their child is associated. One mother who is raising three children herself recently told me:

All of my children are superior in school, and they should have a bright future if I can keep them out of trouble. But the children in this neighborhood are cruel and destructive. They delight in breaking or stealing other children's toys. Their language is foul; their attitude is rebellious and beligerent. They have taught my children some horrible habits and to do some things they wouldn't even think of by themselves.

The working mother's job becomes especially difficult if what she is trying to teach her children is undermined by peer influences. Many children who are brought up by fine parents do become delinquent because of friends who get them into trouble.

Research findings generally indicate, however, that as children get older, usually by their middle teens, they tend to select friends whose values are in keeping with those of their parents. This doesn't always happen, but it is likely to, provided that the children like their parents and try to be like them, and provided that there is some opportunity for choice. But before children can travel very far from their neighborhoods, or before they can drive a car to a friend's house, they are stuck with those playmates that live nearby. Mothers can encourage their children to pick and choose their friends wisely if the children have a choice.

Individual Responsibility

The first thing parents ask when their children get in trouble is. What did I do wrong? I suppose it's natural to blame oneself. But with so many other persons exerting influences, the mother or father may not be at fault. They may have done everything right, and their children may not turn out well in spite of their best efforts. For this reason, I think we as parents have to learn to be quite philosophical and, above all, to teach our children that they are responsible for themselves and that what they do is ultimately up to them, but that they have to accept the consequences. The best parents tell their children: "If something goes wrong, don't blame me, you are responsible for yourself. I can't live your life for you. Only you can do that."

PRINCIPLE NUMBER SIX

Early Influences

The last important principle of child development emphasizes that *early influences on children are less important than once thought and that the effects are not irreversible.* Freud, more than any other writer, believed in the importance of early experiences, so much so, in fact, that he believed that negative influences in children's first few years of life would warp their personalities for the rest of their lives. This gospel of child development influenced thinking about raising children for the next 50 years. This view is reflected in the often quoted remark: "Give me a child for the first five years of his life, and you can have him after that." The implications are that nothing that happens after the first years is as influential as what happens before that and that nothing can offset early influences.

The latest research with children indicates that the importance of early experiences has been overemphasized and that much can be done to offset early, negative influences (Ainsworth, 1967). One such example is that of infants who were raised in a creche in Lebanon (Dennis, 1973). These infants were placed in cribs with solid sides so that they could not see what was going on around them. They were given little adult attention and few toys, and they were left all day in bed in the bare room. When tested at the end of the first year, they were found to have developed intellectually at an average of about half the usual rate, even though at birth there were indications that they were normal. Those children who were subsequently adopted showed a remarkable recovery, with an IQ average of 85. Those adopted before 2 years of age had an average IQ of 96. The girls who remained in the institution, with its restricted, impoverished environment, were tested at ages 12 to 16 and found to have an average IQ of 54.

This research indicates that intellectual or social deprivation early in infancy does not necessarily have irreversible consequences. Early experiences are incorporated into adult personality only if these experiences are repeated throughout the childhood years. The greater the intensity of the influences, and the longer they are felt, the more permanent effects they may have on adult personalities.

Implications

This principle has important implications. One is that parents can make mistakes without ruining their children for life. This comes as quite a relief to those parents who know they did some wrong things, especially when they were first learning how to bring up children. Early mistakes can be corrected, and the children may not only survive, but thrive.

This means that the early years are not the only important

years in forming adult personalities. One woman who went to a counselor because she was having problems explained:

> *My psychologist keeps asking me what happened in my childhood that caused me to be the way I am. Nothing happened, except that I had a very happy childhood. It's my adulthood that's creating my difficulty. My problem is that I married the wrong man.*

Problems can be created and, usually, corrected at any point in life. Some children get along beautifully until their teens, at which time everything seems to go wrong. I once testified at the court trial of a college student who, with a friend, had committed armed robbery. The boys had hit a cab driver over the head and had stolen his wallet containing $4.73. Numerous witnesses, including myself, testified to the boy's fine character. He was an Eagle Scout, had attended Sunday school and church all his life, was a model student in school. He had never done anything wrong before. But the judge sentenced him to one year on the state farm. The judge's argument was that any boy who had all the advantages of this one should never have committed such an act. He was even more at fault than a boy who had two strikes against him from the beginning. The judge felt that the privileged boy deserved more punishment. But the difficulty was that admission to the state farm became the first of a whole series of events which completely changed the boy's character and life. Were the parents to blame? Certainly not. Could the problem be traced back to the way the boy was brought up? Not as far as we could determine. Nothing went wrong until this unfortunate event during the boy's college years and until he was punished by a vengeful judge. If anyone were to be blamed, it would be the older friend of the boy, who thought up the whole idea of the robbery, and the boy himself for going along.

Working mothers are usually more concerned about young children because they are more dependent, but just as many ought to be concerned about their teen-agers as well. A psychology professor made the observation that as far as he could determine, age 13 for girls and age 15 for boys were the most crucial years of their lives, since during these periods they were at the height of their rebellion and were not yet mature enough to make wise decisions. He felt that if they didn't get into difficulty by this time, their chances of having problems became much reduced. Statistically, he was right, but, as we've seen, every age is important and ought to be so considered by conscientious parents.

2

The Development of Attachments

MEANING AND IMPORTANCE

Meaning

Attachment means the feeling that binds a parent and child together. It is the emotional bond between them, the desire to maintain contact through physical closeness, touching, looking, smiling, listening, or talking. Young children who have developed a close attachment to their mothers run to them when frightened, seek the comfort of their arms when upset, and otherwise derive pleasure and security out of just being near them or of being able to see or communicate with them.

Importance

All infants need to form a secure emotional attachment to someone: to a mother, father, other family member, or to a substitute care-giver (Bowlby, 1969). They need warm, loving, stable relationships with a responsive adult on whom they can depend if they are to feel emotionally secure. Ordinarily, the person who is closest to children from birth is the mother. If for some reason she can't be close, the child needs to form a similar attachment to whomever is the primary care-giver. The formation of such an attachment is vitally important to children's total development. It gives them security, but it also makes their socialization possible. They begin to identify with, imitate, and learn from the person(s) to whom they feel closest. Through such contacts, children learn what society expects of them. Such relationships become the basis for personality and character formation. We know, too, that mental growth is accelerated if children have secure relationships from which to reach out to explore and to learn.

TO WHOM ATTACHMENT DEVELOPS

Multiple Attachments

Can children develop close attachments to more than one person?

Most assuredly they can. Most studies show that young children can and often do become equally attached to their mother and father. This represents two significant attachments. Then, if there are other relatives, such as a grandparent in the home, or older children, strong attachments may also be developed with these persons. Two investigators found that by 18 months of age, 87 percent of a group of infants had formed multiple attachments, with a third of the children having five or more attachments (Schaffer & Emerson, 1964).

Anthropologists have emphasized that in some societies children are regularly cared for by a number of persons and that such children enjoy healthy interpersonal relations with all the family members. In fact, in such families, the loss of the mother is not completely disastrous to the child, since there are already other adults to whom the child has become closely attached. The same thing holds true in our own society in extended families. One woman told me that when her father deserted the family she was not very upset because she had her grandmother, grandfather, aunt, mother, and older sisters and brothers in the household, all of whom were very close to her.

We should not assume, however, that, because children can form multiple attachments, it is all right for care-takers to be constantly changed. Stability of care, whether by a parent, relative, or baby sitter, is one of the most important elements in the maintenance of emotional security. It *is* upsetting to a child who has formed a close attachment to one person to have that person leave only to be replaced by another and then by another. One of the hardest problems working mothers face is to get dependable substitute care that will not be constantly changing, yet this is one of the most important keys to the overall effect of substitute care on children. When substitute care is obtained, it is also important that a child have a chance to form a close attachment with the substitute before he or she is separated from the primary attachment figure.

Physical Care-takers versus Others

Someone told me that babies are close only to those who feed them, change them, and bathe them, and to those who are responsible for their physical care. Is this true?

No, it is not true. Feeding and physical care are only two of the ways through which attachment develops. It's true that children begin to feel dependent on those who satisfy their hunger or alleviate their physical distress. But they also develop attachments to those who cuddle them, rock them, soothe them, talk or sing to them, or play with them. Sometimes babies develop a closer relationship to their fathers than to their mothers, even to a father who doesn't feed and diaper them. The reason may be because the father has more time just to play with them than do some mothers. I've seen babies squeal with delight every time their fathers come into the room. Even though these fathers were home only a couple of hours a day, they devoted much attention to their children during that time.

The important factor in attachment development is the total dialogue that goes on between mother and child. Some mothers are supersensitive to their children's needs. They seem tuned to their children's signals and respond fairly promptly and appropriately to their babies' cries. They are able to interpret behavioral cues to discover what their infants are trying to communicate. They like their babies, are interested in them, spend time interacting with them, and are understanding in their responses to them. As a result, their babies often smile, bounce, and vocalize in interaction with their mothers and show in other ways that they enjoy the social contacts with their mothers.

Attachment is also more likely to develop with those persons who initiate contacts with their children. Sometimes children become very attached to a grandmother who comes to visit only once a week. The reason is that grandmother goes out of her way to pay attention to them. Mothers, or other adults, who are so preoccupied with their own interests or worries that they don't initiate contacts with their children, make it harder for closeness to develop. Some fathers in the United States are only minimally involved with their preschool age children. Such fathers only talk to their young children for a few minutes a day. It's hard to develop attachment with such minimal contact.

Fathers

What do you think of allowing fathers to hold their newborn infants and to participate in their day care while they are in the hospital?

I think it's a wonderful idea and one that contributes positively to paternal-child relationships and attachments. Fathers who only get to peek at their infants through nursery windows, or who are asked to leave their wife's bedside during feeding time, do feel excluded and not a part of the total experience. This may carry over into the family situation at home, particularly if the mother also continues to exclude the father. Fathers who are involved in prenatal classes, who attend their wives during labor, and who are involved very early in the ongoing postpartum care of their children are the ones who see themselves as part of their children's lives and who are more likely to be close to their children as they grow.

Baby Sitter or Teacher

Is there a possibility that a year-old baby will develop a closer relationship to a baby sitter or to a day-care teacher than to his or her mother?

Not if the mother also takes an active part in caring for her child. If she lets a live-in baby sitter take complete responsibility for the baby's care—which is almost impossible, since a 1-year-old will protest, at least initially—there is a remote possibility that the baby will prefer contact with the sitter over that with the mother. More often, the baby forms multiple attachments but still prefers the mother. Actually, if the mother goes to work full time, it is far better for her baby to develop a close attachment to the baby sitter; otherwise, the child will be insecure with the mother gone. Instead of resenting such an attachment, the mother should welcome it, since it is necessary for her child's secure development.

One investigation of the attachments of 9- to 31-month-old infants who were enrolled in an infant day-care center showed that the children were more attached to their mothers than to their teachers in spite of the fact that the majority of the children went home to relatives or neighbors because their mothers worked or because the mothers were in school at night or were not home for some other reasons (Farran & Famey, 1977). A majority of these children had lived in three or more homes prior to the study. The amazing thing about these results is the strength of the bond that exists between mother and child even when a mother is forced by circumstances to share the care of her child with others.

DEVELOPMENTAL TRENDS

Specific Attachments

On the average, attachments to specific persons do not develop until about 6 or 7 months of age. Before this age, we find no upset at separation, whether it is a major one, such as hospitalization, or a minor one, such as the mother leaving the room. It is true that babies left alone in a room may begin to fret, but they may be comforted by anyone. They seek attention in general rather than the attention of a specific person. Consider the following two observations:

A ten-week-old baby is lying in his crib. His mother, tidying the blankets, leans over him, talking and smiling, while the baby coos and "talks" back. The mother leaves the room to greet a visitor. The baby cries. The visitor, who has not seen the baby before, comes over, leans down, smiles, and talks to the baby. The baby stops crying and smiles as the visitor picks him up.

An eight-month-old baby is playing on her mother's knee, when her mother puts her down and leaves the room to answer the door. As the visitor enters, the baby cries. When the visitor attempts to comfort her by picking her up, the baby cries more frantically until the mother returns and holds her. Then the baby calms down. From her mother's lap she first stares and later smiles at the visitor [Dunn, 1977, p. 29].

A crucial change is demonstrated in the above two situations. Both the 10-week-old and the 8-month-old babies protested at being left, but the older child protested at her *mother's* departure. The visitor seemed to upset her more. She no longer treats people as interchangeable companions; separation from her mother has taken on new meaning because she is now attached to her.

Maturation

Before attachment to the mother can take place, three things must occur. One, infants must learn to distinguish human beings from inanimate objects in the environment (Cohen et al., 1977). This ability comes early. By 3 weeks of age, a live human face elicits more excitement from an infant than a drawing of a face. Babies will smile readily at the sight of a human face by 5 or 6 weeks of age. Two, an infant must learn to distinguish among different human beings so that he or she can recognize his or her mother as familiar and strangers as unfamiliar. Some infants are able to recognize their mothers by 1 month of age; 81 percent can do so by 3 months; and all normal infants can by 5 months (Fagan, 1977). Three, infants must develop a specific attachment to one person. As suggested, infants develop attachments to persons in general before they develop attachments to individuals. Before specific attachments develop, children would just as soon have a loving, attentive baby sitter care for them as a mother. Even though an infant knows his or her mother, he or she is still content with the attention offered by others.

Reaction to Separation

There are important implications to these findings. Separation between mother and baby is usually not serious before the vulnerable age at which specific attachment is reached, as long as adequate substitute care is given. If it is possible to choose the time of hospitalization for elective surgery, it should be done before the child is 6 months of age, if feasible. Adoption and other procedures involving a change of motherfigure should also be carried out, where possible, within the first half-year of a child's life. The second half of the first year of life is crucial as far as attachments and separation are concerned. Twelve to 13 months of age is probably the most vulnerable time, when specific attachments are at their maximum.

Decreases in Attachment Behavior

Generally, we see a decrease in the attachment behavior of children over the course of the second year, indicating increasing independence and maturity. Also, contact, which is sought primarily through physical closeness and touching at 1 year of age, gradually expands at 3 years to wanting contact by looking and talking across a distance. Nursery school children may want to be close to their mothers or teachers, but they also seek other forms of comfort, reassurance, and attention. The older children get, the more they seek verbal soothing and re-enforcement. Also, as their social contacts expand, so do the number of attachments they form.

Sensitive Period

Isn't there supposed to be a sensitive period right after a baby is born when contact between mother and child is important if a close relationship is to develop?

Yes, such a sensitive period does, in fact, exist (Blehar et al., 1977). Science has not yet defined how long that period lasts, but it begins immediately after birth and continues for an unspecified length of time, certainly at least as long as the hospital stay. Mothers who are given their naked babies immediately after birth and who are allowed more time to fondle them, kiss them, look at them, feed them, and hold them close than is permissible with the usual hospital routine show a greater tendency afterward to pick up their babies when they cry and to spend more time looking at them and being close to them than do other mothers. Those who are breast-feeding are more likely to continue nursing longer after birth than are nursing mothers who have not had extended contact.

One group of mothers of low socioeconomic status who had extended contact with their newborn babies showed more interest in their children as long as two years after birth than did mothers who had not had the extra contacts (Kennell, 1974). The extended-contact mothers spent more time helping the doctor during office visits and soothing their children when they cried. They talked to their children more, and they used more questions and fewer commands than did the limited-contact mothers. The fact that the effects of extended contact lasted so long indicates that such early contact is very important for mothers in poor social circumstances. The generally superior environment in middle-class homes can partially compensate for any lack of early attachment in these families, however, so that there may be few noticeable differences among extended-contact and limited-contact babies after 3 or 4 months have passed. However, even in these middle-class homes, babies who are separated from their mothers show greater stress: They cry more and more often than do those who are not so isolated.

My baby was born prematurely and was in an incubator for three weeks, during which time I didn't have much contact with him. Will this affect our closeness later on?

It may, at least for a while, but the mother can make up for the lack of early contact if she tries to maintain a closer than average relationship for a period of time after incubation is over. One investigator in a London hospital found little difference during follow-up between the mothers of premature babies and those of normal, full-term babies (Macfarlane, 1977, p. 105). But at this hospital every attempt was made to minimize the separation. Parents were allowed to see, touch, hold, and care for their babies as much as conditions permitted. Even brothers and sisters were allowed to visit, which, incidentally, helped the siblings to feel closer to the new baby, too.

ATTACHMENT AND THE WORKING MOTHER

Quantity versus Quality

If the mother has a full-time job and is gone all day, can she be as close to her children as the mother who is home all the time?

Yes, she can. Some working mothers are even closer to their children than those not employed outside the home. Whether or not the mother is employed is not the crucial factor in whether or not she and her children are close. The *quality* of the mother-child relationship is more important than the *quantity* of time mother and child spend together. However, the longer the mother and child are separated, the more important it is for the mother to devote enough exclusive time to her children when she is home. If, when she gets home, she has to spend all of her time housekeeping, cooking, and catching up on the chores, her children may very well feel rejected. If her baby sitter, housekeeper, husband, or older children can do the household chores and have dinner prepared when she arrives home, so that she can devote herself exclusively to the children, they may feel much closer to her than to the mother who is home all the time but who virtually ignores them.

The total amount of care any mother gives her children is important, however. If employment prevents the mother from giving her children sufficient attention, then she does have a problem. But a lot of other things besides employment also prevent mothers from being close to their children: too many social activities, too much work in the home, worry and depression, even preoccupation with themselves and their own thoughts. Most mothers who are employed realize that they have to cut back on their activities in order to be able to have enough time to be good mothers as well. Some mothers who are not employed have so many activities that they are not attentive, and they know little about their children's special ways of behaving; they and their children are strangers to one another.

Children in Day Care

What about children who are looked after in day-care centers? Are there any differences in parent-child attachments between children cared for in centers and those cared for by mothers at home?

There may or may not be differences, depending upon a number of factors, especially upon the quality of care given at the center (particularly in relation to teacher-child ratios and the continuity of the teaching personnel) and the quality and kind of care the mother gives her own children when they are home. Probably the most important factor is the quality of care in the center. If there are very low staff-children ratios (1:3 or 1:4 is considered low) and a highly trained staff, the effect on young children is more likely to be positive. In one high quality center where $2\frac{1}{2}$-year olds had been enrolled since they were about a year old, no significant differences were found in the ratings of the children's attachments to their mothers when compared to other children, but the day-care children were also more dependent on other people than matched children not enrolled in the center (Caldwell, 1970). But this finding is generally true of children from low socioeconomic status families: The children become more dependent upon others because they generally receive less adequate care from their mothers. Another study of children from 5 to 30 months of age revealed no evidence of a weakened or insecure attachment to the mother despite daily separation in a day-care center (Doyle, 1975). This center had an adequate staff-child ratio of 1:4. In contrast, comparison of 2- and 3-year-old day-care children with home-care children showed that the former had more disturbances in the attachment relationships with their mothers (Blehar, 1974).

It is very unwise to generalize from the results of any one investigation. A completely inadequate, hostile, or rejecting mother who sends her baby to a high-quality infant-care center may be doing the child a favor if he or she is able to have better care and closer attachments at the center than would be possible at home. A very adequate, accepting, competent mother who enrolls her infant in an inferior infant-care center may be harming her child. The net effect depends partially on the quality of care at the center versus the quality of care at home. Certainly, no mother can put the entire responsibility for care of her child on a day-care center. The child will ordinarily be returned to the mother each afternoon after work and on weekends. More will be said about day care in Chapter 14.

Nonattached Children

I have seen some young children who are very distant and unemotional and who don't even seem to notice when their mother comes home in the evening or after taking a trip. Is this normal?

Sometimes children are preoccupied with what they are doing and don't notice, but if this happens frequently, it is not normal, and it may indicate a lack of attachment to the mother. Young children may show marked differences in the degree of attachment to their mother. "Nonattached" children, or those whose attachment development is delayed, may make no distinction between their own mothers and another member of the household or a caretaker. They accept the attentions of one person as readily as they accept their own mothers. They do not cry when the mother leaves the room nor do they attempt to follow her, and they are sometimes precociously independent. This is not normal behavior for children who are old enough to have developed attachments to their mother.

Insecure Attachment

I know a 2-year-old boy who is so dependent on his mother that he won't let her out of his sight at all. If she has to leave him, he screams. Isn't it possible for some children to be too dependent on their mothers?

Yes, it is. These are what we call insecurely attached children. Their clinging, dependent behavior is a symptom of their insecurity. Insecurely attached infants are fussy babies. They cry not only when they are parted from their mothers but even when they are in close proximity. They cry to be picked up, or they cry when their mothers put them down. They seek almost continuous physical contact and are unable to tolerate even a little distance between themselves and their mothers.

There are various reasons for this overdependent behavior. Children who receive insufficient food and who are chronically hungry may develop these symptoms. This sometimes happens if a mother is trying to nurse her baby and has insufficient milk over a long period of time. Of course, it can happen if she just doesn't feed her baby. Children who are chronically ill may become overly dependent. Children who are rejected and neglected may develop an excessive need for attachment. Or if their mothers are highly anxious, nervous, neurotic persons, this anxiety is felt by their children, who seek constant reassurance as a result. Also, mothers who become depressed, mentally ill, or preoccupied and worried about marital difficulties or their own personal problems are not able to give their children the attention and assurance they need. Any one or a combination of these conditions may result in children who are overly dependent and insecurely attached.

Response to Crying

If I go in to see what is the matter as soon as the baby cries, isn't he more likely to cry even more the next time? Shouldn't I let him cry it out to show him that he can't get my attention any time he wants?

Some experts, the *social-learning theorists*, agree with this mother. They feel that responding promptly to babies' cries rewards their crying and encourages them to cry more. Other experts, the *attachment theorists*, believe just the opposite. They say that babies whose crying is ignored early in life tend to cry more persistently thereafter. Furthermore, this persistent crying aggravates the mother and discourages her from responding.

Who is right? Both are. This is not as confusing or impossible as it sounds. Generally speaking, a sensitive and prompt response of the mother to the baby promotes a harmonious relationship with a child who is secure and content. Mothers who respond promptly to distress tend to have children who are among the least fretful. This view supports the attachment theorists. However, overanxious mothers who respond unnecessarily to fretfulness when the baby really doesn't need the mother are encouraging excessive crying and demands. In other words, some of the most fretful babies may have mothers who are overly anxious about responding. This view supports the social-learning theorists.

As in many other instances, avoiding extremes in raising children is often the wisest thing. If a mother never responds to her baby's cries of distress, one reaction is for the child to give up crying entirely and become very withdrawn, but no one would say that because such a child is quiet, he or she is well adjusted. The other extreme is for the mother to respond anxiously to every whimper. Unnecessary "smothering" also creates problems, since it makes tyrants of small children. I do feel, however, that it is better for children if a mother is very sensitive, even if she is sometimes overindulgent, than it is for her to be a rejecting, neglectful mother.

3

Separation Anxiety and Strangers

SIGNS AND EFFECTS OF SEPARATION ANXIETY

Symptoms

Signs of separation anxiety vary somewhat according to individual children, to their ages, and to the length of time they are separated from the attachment figure. After infants develop attachments to specific persons (usually by six months of age), they begin to show signs of distress when these persons leave them (Ross, G. et al., 1975). The simplest manifestation is a baby crying when the mother leaves the room. Observers have found that some babies as young as 15 weeks will cry when their mothers leave. Most certainly will by 30 weeks. Those who have been most closely attached to their mothers are more likely to protest at their mothers' leaving than are those who are not so attached (Dunn, 1977, p. 64). The most common separation is a mother leaving a child alone in a room and closing the door. Infants may cry, and their play may cease soon after the mother leaves. If they are old enough to creep or walk, they may try to follow and to search actively for her. If the mother leaves the room but the child can observe her in the adjacent room, anxiety is minimized. One observer discovered that young children in a park commonly "froze" when the mother walked away from them, but they did not cry or attempt to follow. A group of infants in a laboratory experiment played contentedly for several minutes before following the mother, who had walked out of sight (Corter, 1976).

Effects of Long-term Separation

If separation continues for very long, usually over a period of days, symptoms become more serious. The initial phase of protest and searching is followed by a period of despair, during which children become quiet, apathetic, listless, unhappy, and unresponsive to a smile or a coo. Finally, if separation continues, the children enter a period of detachment and withdrawal when they seek to sever the emotional ties with the attachment figure. They appear to have lost all interest in the person to whom they were formerly attached. In extreme cases, they seem to lose interest in almost everything going on around them. There is no attempt to contact a stranger and no brightening if strangers contact them. Their activities are retarded: They often sit or lie in a dazed stupor. They lose weight and catch infections easily. There is a sharp decline in general development.

The trauma of long-term separation without an adequate substitute attachment figure is best illustrated by the following description of a 2-year-old child who had a good relationship with his mother at the time he was hospitalized. He was looked after by the same mother-substitute and visited by his mother during the first week, but his behavior deteriorated when the mother reduced her visits to twice a week and then gave up visiting him.

He became listless, often sat in a corner sucking and dreaming, at other times he was very aggressive. He almost completely stopped talking. . . . He sat in front of his plate eating very little, without pleasure, and started smearing his food over the table. At this time, the nurse who had been looking after him fell ill, and Bobby did not make friends with anyone else, but let himself be handled by everyone without opposition. A few days later he had tonsillitis and went to the sickroom. In the quiet atmosphere there he seemed not quite so unhappy, played quietly but generally gave the impression of a baby. He hardly ever said a word, had entirely lost his bladder and bowel control, sucked a great deal. On his return to the nursery he looked very pale and tired. He was very unhappy after rejoining the group, always in trouble and in need of help and comfort. He did not seem to recognize the nurse who had looked after him at first [Bowlby, 1965, p. 30].

The trauma of extensive separation without an adequate substitute can be quite severe.

Age Factors

Generally speaking, distress over separation is greatest after 6 months and until about 3 years of age. It is most evident in young children who have had a close relationship with their mothers and who are separated suddenly without an adequate substitute care-giver provided, to whom the child has already become attached. Protest over temporary separation begins to decline most sharply around age 3. The decline in anxiety accompanies the increase in the power of recall: Children are able to remember their mothers and a promise that they will return; also, increasing autonomy and mobility make them less dependent ("A Child's Second Birth," 1978).

Preschool children from 3 to 5 years of age can still experience a great deal of separation anxiety, however, as every nursery teacher knows. The following account of the reactions of a 5-year-old to his first day in kindergarten was given to me by the teacher.

> Alan was extremely upset when his mother left him in school that first morning. He cried and screamed as she went out the door. I had to hold onto him bodily to keep him from running after her. He kicked me and tried to bite me because I wouldn't let him go. After this initial protest, he insisted on staying in the hallway, so I got him a chair and he sat in it facing the door the entire morning. He wouldn't join in any of our activities or come into the play room no matter how I urged him. He kept his vigil until his mother arrived, and then screamed and laughed and hugged her when she came in the door. You would have thought that she had been gone for a week. Actually, it was only two-and-one-half hours.

The older children become, the less they are upset at separation, partially because they are more independent and partially because they will take more readily to mother substitutes. Between the ages of 5 and 8, the risks of upset decrease even further. Contrary to what we find in younger ages, the children of this age who have the happiest relationships with their mothers are better able to tolerate separations than those who are only insecurely attached. A happy child, secure in his or her mother's love, is not made unbearably anxious. The insecure child, already anxious in his or her attachments, may become even more troubled by forced separation.

We are not to assume that school-age children, or even adolescents, remain untouched by separations. Surveys of children between the ages of 5 and 16 who were evacuated from the city of London during the war confirm the finding that children are not yet emotionally self-supporting. Teachers reported that homesickness was prevalent; that the power of concentration on schoolwork declined; and that bedwetting, nervous symptoms, and delinquency increased. In most cases, there were no serious aftereffects following the children's return home, but in others, the problems persisted for a while afterward (Bowlby, 1965). Young people as old as college age may go through a period of extreme homesickness when first away from home. They get over it, but it's very upsetting for a while.

Factors That Affect Separation Anxiety

What factors affect how children react when you leave them, and what can you do to keep them from being so upset?

There are a number of factors which affect children's reactions to separation. They include the following.

Temperament and individual personality differences in children affect their separation responses.

The age and sex of the children are important. There is some evidence that boys are more disturbed by separation experiences than are girls.

Previous experiences of unhappy separation make subsequent separations more upsetting. The more unhappy separations are and the more often they are repeated, the more likely it is that each experience will also be upsetting. This is why it is very important that the first experiences with baby sitters or day care be happy from the beginning. Children can become so negatively conditioned to unhappy separations like going to the hospital that repeated admissions are very difficult. However, children can also be habituated to happy separations so that they can actually look forward to them.

The length of separation is also a factor in the degree of upset. Other things being equal, children who are separated for the longest periods of time experience the greatest upset. This is why it is better for mothers to leave their children only for a few hours at a time in the beginning and then to increase gradually the time they are gone. Short-term separations of a night or so seem to have little serious effect, and children recover fairly quickly. If a mother of young children has to go to work daily, she and her husband can try to stagger their hours so that one or the other is home for at least a few of the waking hours of the day. That way, the separation period is shortened and is not continuous throughout the day. Even going home for lunch, if that is possible, helps to alleviate separation anxiety.

The most crucial factor in the degree of upset is the substitute care that is given while the mother is gone. The person who is closest to the children, other than the mother, is usually the father. If the children are strongly attached to the father, they may stay with him for a considerable period of time while the mother is gone. In fact, millions of children stay with the mother all day without upset while the father is gone, so why not the other way around? It's the same principle. Children can also stay either with a relative to whom they are attached or with a baby sitter, provided that they are close to her. The important thing is to be sure that the children have developed attachments with the substitute care-givers before you ever contemplate leaving them for very long.

If the children don't know the sitter, there are several things the mother can do to eliminate separation anxiety. Initially, she can have the baby sitter over to care for the children and play with them while she is home. The presence of the mother will partially moderate any negative effect a stranger's presence might have. After the child gets to know the sitter, the mother can leave for brief periods, gradually increasing the time as the children become adjusted. Eventually, she can go to work during the day with only a minimum of upset or with none at all.

Another factor helps to moderate upset: keeping the children in familiar surroundings while the mother is absent. In other words, it's less traumatic to baby-sit the children in their own home than it is to take them to a next door neighbor's house or to a day-care center. Unfamiliar surroundings increase the problems of adjustment even though the difficulties can be overcome.

PRACTICAL PROBLEMS AND QUESTIONS

Part-time Work

If I leave my 8-month-old to get a part-time job for four hours a day, will it affect her?

It can be a very upsetting experience, or it need not affect her negatively at all, depending upon the arrangements that are made. I feel that the least upsetting arrangement is care by the other parent in the child's own home while the mother is gone or substitute care by a close, dependable, capable relative in the child's own home. If neither of these alternatives is possible, then I prefer a dependable, capable baby sitter in the child's own home, provided that the necessary precautions are taken to get the child acquainted with the sitter over a period of days before the mother has to leave. It is also vitally important to young children that they have the same sitter every day, unless there are alternate sitters to whom a child has also become attached. It is perhaps a good idea to help children become attached to several substitute care-givers in case one is absent and can't show up. The worst arrangement is to spring a complete stranger on a child and then for the mother to be gone for several days or longer without warning.

Going on Vacation

What do you think of leaving a 2-year-old at home for two weeks so that my husband and I can take a vacation?

This mother and her husband certainly deserve time alone and, if they are like most couples, probably need a vacation. However, real upset can occur unless the precautions already described are taken. If the couple find that a familiar attachment figure whom they have employed to baby-sit cannot make it at the last minute, and if another familiar person is not available, then the couple ought either to take their baby on the vacation, perhaps taking a sitter with them, or postpone the trip to another time. The following account from my counseling notes shows what happened when a stranger was employed to baby-sit an 11-month-old child while a couple took an extended vacation.

> *I told my husband that the only way I could have a real vacation would be to get someone to take care of the baby and for us to go away together. So that's what we did. We hired an older woman down the street, and left for Hawaii. It was a wonderful trip, but I did worry about the baby. When we got home, she acted as though she didn't even know us. The baby sitter said she wouldn't eat right, or go to bed, that she had awful temper tantrums, and wouldn't do anything she said. Since we've been home, she clings to me every minute, fusses over everything, and won't let me out of her sight. If I tell her I have to go shopping, she screams and doesn't want me to go. I have to take her with me everywhere.*

Dependent Behavior

My 13-month-old doesn't want to let me out of his sight. No matter where I am or in which room I'm working, he tries to follow me. He won't play outside by himself unless I'm along. Is there something wrong with him? What can I do to keep him from being such a baby?

Actually, the behavior of this toddler is fairly normal for his age. The fact that he wants his mother in sight at all times doesn't mean that there is anything wrong. The best thing the mother can do is to let her son keep her in sight as much as is practical. As long as they can see her, most children are quite content to play in the same room or in an adjacent area where the mother is working. Sometimes toddlers go off by themselves and are content for a while, only to come back periodically to check to see if mother is still there. If the mother goes out, she can put her baby in a backpack, papoose style, and do her shopping with both hands free. Such arrangements are becoming much more common as modern women learn that children in primitive societies whose mothers carry their babies around with them grow up much more secure than do children whose mothers are always trying to get rid of them.

The worst thing the mother can do is to punish her child for "clinging" or for "being a baby." He *is* a baby, and he deserves some time to be dependent before he is pushed out in the cruel world to fend for himself. If the mother puts her baby outdoors and locks the door or if she tries in other ways to force him not to be so dependent upon her, his dependent behavior usually becomes worse, not better. The more she tries to "push him away," the more anxious he becomes about the separation. Children have to become independent at a rate they can accept without undue forcing.

Leaving a Newborn

I have a neighbor who went back to work two weeks after her baby was born. What do you think of doing this? Won't this harm her baby?

Actually, if competent substitute care is obtained, there is far less upset at 2 weeks of age than there will be later on. All of the upset at 2 weeks will be the mother's, not the baby's, particularly if the mother worries about her baby while she is at work. Usually, the mother can expect protest from her baby only after attachment development. The usual experience is for everything to go along fairly smoothly for six months or so, if the baby is healthy and if competent substitute care arrangements are made, only to find that the baby then begins objecting to the mother leaving. In this case, the separation anxiety can be minimized by spending extra time with the baby before and after work and by following some of the precautions already given (the most important of which is regular care by the *same* person). Sometimes a baby becomes very attached to a substitute person who, for some reason, can't baby-sit any longer. In such cases, the mother or father may have to care for the baby themselves until new attachments can be formed.

The question of the long-term effects of substitute care on children from birth onward is a very controversial one. So much depends on the total circumstances and on the mother's reactions as well as on the children's reactions. As far as we know, there is no evidence to suggest that mothering can't be shared from the beginning of life by several people, provided that the child can form fairly deep and stable attachments to these multiple mother figures. Leaving a child daily in the care of a father or a live-in grandmother so that the mother can go to work, even over a period of a number of years, is far different than leaving a child to be cared for by a procession of baby sitters with whom the child has only superficial attachments. Also, leaving a child in a well-run, well-staffed, superior infant-care center is far different than leaving a child in an overcrowded, understaffed nursery where care is completely inadequate and where the personnel cannot give sufficient individual attention to each child. The effect on children of a mother working is far different if she is a happier, better adjusted, and better mother when she gets home than if she is an overtired, distraught, impatient, and rejecting mother when she gets home, *because* she has been at work all day. Working affects mothers differently, just as it affects children differently.

Leaving Children with Neighbor

I have a neighbor who is willing to baby-sit, but I have to take the baby over to her house, since she has other children to care for. What do you think of this arrangement?

The situation raises some important questions: How old is the child? How competent is the neighbor? How many other children does she care for and how old are they? The younger the children, the fewer any woman can manage. The basic guidelines for group home care are given in Chapter 14. The child may protest being left at the neighbor's house if he or she hasn't been there before and doesn't know the woman. In such cases, the mother should try to stay with her own child over at the neighbor's house until her child becomes more used to the situation. Or she can shorten the time during which the child is left and then gradually increase the total time she is absent. Or if an older brother or sister can stay at the neighbor's house with the baby for several days, the upset is kept to a minimum. The general rule is to introduce a child to a new situation and to a stranger gradually.

Nursery School

I have a $2\frac{1}{2}$-year-old who's starting to nursery school when I go back to work. What can I do to keep her from being upset?

The same principle applies here: Introduce the child to nursery school gradually. The best schools allow the mother to first bring the child to the room to play when there aren't any other children around. If the child can become used to the room and become attached to a familiar toy, then he or she will feel more secure the next time. Also, it's important for the child to become acquainted with the teacher, so when school opens the child knows that Ms. Smith is going to be there. Also, having shortened sessions during the opening few days of school can help, as does the practice of allowing the mothers to stay for the first few mornings. The mothers' presence helps to alleviate the children's anxiety. Gradually, they begin leaving their mother's side and entering in the play, forgetting that they are in a new situation (Fein, 1975).

When it is time to leave, the mother should *never* sneak out. Instead, she should say, very simply, "I'm going to go shopping (or I'm going to work), and I'll be back at 11:30 to pick you up." Then kiss the child and leave. Introduction to a school bus can also be done gradually, school policies permitting, with the mothers or older brothers and sisters riding the first few mornings, if necessary, until the children become familiar with the bus, the driver, the other children, and the whole procedure. There is no need for the introduction to nursery school to be a frightening experience. If properly handled, separation anxiety can be kept to a minimum, and the child can very much look forward to going to school.

Going to the Hospital

My 4-year-old may have to go to the hospital for a major operation, and he will probably have to stay ten days. What should I do to minimize the emotional upset?

I would stay with the child, making arrangements to sleep in the hospital and in the same room as the child, if possible. If the mother can't stay all the time, the father, older relatives, and/or teen-agers can rotate so that a family member is present all the time. Such arrangements can be made in many hospitals, and I feel that such arrangements are vitally important to children's emotional health. Going to the hospital is frightening enough, but having to stay there for ten days is far more of an upset than most children, even the best adjusted ones, can handle. All of the symptoms of separation anxiety—upset and protest, followed by despair, withdrawal, and detachment—are frequently seen after a few days of hospitalization. In addition, children fear being hurt or mutilated or being left alone. Also, they may interpret being sent to the hospital as punishment for wrongdoing. "I will be good, don't make me go" is the way some children feel. One $7\frac{1}{2}$-year-old boy who had been in the hospital three times since the age of 3 recalled: "I thought I was never coming home again because I was only 6 years old. I heard my sister say they were going to dump me and that I'd never come home again" (Bowlby, 1965, p. 34).

The worst hospitals are those that not only won't let parents stay overnight but those that enforce strict visiting hours, so that children are separated from the parents for much of the day. I would refuse to send a small child to such a hospital.

Reunion Behavior

Sometimes my preschooler is impossible when I get home from work. Do most children act terrible when the mother comes home after working all day?

All children don't, but many do. Investigations of reunion behavior of children reveal various reactions.

Some children become very dependent and possessive, clinging, whining, and crying for attention, almost insatiable in their demands upon the mother. In such cases, it is helpful if the mother can devote herself exclusively to her children after she gets home. (This is why it is so wonderful to have someone else cook supper.) If she tries to rebuff her children, their attachment behavior is only increased.

Some children are quite angry at the mother and resist (at least initially) her efforts to hug them or to pay attention to them. It is evident that the children have ambivalent feelings toward her. On the one hand, they want her love and attention. On the other hand, they resist it because they are mad and fearful. If a separation has been long and upsetting, any withdrawal behavior of children is their effort to keep from being rejected or deserted again.

Sometimes, upon reunion, children are emotionally frozen, unable to speak or express their feelings until tearful sobs finally burst forth, accompanied by accusing questions: "Why did you leave me, Mommy?"

The important thing is to be sensitive to children's reactions and to recognize that the worse they behave upon the mother's return, the more evident it is that they have been upset by her leaving. A sensitive mother can try to offer extra opportunities for contact with her children after returning home.

STRANGER ANXIETY

Age

Fear of strangers ordinarily begins at about 6 or 7 months of age, rarely before then. Usually, this fear begins after the onset of specific attachments (Skarin, 1977). Children who are very frightened may cry or cling to their mothers. Less upsetting reactions include general wariness or an active turning away and avoidance (refusing to be picked up, refusing to speak, or running away) (Klein & Durfee, 1976; Waters, 1975). Generally, fear of strangers increases from 6 months of age to about 2 years, after which it declines (Belkin, 1975).

Individual Differences

Children differ considerably in their reactions to strangers (Ross & Goldman, 1977). Some never seem to show much fear at all. They smile readily, seldom turn away from being approached, and may even approach the strangers after only a few minutes of contact. Individual differences relate to how secure children are and to their background of social experiences. Some children are more used to having pleasant experiences with a variety of persons. However, children who have suffered repeated and upsetting exposures to strangers become even more wary and frightened the next time they are approached. Several studies have shown that some day-care children are more wary of strangers than are home-reared children, indicating that the former may have learned to be afraid because they associate the presence of a stranger with separation from the mother (Blehar, 1974; Tizard & Tizard, 1971).

Overcoming Fear

What can I do to help my son get over being afraid of other people?

We know that, if children are with either or both parents at the same time that they are in the presence of strangers, they are less frightened than when they are alone with strangers (Feldman & Ingham, 1975). Children are less frightened of strangers in familiar surroundings than in surroundings to which they have not become accustomed. This means that parents who invite friends over to their own home and let the children stay around during the socializing are helping the children get used to other people in an environment that is the least stressful of any. Or if the mother takes her children with her when she goes out and stays with the children the entire time, she is getting them used to other persons at the same time that she is giving them the security of her presence. The most frightening situation is to leave children with strangers in an unfamiliar setting. This is why I've urged introducing children to new people and to new situations gradually. Also, it's wise to avoid separations and frightening experiences at a time when the fear of strangers is developing or is at its peak. From 1 to 2 years of age is an especially bad time. Either before fears develop or after children begin to lose their fear of strangers are better *times* to expose children to new people.

Fear of Men

My 1-year-old likes women but is terrified of men. Is this quite common?

It certainly is quite common, particularly in homes where the father is seldom home, where he has little contact with young children, or when contacts with him tend to be upsetting. Some men are rougher with their children than are women, they have gruffer, louder voices, so that children become frightened of them. This is not always true, of course. Some mothers comment: "Our child is crazy about men."

But it's important to understand that children develop differential responses to different people. Some children develop a specific fear or dislike for a particular person. It's sometimes hard to understand why, except that the response may have been conditioned by a previous association which a child found frightening, or the child may be frightened simply because the other person was different. Interestingly, most children are not afraid of other children—even strangers. Apparently, a child stranger is recognized by infants as being like themselves and therefore not threatening. One study of the responses of infants from 7 to 24 months of age to an adult female, to an adult female midget, and to a 5-year-old male and a 5-year-old female showed that the infants were most frightened of the adult and least frightened of the children, with their reaction to the adult midget somewhere in between (Brooks & Lewis, 1976).

4

The Development of Love and Security

FEEDING AND SECURITY

Regular and Adequate Feeding

One of the important requirements to ensure not only physical health but emotional security as well is for children to receive regular and adequate feedings (Barman, 1972). The chronically hungry child becomes an anxious child.

Several years ago, a student in our Upward Bound program at the University of Maine told how her mother would leave her and her brother alone in the house, not returning for days at a time. The girl was 4 years old and active enough to climb up on cupboards to obtain some food. But her younger brother, only an infant, could not. The girl tried to give him some food, but she was not able to feed him properly. As a result, her brother became mentally retarded from malnutrition. He spent his childhood in an institution. The girl ate enough to sustain her physical health, but she grew to be a very insecure, anxious young woman who was completely distrustful of most people.

Children need to be fed regularly when they are hungry. Hunger creates tension throughout the body. If the tension mounts too high, infants cry, wiggle, and make known their distress to others around them. Ordinarily, they get relief. If they do not, at least in a reasonable period of time, they become anxious, fretful, and more and more uncertain that their basic needs will be met. Some children react by developing a pressing, clinging attitude, demanding attention and reassurance all the time. Others, who are quite deprived, and who are not successful with demands, may begin to withdraw and lose interest in what is going on around them.

Actually, in the first couple of weeks, breast-fed babies may be more restless and cry more than those who are bottle-fed (Dunn, 1977, p. 8). This is because it takes a while before the mother's milk comes in, so the supply may be insufficient in the beginning (Spock, 1977, p. 107). Also, human breast milk actually contains less protein than does cow milk, so breast-fed babies need to be fed more often than do bottle-fed babies (Dunn, 1977, p. 93). However, the more often the baby suckles, the more the flow of milk is stimulated, so the mother's body ordinarily regulates the milk supply according to the baby's need, provided that the mother doesn't get panicky. If, after two weeks, the supply is still inadequate, she should consult her doctor, who may want to supplement her baby's feeding with a bottle. She should not turn to a supplement too soon, however, or the decreased time the baby is at her breast will actually inhibit further milk production.

Breast- versus Bottle-feeding

Much of the controversy over bottle- versus breast-feeding is over their long-term psychological effects on the emotional development of children. Do breast-fed babies grow to be more emotionally secure than bottle-fed babies? Is breast-feeding superior from a psychological point of view? The evidence seems quite clear that there are no unvarying psychological effects on children from either breast-feeding or bottle-feeding which are manifested in adult years (Schaffer, 1977, p. 10). In other words, it doesn't really matter, years later, whether a child has been breast-fed or bottle-fed (McClelland et al., 1978). Children may grow up to be emotionally secure or insecure, whether bottle- or breast-fed.

Working and Nursing

I would really like to breast-feed my baby, but how can I possibly do it when I'm working?

It is more difficult to nurse and work, but it's not impossible. There are several possibilities. One is for the working mother whose job is close enough to her living quarters to go home in the middle of the day for a quick nurse and lunch. This not only allows her to feed the baby but to spend time with the child, which is helpful to the baby's security. If the mother works a full eight-hour day and nurses her baby before leaving for work, then at noon, and then right after work, the arrangement is possible if her baby is satisfied with a four-hour schedule. Obviously, this may not work in the early weeks, since many tiny infants require feeding on a two- or three-hour schedule. If the mother can stay home until her baby starts eating cereal and other solids and is satisfied with a four-hour feeding schedule, it is possible.

Even if the mother can't come home in the middle of the

57

day, and if the baby is on a four-hour schedule, only one supplementary bottle is required during the day. Even if two are needed, there's no problem, provided that the baby has become used to both the bottle and the breast. This may require some careful planning. If the mother knows she is returning to work, and if she wants to nurse, she should introduce a "relief" bottle once or twice a week, so that the baby will get used to it ahead of time. If the mother gives the bottle too often, especially in the early weeks, the baby may start refusing the breast. If this happens, the milk supply will diminish, and to continue nursing at all will become difficult. If a bottle is not introduced before the mother goes to work, so the baby is not used to it, the child may have a more difficult time adjusting. The secret seems to be to offer only enough bottles to get the baby used to them and to depend mostly on breast-feeding to keep the milk flowing. Then a supplementary bottle or two daily becomes a necessity when the mother returns to work. Some mothers may not care to bother with breast-feeding at all, which is certainly easier, but which also deprives them of an experience that they desire and cherish.

Making a Decision about Nursing

Each mother has to decide for herself and according to her own personal feelings what she wants to do. Some women have a strong desire to breast-feed but succumb to pressure from doctors, nurses, relatives, or friends to use a bottle instead. Later, these mothers regret that they did not breast-feed their babies.

I would like to nurse my baby, but I am afraid that I can't because of small breasts and inverted nipples. Will I be able to nurse?

Actually, the physical conformation of the breasts need not

prevent the mother from breast-feeding. Small breasts usually contain as many mammary glands as large ones. The extra bulk in the latter is made up of fatty tissue, which is nonmilk producing anyhow. Even if a mother has no protruding nipples at all, she can squeeze the areola (the dark ring around the nipple) together and put it into the baby's mouth. Babies who develop the habit of sucking only the nipple may also chew the nipple, causing pain, so all babies should be taught to take the areola in their mouths.

Some mothers have trouble with cracked, sore nipples and have to give up breast-feeding. Many such problems could have been prevented if the nipple had been conditioned by massaging before the baby was born. If massaging was not done, the doctor may be able to help the mother overcome the problem if it should develop. But the important thing is for the mother not to be upset or disappointed even though she discovers that she cannot breast-feed her baby. The child will certainly not suffer any ill effects from being bottle-fed.

Some women discontinue breast-feeding because they find it sexually stimulating and are embarrassed by their feelings. Other women enjoy the sensation. In fact, women who breast-feed generally want to resume sexual intercourse sooner after childbirth than do nonnursing mothers (Masters & Johnson, 1966, p. 162).

Many other arguments can be given for and against breast-feeding. But for women living in good hygienic conditions, it seems to me that personal feelings are the only sensible criterion for deciding between breast and bottle. In primitive societies, where sanitation is unsatisfactory and milk is either expensive or difficult to obtain, breast-feeding may be the only safe or possible way to nourish a young baby (Stone & Church, 1968, p. 128). In our society, women have a choice, and that's the important thing.

OTHER EMOTIONAL REQUIREMENTS

Sucking

With whatever method of feeding, it is important that babies get sufficient sucking. Most need several hours a day in addition to their nutritional requirements. One of the real disadvantages of bottle-feeding is that babies usually have to do only a minimal amount of sucking to obtain an adequate amount of milk. This is especially true if the holes in the baby's bottle are too large. This may be remedied by offering nipples with smaller holes. Since sucking is a source of comfort and emotional security, feeding time should be a relaxed, unhurried experience, allowing the baby ample opportunity to suck. Most babies can empty the mother's breast in a short time, but they continue to suck for a period afterward. Experiments have shown that babies continue their mouthing motions long after they have been fed (Schaffer, 1977, p. 33). A pacifier is a highly effective way of meeting children's emotional needs apart from nutritional requirements.

Physical Contact

Another important emotional need of children is for cuddling and physical contact. They have an emotional need for fondling, touching, stroking, warmth, the sound of a pleasant voice, and the image of a happy face. There are actually three most effective ways of calming babies who are upset. One is by swaddling them in a soft blanket and holding them close so they feel more secure. Another is by giving them something to suck on. The third is by rocking them gently. Mothers who breast-feed have to hold their babies close to themselves, and they often rock and talk to them during feeding. Mothers or fathers who bottle-feed should do the same. It is the physical contact with their children and the gentle rocking during or after feeding which helps them to feel loved and secure. Unfortunately, it is possible in bottle-feeding to put the bottle in a holder attached to the baby's crib and to go into the next room and read a book! The baby gets plenty to eat but not plenty of love. Because of this need for physical contact, parents should hold their babies close to them during feeding. And, as the children grow, they should hold them on their laps, rock them, cuddle them, and hold them close. "Loving time" is especially helpful if parents have been separated from their children for periods of time during the day.

There are marked differences, however, in the amount of cuddling which different children need. Some babies will actively resist and protest at being embraced, hugged, and held tight, even when they are tired, frightened, or ill. These "noncuddlers" are more active, restless, and intolerant of physical restraints than are "cuddlers," who tend to be more placid, sleep more, and to play with more cuddly toys. These differences often do not stem from the way different babies are handled, but they are evident from the early weeks on (Schaffer, 1977, p. 5). This means that mothers have to learn to be flexible, to sense individual needs and differences in their children, and to treat each one according to that child's needs.

Love and Warmth

One of the most important requirements in helping children grow as loving, secure persons is the amount of affection a mother shows her children—her "mother warmth" and attitudes toward them. Some mothers thoroughly enjoy their babies. The mothers are happy, laughing, and tender with them. They smile at them a lot, talk to them lovingly and kindly, and indicate by word and action that they adore them. Other mothers resent it that their babies require so much care, and they become angry when their babies cry. They become impatient for the baby to finish feeding. They handle their babies roughly and hurriedly and, as the children grow older, may even abuse and mistreat them. Here are some common examples of mothers who create insecurity in their children.

> *I'm not going to spoil my kid. I tend to him when I'm good and ready and not before. It's good for babies to cry it out. The other night my baby cried for over an hour. I turned the radio way up and went into the other room and slammed the door so I couldn't hear. It worked. He hasn't pulled that crap on me since.*

> *I've had trouble weaning my baby from the breast, so I pinch her while she's nursing. She's getting so she doesn't like it.*

> *My 2-year-old refuses to eat his vegetables, so I squeeze his cheeks to make him open his mouth and I stuff them down his throat. It's the only way I can get him to eat it.*

One wonders how some mothers can be so unfeeling and cruel.

SOME CAUSES OF INSECURITY

Gaining a sense of trust is the most important development in children's early years of life. When they do not grow to trust, their distrust usually stems from one or several different causes.

Maternal Deprivation

The effects of young children being separated from their mother or mother substitute after close emotional attachments have been formed have already been discussed in Chapter 3. The longer the deprivation continues, the more pronounced the effects. Such children are typically described as emotionally withdrawn and isolated, with an air of coldness and an inability to show warmth and sincere affection or to make friends in a caring way. One woman who adopted a 5½-year-old girl who had been shifted from one relative to another described her daughter as not being able to show affection. The mother complained that she "would kiss you but it would mean nothing." The adoptive father explained that "you just can't get to her." A year and a half after the adoption, the mother remarked: "I have no more idea today what's going on in that child's mind than I knew the day she came" (Bowlby, 1971, p. 37).

But what is significant is that children can remain with parents and be similarly deprived if their parents are not able to fulfill their needs for affection, for loving care, for understanding and approval, or for protection from harm. Mothers who have babies they don't want and who reject them or fail to care for them properly are exposing their children to maternal deprivation just as surely as if they went away and left them. Such deprived children may evidence some of the same physical symptoms—poor appetite and sleeping habits, restlessness, bedwetting, allergies, or severe debilitation—as do children who are separated from parents. They may evidence the same emotional coldness and anxiety. As they grow older, they may become hostile, overactive and aggressive, noncooperative and rebellious. Some become deceitful, prone to stealing or to other delinquent acts. Sexual promiscuity is common (Bowlby, 1971, p. 38).

Intellectual retardation often accompanies emotional deprivation. Deprived children lag behind in language development and cognitive and intellectual growth. They often measure well below their chronological level in intellectual ability, and they have difficulty keeping up with their grade level in school. If deprivation begins during the first year of life and continues for three or more years, some children suffer major intellectual and personality impairment that is difficult to reverse completely, no matter how favorable the subsequent environment may be (Weiner & Elkind, 1972a, p. 55).

Tension

Another important cause of emotional insecurity is to be cared for by a mother who is a tense, nervous, anxious, irritable person herself. One mother remarked:

> I've been very nervous lately, and my two children have been impossible. They know when I'm upset, and they become much harder to deal with.

Tension in infants may erupt into symptoms such as colic, eczema, diarrhea, or crying or fussing, which are the infant's primary signals of trouble (Janov, 1973, p. 98). One of the principal requirements for successful breast-feeding is for the mother to be calm and relaxed. Tension interferes with the "let-down reflex" that allows the milk to flow freely from her breast. If this occurs, the baby becomes upset because of insufficient food, which, in turn, upsets the mother even more. Such an increasing cycle of tension is not in the best interest of a warm, gratifying parent-child relationship. Salk writes:

> In the old days mothers used to be encouraged to drink beer when they were breast feeding. The supposition was that beer increased the production of milk. Actually, it was not the beer itself, but the effects of the beer on the mother that increased the flow of milk. The alcohol in the beer tended to relax the mother. When she relaxed, the let-down reflex facilitated the milk flow [Salk, 1975, p. 40].

Parents have to be aware that quarreling between family members upsets children, especially if the quarrels are frequent and violent. A husband and wife start to shout at one another; the baby begins to cry. Even the dog hides under the table. Children who are forced to listen to repeated parental fights become more and more anxious themselves.

Exposure to Frightening Experiences

The effects of isolated exposure to frightening experiences are usually temporary, unless the experience is quite traumatic. A friend related the following story.

> We had to go out and leave our son Peter (age 5) with a baby sitter whom we employed from a local Bible college. When we returned Peter was cranky and upset and refused to go to bed. He screamed if we tried to make him stay in bed. Several days later we learned from Peter that the baby sitter had told him that if he wasn't good that he would be burned by fire in hell. Peter was so frightened that it took him several weeks to get over the experience.

One mother reported that her 2-year-old wouldn't lie down in his crib and go to sleep. If the mother put him down, he immediately sat up. Finally, he would fall asleep sitting up, in spite of his efforts to stay awake. In trying to get at causes, I discovered that the mother was spanking him soundly every time he wet the bed. The prospect of another accident was so frightening that the boy refused to go to sleep.

Most adults can recall other frightening experiences: being locked in a closet, being chased by a dog, getting lost on the way home from school. These experiences are not forgotten, but the long-term emotional effects are often not disastrous. Children gradually overcome their fear. Occasionally, however, experiences are traumatic enough or repeated often enough to cause more permanent harm. A small child who is sexually molested on one occasion may get over it quickly if adults around her aren't too upset, but another who is repeatedly molested may be permanently scarred. The following account was given by a nursing student:

> My own father first molested me when I was five years old. From that time on until I was fourteen he had intercourse with me regularly. You can imagine what it first felt like when I was young. My vagina was completely undeveloped. I felt as though I was being torn apart.
>
> My first marriage ended in divorce. I couldn't let my husband go near me. All I could think of was those times my father raped me, and how much it hurt.
>
> I'm happily married now, though, and was able to overcome my problem. Before we ever had intercourse, my husband just lay beside me, holding me close to him all night. He did this for several nights, until I began to feel warm, loved, and less frightened. Gradually we began love play, and finally one night I asked him to make love to me. He was wonderful. After that I was never afraid again [Rice, 1978b, p. 93].

Criticism

Frequent disapproval and criticism may make children very unsure of themselves. Actually, such parents are showing their children that they actually hate them. Two psychiatrists describe the life of a boy whose parents hate him.

> From the time he awakens in the morning until he goes to bed at night he is nagged, scolded, and frequently slapped. His attempts at conversation are received with curt, cold silence or he is told to be quiet. If he attempts to show any demonstration of affection, he is pushed away and told not to bother his parents. He receives no praise for anything he does no matter how well he has done it. If he walks with his parents and lags a little, his arm is seized and he is yanked forward. If he falls, he is yanked to his feet. . . . At mealtimes he is either ignored or his table manners and inconsequential food fads are criticized severely. He is made to finish whatever is on his plate. . . . The

child soon realizes that he can expect nothing but a hurt body or hurt feelings from his parents, and instead of feeling love for them, he feels fear, loathing, and hatred [English & Pearson, 1945, p. 108].

If criticism continues over the years, the results can be devastating. Here are some examples.

No matter what Marilyn did while growing up, her parents never approved. She was an honor student in high school, but if she got all As and one B, her parents would say: "That's fine, dear, but you'll have to raise that B." Once she sewed an apron and showed it to her mother, but all her mother could do was to point out all the things that were wrong with it. Marilyn continued to struggle for approval until her sophomore year of college. She was never able to please her parents. She finally quit trying. Her grades dropped drastically, primarily because she didn't hand in her written assignments. Actually, she wrote several fine papers but tore up each one, fearful that they were not good enough and that they would be rejected. She flunked out of college and now lives in fear of criticism and disapproval of any kind, so she has not been able to fulfill even a fraction of her potential or to use her brilliant mind.

As far back as she can remember, Nancy's father always criticized her and called her stupid. Consequently, her greatest fear while growing up was that others would think she was dumb. In each grade in school, she always managed to believe that one teacher didn't like her. After graduation, she went from one job to another because "her boss didn't like her." If things went wrong at work, she hesitated to complain, because she was afraid that her boss would fire her. If she didn't understand something, she wouldn't ask, because she was afraid that her boss would think she was dumb. She liked one college boy but quit going with him because she thought him brilliant and felt he couldn't be serious about her because she hadn't been to college. She's a beautiful girl, but when others stare at her she wonders whether there is a spot on her dress or if her hair is messy. Her lack of self-confidence is keeping her from attempting things she can easily do and from significant achievement.

The opinion that children form of themselves is usually a reflection of the feelings which parents manifest toward them over the years. If parents tell the most handsome son that he is ugly, and if they tell him often enough, he may end up believing them. Repeated criticism will destroy whatever self-confidence children have in themselves and may so damage their self-concepts that it may take years to overcome.

Overprotection

Parents who are filled with fears and anxieties themselves, and who are fearful for the safety and well-being of their children, may not permit them any activities in which there is an element of danger. One girl remarked: "My parents would never let me go to dances because they were afraid I'd get involved with boys." Another commented: "I was never allowed to ride a bicycle, consequently I never knew how to do anything that other kids did." A boy explained: "My parents wouldn't let me go to Scout Camp or go away to college. I'm 26 and have never been away from home."

Overprotected children whose parents never let them develop autonomy as independent persons may become so fearful of making decisions or of doing things on their own that they have difficulty establishing themselves as independent adults.

Overindulgence

Children who are permitted every satisfaction and liberty, whether these things are good for them or not, are inadequately prepared to face the frustrations and disappointments of life. Such children are not disciplined or taught to consider others, so they become selfish and demanding, quite inconsiderate of the feelings of others. If they are overindulged with material possessions, they come to expect them without the necessity of hard work or individual effort. Some children are overindulged by parents who never place any restrictions on them, who never establish limits and rules to control their actions or necessary guidelines by which they are to conduct themselves. Anxiety results when these persons get out into the world because they discover that other people resent them or dislike them because of their selfish behavior. They are puzzled that others don't indulge them as their parents have done, and they become more and more anxious that they won't be successful in their social relationships.

One of the chief causes of insecurity in young children is poor impulse control and consequent guilt and anxiety over their own behavior. The following account was given by a kindergarten teacher in the school I directed.

Bobby, age five, seemed withdrawn and at times hostile and destructive in school. He seldom entered into school activities or played with the other children. On a typical day he would wander around the room mumbling: "Yah, yah, yah," and would kick another child's blocks or hit him over the head with a toy. I spoke to the mother and told her that he was either mentally retarded or quite disturbed emotionally. We decided to have him tested at the child guidance clinic and imagine my surprise when he was tested and found to have superior intelligence: Bobby's problem was that he was never disciplined at home. His mother was the kind of person who could never say "no," no matter what Bobby did. She was afraid that if she disciplined him that he wouldn't love her. She was very afraid of his rejection. The clinic suggested firm, consistent discipline. Whenever Bobby was destructive, I was told to isolate him from other children by making him stand in the hall. He really screamed bloody murder. This kept up for several weeks. In the meantime, the mother was given counseling to help her learn how to control Bobby. Gradually, he began to come out of himself and to cooperate. The more control we were able to establish over him, the more he was able to control himself. He actually had become extremely fearful of his own destructiveness so that the only way he could cope was to withdraw into himself.

This case illustrates the role that discipline can play in building security. Children need to know what is expected of them and to feel that they are pleasing adults. Children who are overindulged by parents begin to resent them even more because they will not give them the help they need in learning how to get along with others.

Child Abuse

Child abuse takes two main forms: neglect and attack. Parental neglect has already been discussed. Parents who physically attack and hurt their children may have a devastating effect upon them—both emotionally and physically. The battered child may suffer burns, lacerations, fractures, hemorrhages, and bruises to the brain or the internal organs. A case in point is that of an 18-month-old infant whose mother sat him on the red-hot burner of the stove because he wouldn't stop crying!

Battered children are often premature, sickly children who make extra demands upon parents who are not able to cope. Parents who batter their children expect and demand behavior from them that is far beyond the children's ability. Such parents are immature themselves, with poor impulse control, and in great need of love. Often they were neglected and abused while growing up. One such example is that of Kathy, the mother of a 3-week-old boy, Kenny: "I have never felt really loved in all my life. When the baby was born, I thought he would love me, but when he cried all the time, it meant he didn't love me. So I hit him" (Smart & Smart, 1972, p. 178). Not only do battered children suffer the pains of physical abuse, but they are deeply scarred emotionally by the rage and hatred directed at them. Pathological fear, deep-seated hostility, and a cold, indifferent ability to love are often the results. How successful emotional rehabilitation can be will depend upon the damage done. There are cases of battered children blossoming into happy persons after being adopted by loving parents.

5

How Does Working Affect Children?

How will my going to work affect my children?

The most honest and complete answer is: The effects vary with different mothers, different children, and different types of substitute care, but, overall, the mother's working outside the home need not have any negative long-term effects on children's normal development (Corenelius and Denney, 1975).

THE MOTHER'S REACTIONS AND FEELINGS

There are, however, a number of factors that are important in determining these effects.

Attitude toward Work

One of these factors is whether or not the mother is able to satisfy her desires about working (Weaver & Holmes, 1975). One investigation showed that the worst mothers were those who stayed home to take care of their children when they actually preferred being at work (Murray, 1975). Mothers who worked were considered much more adequate as mothers than those who stayed home against their wills. The highest scores for adequacy of mothering, however, were given to full-time homemakers who preferred this role. Thus, a mother who prefers *not* to accept the full-time maternal role but assumes that role due to social pressures may do a greater disservice to her children by maintaining close contact than she would by leaving them in the care of others. Had she worked rather than accepted the maternal role, she may then have been a more adequate mother than before, although not as adequate as the satisfied homemaker (Murray, 1975, p. 780).

The quality of mothering is also affected by whether or not the mother is satisfied with the outside work in which she is engaged. If she is engaged in work she enjoys and which she finds fulfilling, if she feels she does a good job, and if she comes home in a good frame of mind because of it, these factors will enhance the quality of her interactions with her children (Harrel & Ridley, 1975, p. 562).

Guilt, Ambivalence, Anxiety

Many mothers who work experience a great deal of guilt (Francke, 1978). Society, at least in part, has tried to make mothers feel that if they don't bring up their own children, full-time, they aren't good mothers. Although these attitudes are changing slowly, enough elements of this "pernicious doctrine" exist to make many mothers feel very guilty about working (Callahan, 1971, p. 134). As a result, they are torn with conflict between their economic or personal need to work and their feelings of adequacy as mothers (Powell & Resnikoff, 1976). The resulting tension and frustration are hardly conducive to being a happy mother. An insecure mother makes insecure children.

One of the effects of guilt and ambivalence of feeling is to come home laden with gifts as a way of saying, "Please forgive me for being gone all day." The mother who continually apologizes for leaving her children ends up with children who object even more. Or she may relax rules and discipline as a way of trying to win the children's affection. This leads to further demands on the part of the children that the mother prove her love and interest. A cycle of guilt, anxiety, overindulgence, and excessive demands is stimulated, a situation which is harmful to the children. Thus, it is not working, as such, which creates the problem, but the mother's anxiety about it. One woman writes:

> *If the mother is completely comfortable about working, her children will be, too. If she feels guilty, the children will be upset* [Callahan, 1971, p. 136].

One teacher summed up her observations by stating that "being a working mother's child is not so very different from being a housewife's child. If a child knows absolutely that he is important, if he has faith that he is loved, he will probably be okay—here, or anywhere else" (Scott, 1977, p. 23).

Personal Factors

The mother's own personality—her physical stamina, emotional stability, and ability to withstand pressure and frustration: All influence her relationship with her children.

Some mothers love to be busy; they thrive on twelve-hour work days. They have a high energy level, a lot of drive, and a high tolerance to frustration. They enjoy the challenge of being a superior career woman, wife, and mother. Other women are barely able to manage a minimum of care of house and husband, never mind a child and a career. Some women come home from work completely exhausted and physically and emotionally unable to respond sensitively to their children. They feel like screeching when their children start making demands as soon as they get home. Thus, the personality of the mother herself will have to be considered in determining how she reacts to her work and to her children.

Mothers who go to work when their children are small may differ considerably in personality from mothers who prefer to stay at home (Hoffman, 1974; Moore, 1969). The stay-at-home mothers in one study were more self-confident in handling their babies and more personally involved in mothering activities than the working mothers. They expressed more affection, spent more time playing with their babies, and were more tolerant of irritating behavior than were the working mothers. The working mothers were more detached from their infants and took less interest in them.

But the real question arises: Would the working women have been more motherly if they had stayed at home? It is doubtful. Staying home does not force women to be maternal. Some women are, and some aren't. Those who definitely aren't would do well to hire a maternal baby sitter or decide not to have children at all. And as far as scheduling is concerned, it is helpful if the individual mother knows her own capabilities and tries to do only as much as she knows she can manage. To take on more results in internal pressure, conflict, and frustration, which are certainly not conducive to the personal happiness of the mother or to the well-being of her children.

ONE'S FAMILY AND ONE'S JOB

Ages of Children

The working mothers who worry about their children the most are those with young children. It's hard to go out the door when the children are pleading, "Please don't go, Mommy." However, as discussed in Chapters 2 and 3, this does not mean that children are being damaged by the mother's absence, *if* she takes into account important factors in relation to attachment and separation anxiety and is able to get competent substitute care. What it means is that the more and younger her children, the more she worries about them when she is gone (Nevill & Damico, 1977). As one mother said:

> I do feel badly leaving my two little children who are not yet in school. My big children hardly know I do any outside work since they are at school when I am at school and I am home when they arrive. But the two little ones, three and four . . . say frequently "Don't work" and "Stay with us" [Callahan, 1971, p. 148].

It is precisely this concern about younger children which leads some mothers to conclude: "I wouldn't think of leaving my children until they are three." Or, "I'm going to wait until they're in school before going back to work." However, the mother who decides to work or who has to work when her children are small can arrange things so her children are not affected negatively over the long term.

Numbers of Children

One of the things that happens, of course, is that women who want to work, especially those who want full-time careers, decide to restrict the number of children they have.

Career women have fewer children, and they wait longer after marriage to have them than do other women (Holmstrom, 1973; Rapoport & Rapoport, 1971). An investigation of the relationship between female employment and fertility among 388 working mothers in North Carolina showed that the longer the women were employed after marriage, the more they used birth control, and the longer they waited to have their first child, the smaller were the numbers of desired and expected children (Clifford & Tobin, 1977). It certainly is a lot easier to take care of one or two children and to work than it is to take care of a larger family. In fact, the easiest solution to combining a career with child rearing is not to have any children, which is precisely what increasing numbers of women are doing. Some women don't want any, and, in fact, shouldn't have them, and they should not be made to feel that something is wrong with them because they have opted for voluntary childlessness.

Days and Hours of Work

How long a woman works each day and week and the hours she works are important factors in determining the overall effects of a working mother on children. There is a world of difference in going to work part-time, or working during the hours when children are in school, and being engaged in a full-time career that requires extra time evenings or weekends or that requires a lot of out-of-town travel. The higher the position the woman has achieved and the more responsibility she has assumed, the greater the strain upon her and the more time she will have to spend away from her children. One investigation of 20 dual-career couples in the Boston area where the wives held very responsible positions showed that six of these wives traveled alone on business trips to Europe, Africa, or Asia for periods of time from three weeks to almost a year (Holmstrom, 1973, p. 43). Five out of six of these women had preschool or grade-school age children whom the husband cared for while the wife was away. During the longest separations, the family was periodically reunited. But some of the husbands traveled more than the wives, so they were also away for long periods of time, during which the children were cared for by substitute caretakers.

Contrast this situation to another I know where the wife is a veterinarian with a small animal clinic in the basement of her home. She schedules her own office hours, part time, and is able to spend several hours each day taking care of her two small children. In this situation, one could say that her preschoolers are not at all affected negatively by her career. In the case of the career mothers who were absent for long periods of time because of work, it's hard to imagine that the children were completely unaffected, particularly during periods when substitute care was inconsistent or incompetent, or when the father could not take over part of the responsibility.

There are several important things that the mother can do to minimize or completely eliminate any negative effects on the children.

1. She can try to select and schedule her job to allow the maximum amount of contact with preschool children during the day. An hour or so in the middle of the day helps tremendously. Contact before and after work is important to children of all ages. Time at bedtime also builds security and a feeling of being loved and cared for.
2. She should try to devote some exclusive time to her children after coming home from work. The children will be demanding for the first hour or so, but this tapers off once their immediate needs for her attention and affection

(which she should give in abundance) are satisfied. She and her husband should also try to be with the children as much as possible on weekends.
3. She can involve her husband as much as possible in caring for the children when she cannot. At other times, substitute care ought to be selected carefully, and young children should be given the opportunity to develop attachments to the sitters before being left alone with them.

Quality and Consistency of Care

The most difficult problem working mothers face is finding adequate substitute care. And no matter how careful the mother tries to be, it is not always easy to control the quality of care. Sometimes, one can only guess what goes on between baby sitter and child when the mother is gone. I have worked for years in an academic community where there have always been plenty of students who wanted to baby-sit. But even then, this does not assure competent help. One of the graduate students we hired (a male) was later convicted of child molestation. Fortunately, he had no such inclinations toward our daughter. A female senior whom we had hired several times was later convicted of arson for trying to burn down the school dormitory. She certainly showed no such inclinations when in our home. In contrast, we found an elderly, grandmotherly woman who was very warm and extremely competent and whose services we were able to employ for several years, to the benefit of our children.

Part of the problem of substitute care arises from the fact that public philosophy and sentiment in this country emphasizes the responsibility of the individual mother in caring for her own child, so only a limited amount of public child-care facilities are available, and these are available only to the poor and problem families or, if private, to the wealthy who can afford the high fees. Middle-class working mothers aren't poor enough to have welfare help nor rich enough to hire governesses, so they make do as they are able.

In the old days of the extended family, when several generations lived together in the same household, there was always some adult at home to care for the children when the mother was busy. But in these days of the nuclear family, where sentiment supports a "Molly and me and baby makes three" philosophy, the working mother has no help to turn to, unless she's fortunate enough to have relatives nearby who are able and willing to assist in the care of children, which many, understandably, aren't. As a result, the mother has to hire a private sitter, which is expensive and unpredictable, or park her children at a neighbor's house, where she cannot be certain what goes on between the children of various ages and temperaments. Various types of individual and group care arrangements are discussed in Part II of this book.

SOCIALIZATION OF CHILDREN

One of the inevitable results of going to work is the increased influence of other persons in the lives of one's own children. This can be either advantageous or disadvantageous. Once children get over the stage of being afraid of strangers (and having a series of baby sitters while the children are young may increase their anxiety), they begin to reach out more to the many other persons with whom they have contact. One mother reports: "Our children are quite sociable. They are not shy and they enjoy meeting people." This mother attributed this social behavior to the happy baby-sitting experiences of her children.

Similarly, older children who are quite used to group care feel much more at ease in social groups than those who are reared in a nuclear family with only limited social contacts. Older students who have the hardest time making social adjustments when they first go to college are those who come from isolated nuclear homes or communities where their contacts with others outside their own homes or neighborhoods are quite limited. Exposure to a number of different persons while growing up does build social maturity and develops social poise in older children (Murray, 1975, p. 775).

Disadvantages

One possible disadvantage of substitute care-givers is that other persons take over more and more of the socialization of one's children. This may be of benefit when parents are incompetent, but few good parents want to turn over the entire job to others. However, the more care others give in relation to the care the parents provide, the more likely it is that these other persons will exert an important influence. And this influence may be contrary to the parents' wishes. Substitute care-givers may be more strict or more permissive than parents. One couple found, for example, that their baby sitter was allowing their children to see adult television programs that were filled with violence: programs that were forbidden the children when the parents were home.

Substitute care-givers cannot help but teach their own values and ideas, which may be in direct conflict with those of parents. One couple were shocked when their children began using slang words in referring to minority groups. The parents found out that their school-age children were being influenced by the hateful prejudices of the woman whom they had employed as a baby sitter. Of course it's impossible to keep one's children away from all negative influences outside the family.

Some of the influences at school, for example, or in the neighborhood will be detrimental to the well-being of one's children, but these contacts are not as influential if parents are able to fulfill their own socializing functions.

Even the most conscientious mother who is out of the house a lot will miss out on some of the special moments of her child's world. One mother commented: "I miss out on a lot of his life, the small discoveries he makes when he opens his eye from a nap and discovers how to touch his mobile (Curtis, 1976, p. 198). Another remarked: "I wasn't there when my baby first smiled, when she grew her first tooth, when she spoke her first word, or when she took her first step. I can't help it, but I know I miss out on a lot."

In spite of these precious moments that are missed, the mother needs to realize that no one can ever or will ever take her place in her child's life. Her baby will always need and prefer a part of her, which the caring mother conscientiously gives as she is able. As one woman remarked:

> *When I was growing up, my grandmother, my aunt, and others were always there to take care of me. But when my mother came home from the drug store each day, I wanted her, and she was there when I needed her.*

BENEFICIAL EFFECTS

Most working mothers have less conflict over leaving their children when they realize that their children may derive some real benefits from their being employed (Bettelheim, 1973; Etaugh, 1974; Hoffman, 1974; Miller, T. W., 1975).

Autonomy

One of these benefits is the increased independence that children develop. After the period of extreme dependency of the first several years is over, children actually benefit from increased opportunities to develop self-reliance. The working mother has to encourage her children to do things for themselves while she is gone. From the time the children are 4 to 5 years old, their mother expects them to dress themselves, go to the toilet, and solve minor problems themselves (Kagan, 1971, p. 106). Gradually, they learn to care for their own belongings and their own rooms and to do minor chores. As they get older, they are permitted to play farther from home and to seek a wider circle of friends. By the time they are teen-agers, they should be able to cook supper before mother gets home, to assist in major duties in the house and yard, to assist in shopping and running errands, and to take maximum responsibility in making cooperative decisions regarding the choice of clothes, bedtime, friends, and social activities.

Of course, working does not ensure independence, but it is harder for the working mother to smother her children than it is for the mother who is in the house all day. One of the problems of some children of middle-class families is that they have become so dependent on their mothers for everything that it takes them years to learn how to be on their own. I know high school and college students who can't get dressed in the morning without parental assistance, whose mothers wait on them hand and foot at all hours of the day and night, and who depend upon their parents completely to help them make all their decisions and to support them financially. Very few of these students have mothers who work full time outside the home. Some children need less maternal care, not more, and there is less chance of a completely child-centered, child-dominated family when both parents work (Fisher & Fisher, 1976, p. 187).

Improved Role Model

Another of the benefits of working outside the home is the improved female image that the mother presents to her children (Hoffman & Nye, 1974). The career woman generally has both a superior self-image and a better societal image than does the full-time mother and homemaker. Children of working mothers have a higher opinion of female competence; they see women as less easily hurt emotionally and less in need of security than do children of nonworking mothers (Marantz & Mansfield, 1977; Miller, S. M., 1975). They see women having a wider range of potential careers, and daughters are likely to be oriented toward achievement and toward working outside the home (Gibbons & Kopelman, 1977).

The effect on sons varies. Sons from working-class families may have less respect for their fathers if their mothers have to work, particularly if the fathers are inadequate providers. However, sons of middle-class fathers tend to view their fathers as more nurturant when their mothers work. This is because middle-class fathers tend to assume some of the mother's duties and responsibilities while she is gone, thereby encouraging their sons to view such activities more positively (Wallston, 1973). Certainly, if more and more women are going to assume major responsibilities for family income, more and more men are going to have to assume major responsibilities for family and home maintenance.

Self-esteem

Another of the positive results of the mother's employment is the enhanced self-esteem of the children. This is certainly understandable in the poverty family where the mother's income is the only money that enables the family to have the necessities of life and the self-respect that goes along with these. But it may also be true in other families as well. Mothers who are engaged in long-term employment are more self-assured and self-reliant and so convey these feelings to their children (Lancaster, 1975).

Improved Income

By itself, an adequate or even a high income does not produce happy children, but for a family that would otherwise be impoverished, the mother's employment is of direct benefit in improving the quality of family life and the well-being of the children.

I talked with one family where the husband was laid off from his manual labor job because of a bad back. The mother and father of four children were conscientious parents and were a happily married couple. But it is doubtful whether this family could survive without the mother's income. Certainly, welfare alone was not adequate.

The real question is whether or not the mother's earned income in addition to that of her husband in the average middle-class family really improves the quality of their lives enough to warrant her leaving her children to go to work. A part of the answer is that her additional income does allow them to buy a house; to take an occasional vacation; and to buy better clothes, a better car, or food they otherwise couldn't afford. But these things do not assure happier, more secure children. The remainder of the answer relates to what the mother's employment does to benefit her. If she wants to work, likes to work, and finds personal fulfillment in her work, the children will benefit because they will have a happier, more contented mother and family. Low-income mothers work out of financial necessity. Higher income, better educated mothers work to seek personal fulfillment, and that's important.

Effect on Marriage

One of the considerations in whether the mother's employment is helpful or harmful is the effect it has on the marriage and, in turn, on the children. One woman remarked: "I'm a much better wife—a better person—than I was before I went to work. And our marriage shows it" (Scott, 1977, p. 78). Such positive effects on the wife and on the marriage can't help but benefit the children.

The attitude of the husband is also crucial. If the husband wants his wife to work and she doesn't do so, or if he doesn't want her to but she does, the net effect is a disturbance in the marital relationship, which, in turn, upsets the children. It is difficult for a wife to be happy in her work if her husband strongly objects to it. Most working women agree that the attitudes of their husbands are crucial in determining the overall effects of her working on the family (Holmstrom, 1973, p. 134). The husband's attitudes and roles in relationship to the working wife are discussed in Part III of this book.

6

Mental Development and School

One of the concerns of conscientious parents is how well their children are doing in school. Most parents hope that their children will be smart and that they will bring home good report cards. Or, at the very least, they expect their children will try to do as well as they can and that they will stay out of trouble and do their homework and lessons as expected.

This concern of parents is realistic. They realize the necessity of education in today's world, and they have a genuine desire for their children to succeed. Above all, they want their children to get satisfactory grades so they can get into college and obtain a good job when they graduate.

I know one mother whose chief concern for years has been that her boy go to college. Unfortunately, she's more concerned than her son, who studies only half-heartedly and whose grades are only mediocre. If this boy does not succeed, it will be the biggest diappointment in his mother's life. This mother is not unique. She represents a whole generation of parents who are very worried about their children's education. There is a need, therefore, to take a look at those factors that relate to mental development and school achievement. How can parents contribute to mental growth? What type of family background enhances learning? What are the effects of maternal employment on IQ and on school achievement? How can parents motivate children to learn? What can they do about school adjustments, language lag, reading problems, homework, underachievement, and poor report cards? What about the youngster who is having problems getting along in school?

ENVIRONMENTAL STIMULATION

Sensory Stimulation

One important requirement for mental growth is that children be reared in an intellectually stimulating environment. Infants begin to get acqainted with their world from the moment of birth. They do this by taking in information through the senses of vision, touch, taste, hearing, and smell and by processing this infomation and acting upon it. If infants have a variety of objects to see, touch, or taste; different sounds to hear; or different odors to smell; they learn more than if their exposure is quite limited. Sensory stimulation encourages motor learning and coordination as infants reach out to grasp or as they toddle forward. Auditory stimulation, especially exposure to words, encourages language development and speech.

Variables in Effects of Stimulation

But what children learn, and how much, depends not only on the amount of stimulation but on its type, variety, intensity, regularity, duration, and timing. Children who are regularly given appropriate materials, over periods of time, are going to learn more from their play activities than children whose exposure is more limited. Children who are encouraged to explore the environment around them will learn faster than those who are kept caged up, with little opportunity to move about. Children whose mothers handle them, talk to them, and play with them will learn more than children who are left alone for long periods of time without social contacts. Mothers who take their children with them whenever they go out are going to increase the knowledge and understanding of the larger world in which their children live to a greater extent than mothers who never permit their children out of their own yard.

Maximum mental growth takes place when children are stimulated mentally from infancy on, year after year. No one year, experience, or situation is as important as what happens over several years or as important as the sum total of experiences during years of growth. Mental growth may accelerate when children are exposed to an enriching environment, such as that provided by a superior teacher, but growth then stops or even reverses when children are culturally and intellectually deprived for a period of time.

One example of this comes from a study of a group of children living in an isolated Indian village in Guatemala (Kagan & Klein, 1973). During infancy, the children were kept most of the time in the small, dark interior of their hut, where they were rarely allowed to crawl, were rarely spoken to or played with (though they were always kept near the mother), and where few objects for play were available. When the mother traveled to the market, she left her infant behind, since the outside sun, air, and dust were considered harmful. As a result, these children showed evidence of gross retardation. They hardly moved, were fearful, barely smiled, and were very quiet. Many would not turn toward a sound or smile or babble when spoken to.

In the second year, however, these chidren began to walk, and they were allowed to leave the hut and to participate in life outside it. As their experiences increased, these retarded infants were transformed into active, gay, intellectually capable children. The retardation of the first year was reversed by exposure to a variety of stimulating experiences (Kagan & Klein, 1973).

It is evident that the net effect of sensory stimulation or deprivation will depend upon the age of the children, how long the sensory stimuli are provided or withheld, how often the stimuli are repeated, how varied the stimuli are, and how intense the experiences are.

Overstimulation

Of course, it is entirely possible to expose children to excessive stimulation or to experiences inappropriate to their age level. It has been shown, for example, that in face-to-face interactions with their infants, some mothers try too hard to get their attention, resulting in an information overload and in infants averting their gaze in their efforts to turn away (Field, 1977). Children can tolerate only a certain amount of stimulation. Beyond that point, they want to escape, not to respond. The same principle holds true in the classroom. The teacher who tries to expose the students to too much material in too short a time causes them to become disinterested in further learning. The maximum learning takes place when teachers or parents take their cues from their children and expose them to as much as they can assimilate at a time and no more. I've known parents who were so determined that their children get good grades that they made them participate in endless spelling, arithmetic, or other drills, until the children became so sick of learning that they blocked out all the teaching efforts of the parents.

Some stimulation is inappropriate for a particular age level. Thus, parents who want to help their children learn and who buy their children educational toys that are too difficult for them only succeed in creating frustration. The only thing the children learn is that they can't master the task, so the activity discourages further efforts at learning. I get very annoyed at parents who expose children to adult experiences—like attending adult church services, for example—expecting the children to be quiet, interested participants, and who punish them when they're not. These parents only succeed in teaching children to hate church. The children would be far better off in church school classes appropriate to their grade levels.

Every good teacher knows that there are teachable moments when children hunger to learn and that there are appropriate activities and experiences for different grade levels. Mental growth is accelerated when the stimulation is appropriate for the age group, continues only to the saturation point and not beyond, and is repeated enough to assure that maximum and lasting assimilation takes place.

We know that children learn by being exposed to a variety of people and experiences. But if young children are exposed to too many strangers or to strange environments, they become frightened and withdraw, so all exploratory activity and learning cease. Children can be exposed only as they can accept the unfamiliar without anxiety. Thus, learning must be geared to the child's progress and to his or her emotional readiness to learn.

Individual Differences

Both parents and teachers have to take into account the individual differences in children. Some children are very responsive to visual stimulation, for example, whereas others are not so responsive. Some children are supersensitive to certain sounds; others don't seem to notice. These differences depend partially on the neurological make-up of the children and on the extent to which the children have been conditioned by previous experiences. The differences depend too on the "state" of the children at any particular time. Thus, one experimenter recorded the responses of newborns to the whir of a camera and found activation (startle, increased motion, grimaces, even crying) if the babies were in a quiet state but quieting (decreased crying, less activity, scanning as if to locate the sound) if they were highly aroused (Korner, 1969). The response depended on the baby's state. A touch may produce movement in inactive babies but quiet them if they are crying.

This means that mothers and teachers need to be sensitive to their children's variable states of readiness to learn and to take advantage of those times when interest and motivation are at the maximum. It means, too, that adults can't expect the same response from all children, or even from one child over a period of time. Adults have to learn to be flexible and to take individual differences into account.

FAMILY BACKGROUND AND MENTAL DEVELOPMENT

Language Development

What can I do to facilitate language and vocabulary development in my children?

The best thing this mother can do is to talk and read to her children, since the amount and warmth of a mother's conversation with them influences their vocalization (Wulbert et al., 1975). Mothers who talk to their babies while they are feeding, bathing, changing diapers, picking up, cuddling, and otherwise taking care of them are teaching their children to talk. Mothers who read stories to their children enable them to produce significantly more sounds, and so they learn to talk earlier than other infants (Smart & Smart, 1972, p. 129). Households in which there is a maximum of family conversation also facilitate speech development. Since language is developed primarily by imitation, the more words and conversation children hear, the more likely they are to duplicate what they have heard.

Of course, the quality of language spoken, the correctness of the grammar, and the extent of the vocabulary used all influence the direction and extent of language development in children. Parents whose speech is limited to simple communications about rather concrete ideas or objects are not teaching their children to use more abstract words or expressions. Parents who use incorrect grammar, slang, or swear words will influence these speech patterns in their children.

Maximum language development also takes place within the context of a secure, happy mother-child relationship (Elardo, 1977). Mothers who smile at their babies a lot and who show that they love them and care about them have alert, responsive infants (Osofsky, 1976). Friendly relationships encourage mutual responsiveness and talking (Garrison et al., 1967, p. 168). Children who are comforted and happy because of the sounds mother makes are stimulated to reproduce those sounds. Thus, "words are reproduced if and only if they are first made to sound good in the context of affection, care and attention" (Smart & Smart, 1972, p. 129).

Language is also enhanced by an extensive use of books, pictures, magazines, phonograph records; by supplying age-appropriate play materials; and by providing a culturally rich environment (Elardo et al., 1975). This not only exposes children to a rich vocabulary but also stimulates their thinking and ideas and gives them interesting things to learn and to talk about.

Stimulating Reading

There are several things that parents can do to encourage an interest in reading and to stimulate reading skills. The most important is to read stories to the children from the time they are young. This stimulates their interest in wanting to read to find out what a story is about. It develops a positive association between the words on the printed page and the ideas of a story. By looking at the words while parents are reading, children learn word recognition and pronunciation, which is the first step in beginning to read.

Parents should also provide children with a rich variety of reading materials. If books cannot be purchased, they can be borrowed from the library. If interesting materials are constantly available, children develop the habit of using them at their leisure.

Parents also set an example by their own reading habits. If the parents like to read and often do so, children are likely to imitate their parents' behavior. Unfortunately, many parents, even college graduates, never read a book in any one year. I'm constantly amazed at the number of homes we go into where there aren't any books or bookshelves in the entire house. These are homes of professional people, supposedly educated, intelligent persons, but one would never know it by looking in their homes. If reading becomes a part of life for the parents, chances are that it will be for the children as well.

Of course, all children are different. Some seem to develop a keen interest in reading, even if their parents don't read very much. Some children never do develop an interest in reading even though their parents like to. But parents can stimulate or retard whatever desire is there (Ames, 1970, p. 246).

Encouraging Curiosity and Creativity

Curiosity may be described as a desire to learn, an inquisitiveness, a drive to know and to understand. Children who manifest a high degree of curiosity will certainly learn more and faster than those who have little curiosity.

Even though each child is born with a certain degree of curiosity, this can be stimulated or retarded, depending upon the reaction of parents. Parents who punish their children for being curious and who restrict their mobility and discourage their asking questions may so squelch a child's desire to learn that only a minimum of mental growth takes place.

I remember one child in a kindergarten class who was overinhibited by very strict, stern discipline, so much so that the child didn't dare do anything for fear of being punished. When the children were given an empty tin can to paint, most children painted the outside of the can and then the inside, and, if left long enough to their own devices, they painted the paper on the table and then painted each other. But this boy painted only one tiny spot on the side of the can during the entire period. He reacted in a similar fashion to the use of finger paint, except that, in this case, he sat and looked at the paint, not daring to put his finger in it for fear of getting punished for being dirty.

This does not mean that children shouldn't be disciplined or directed. Completely undisciplined children seldom do well in school because their drives have not been channeled into successful accomplishment. Two investigators found that achievement-oriented sons were those whose parents exercised firm control over them (Nuttall & Nuttall, 1976). But this same study showed that hostile parental control and rejection resulted in decreased academic motivation.

The answer seems to be to find the right combination of firmness and freedom that will give children some direction but that will allow them the maximum opportunities for exploration, within acceptable limits. Curiosity needs to be rewarded and encouraged, and this can be done while parents are also teaching acceptable behavior. In fact, guidance builds security and improves self-confidence, which is certainly needed if children are to become creative, productive persons. The curious child has been described as one who "reacts positively to new, strange, incongruous, or mysterious elements in the environment by moving toward them, exploring them, or manipulating them," as one who "scans his environment seeking new experiences," and as one who "persists in examining and exploring in order to know" (Binter & Frey, 1972, p. 130).

Investigations of the background of creative children and adolescents have shown that such persons are granted early autonomy and independence and are given consistent discipline. The parents engage in many activities and hobbies with their children and are much interested in their achievement. Parents are often interested in intellectual, cultural pursuits. The mothers are often highly educated and have careers outside the home. As a result, the children develop intellectual interests and high aspirations (Smart & Smart, 1972, pp. 544, 545).

MATERNAL EMPLOYMENT

Effects

The crucial question is: What effect, if any, does maternal employment have on mental growth and on academic achievement? Do children of working mothers have as high IQs and do as well in school as those whose mothers are primarily homemakers?

Lower-class Families

Based upon present knowledge, it seems likely that whether the mother works is not the crucial factor in the mental growth of her children or in whether her children do well in school. There is some evidence that, in lower-class families, better academic performance is associated with maternal employment (Cherry & Eaton, 1977; Hoffman & Nye, 1978, p. 163). This does not mean that one is caused by the other. Why there is an association, however, is partly a matter of conjecture. It may be that having an adequate income is important to these women and that the mother is happier and more satisfied and thus is a more adequate mother. Or it may be that the type of mother who works has more ambition and intellectual ability than the nonworking mother, so her children benefit from her superior drive and ability.

Middle-class Families

In middle-class families, there is evidence that daughters of working mothers have higher career aspirations and achievements than do those of nonworking mothers. This is attributed to the less traditional role model provided by the mothers and to a higher evaluation of female competence. If fathers take over more child-rearing responsibilities when the mother works, this should have some positive effects on the children—if the fathers do a good job. Or if working mothers try to compensate for their employment by planning specific activities with their children, this can have a beneficial effect. If working mothers encourage more independence and responsibility in their children, these characteristics can be linked to achievement (Hoffman & Nye, 1978, p. 162).

Cause and Effect

In all these investigations, there is no evidence of cause and effect—that working as such causes superior or inferior academic performance (Query & Kuruvilla, 1975). Some positive and fewer negative associations have been established, but is impossible to sort out all the variables and say that if a mother works, her child will do better or worse in school. No direct effects have been established, although some associations have been established. We do know that there is no evidence to support the idea that maternal employment as such results in maternal deprivation or delinquency (Hoffman & Nye, 1978, p. 165).

SCHOOL

Parental Expectations

One important consideration is that parents have realistic expectations regarding school achievement. In my own contacts with thousands of parents, it seems that the majority tend to feel that their children are of superior intelligence, are advanced for their age, or are smart and lazy. I remember one instance of a parent who insisted that her son be enrolled in the college prep program in high school, in spite of the fact that careful testing and evaluation had revealed that he was not equal to the challenge intellectually. The school acquiesced to parental pressure and placed him in the college program. As a result, the boy failed several of his courses and had to repeat a grade.

The next child in the same family was tested and found to have superior intelligence, so the guidance counselor suggested to the parents that he be placed in the college program. "Oh, no," the mother objected. "I made that mistake once before. He's going to enroll in the vocational program." Again, the school succumbed to parental pressure and put this boy in a program not suited to his ability. He dropped out of school because of lack of interest and motivation.

One of the hardest things in the world is to try to get parents to be objective about their children's abilities, interests, aptitudes, and achievements. Parents may have personal prejudices and emotional hang-ups that prevent them from seeing the true picture of their children. Consequently, it is hard to keep parents from applying unsuitable pressures, which may interfere with their children's academic and vocational achievements. Parents need to get all of the information they can from teachers, guidance counselors, and tests of various kinds, and then to expect their children to work close to their capacities but not beyond. Some parents insist on academic performance far beyond the abilities of their children, thereby creating considerable anxiety, a lowered sense of self-worth, and feelings of frustration and failure. Some parents don't expect enough of their children and are not really interested in them. One boy told me that his parents didn't once look at his report card all the way through high school. His parents just weren't interested. Such indifference certainly discourages motivation.

IQ Tests

So-called IQ Tests, or intelligence tests, are widely misunderstood and often misused. *IQ* originally referred to a score on the Stanford-Binet intelligence test. The score on the test was supposed to measure basic intelligence, with a score of 100 representing average intelligence and scores above or below representing degrees of superior or inferior intelligence.

Today, however, these tests scores should be recognized for what they are: figures that represent comparative evaluations of how one does on a particular test at a specific time. Although the score gives a basic comparison in relation to others, it is not an accurate assessment of native intellect.

For one thing, children who are tested at five-year intervals up to age 18 may show median changes from 6 to 15 points, with individual changes ranging from 0 to 60 points (Rice, 1978a, p. 549). Even a forty point difference may indicate that a child is average at one time and either an idiot or a genius at another time. Obviously, if the scores represented native intelligence, how could it vary so much? It couldn't.

Because of variations in scores, the younger children are at the time of testing, the less predictive are the scores of basic intelligence and abilities later in life. The nonverbal tests for preschoolers are especially inaccurate. "Even the best 'infant' intelligence tests have negligible correlations with test scores obtained with standard tests in later years" (Fisher & Fisher, 1976, p. 130).

For another thing, many of the tests, at least in the early days of their usage, were biased in favor of middle-class children, since the language and examples were drawn primarily from middle-class culture. The tests penalized children from lower classes or from certain ethnic groups: The children did not understand basic vocabulary and the meaning of the questions, not because they were dumb, but because their particular backgrounds did not familiarize them with the things or experiences referred to in the test.

So, although IQ tests may be useful to evaluate a certain type of intellectual functioning (test-taking) at a particular time, they should not be used in a predictive sense to say that a child is or is not capable of going into college or of doing a particular type of work. Subsequent events often prove such prophecies completely fallacious.

IQ scores cannot even be used with certainty to predict academic success and grades, since such scores can account for no more than a third to a half of the variance. Such factors as motivation, work habits, and creativity are certainly as important as test scores (Freedman & Kaplan, 1972a, p. 32).

Of course, efforts to predict may become self-fulfilling prophecies. Children who are told that they are "dumb" may believe it and start acting as though they are, so the very fact of the telling makes it come true. Or because they have been labeled as "slow," they are put into a "slow track" group in school, where they are not given as much work or are not challenged, so they don't learn as fast (Kennedy, 1971, p. 159).

Does all of this mean that children should not be given IQ tests? No. It means that tests should be used cautiously as a diagnostic tool to determine strengths and weaknesses, along with other measurements, such as school grades, so that teachers and parents can discover when and how intervention and remedial efforts will help. For example, the subscales (or scores on particular parts of a test) may reveal specific weaknesses and thus assist teachers and parents in discovering what specific help children need.

When there is a discrepancy between test scores and school functioning, this may be an indication of emotional upset or particular problems at the time of the testing of which adults should be aware. A child who scores high on a test but does poorly in school, or vice versa, is doing so for a reason, so the job of teachers and parents is to discover the reason and correct it.

Report Cards

Bringing home report cards is probably the most upsetting event in the lives of some children. Children who fear they have done poorly or those who have not lived up to parental expectations think up every scheme in the world to keep parents from finding out. They "forget to bring it home"; they "lose it." They are sick, and so they don't go to school that day. They try to erase and change marks. I know one child who didn't go home until midnight because of fear of parental punishment. Another told me that he stole a blank card from the school office, put his own grades in it for each semester (all A's), and brought only that card to his parents. It was the only card his parents saw for one whole year.

Report cards should be a help to parents and their children, not a major source of family disaster. But how?

One, parents should be very cautious about how they react

to a poor report. Some parents become violently upset, resorting to severe punishments, physical or verbal thrashings, or to threatening disciplinary measures that are excessive or unwise. "Grounding" children every night and weekend for a whole semester, for example—not letting them have any social life at all—may create a lot of resentment and not accomplish their purpose of stimulating better study habits or grades. No child can study all the time. Nervous, upset children may do far better when they are studying if they have a chance to relax and have fun in between study times. I've known parents to try to force the overactive child to remain inactive and to study for long hours at a time. It just doesn't improve grades. Other parents may try to push a child of average ability to do better than he is capable of doing. I know one family where the parents won't let their 17-year-old son get his driver's license until he makes the honor roll. It's been two years, and the boy hasn't made it yet—and he may never make it. In fact, such achievement may be beyond his capabilities.

Two, parents should interpret a report card as an evaluation of achievement and progress and as an indication of strengths and weaknesses, and they should give praise and recognition to strengths as well as thoughtful consideration to indications of weaknesses. Do parents compliment their children on the good marks and evaluations? Or do they only notice the low ones? Most children need encouragement, morale building, emotional support, *and* positive help in overcoming problems. Poor marks may indicate the need for special help, tutoring, counseling, or remedial attention of some kind.

Three, reports are more helpful if followed up by parent-teacher conferences to discuss the reasons for the marks and the child's individual needs and to decide on a course of remedial action, if needed. If children are having trouble, what will help most? What should the parents' role be?

Underachievement

The reasons for underachievement are many and varied. Some of the reasons are physical: poor hearing, poor eyesight, various physical illnesses or handicaps. One child did poorly in school for three years before the parents found out that she was seeing images upside down. Another was found to be so deaf that she couldn't hear most of what the teacher was saying. Some children suffer from a brain impairment, such as dyslexia, which causes reading problems. Others are hyperkinetic due to brain injury. Is the child doing poorly in school because of mental retardation or because of other physical impairments? Parents should seek expert advice to see if there are physical causes for problems before they assume that the child is "just lazy" or "not trying."

If the causes are not physical, then they may be emotional in origin. Children who aren't measuring up to their abilities may have emotional disturbances that are interfering with successful achievement. Psychological evaluation should help to get at causes and reveal the dynamics of children's behavior. When parents and teachers have a clear understanding of *why* children aren't doing well, they can take appropriate remedial action. One pediatrician urges parents to get specific answers to the question "why." He writes:

> *"Why is Clara doing poorly in school this year, Miss Smith?" "Because she's lazy." "Okay, but why is she lazy?" "Because that's just her way and she doesn't want to work hard enough." "Okay, but why is that just her way and why doesn't she work hard enough?" "Because she and I hate each other's guts and we don't get along, that's why," or "Because she sits in school all day and worries her head off about whether you're beating your wife at home or not, that's why," or "Because she has a splitting headache in class every day, that's why" or "Because she's a crazy mixed-up kid and needs to see a psychiatrist, that's why." These answers, finally are concrete, simple,*

easy to follow up and may or may not be true. But in any event you have finally found an answer [Homan, 1970, p. 222].

Homan goes on to suggest that parents follow up on what seems to be a plausible answer and, if it still doesn't correct the problem, that they go back to the best expert available until they do find the answer.

Homework

The biggest mistake parents can make is to take over responsibilities for their children's homework. Some parents even go as far as to do their children's homework because they want their children to make good grades. Other parents don't do it but assume responsibility for their children doing it. They do all the worrying about whether their children do their homework or not. They take over the responsibility for the quality of the homework: checking every paper and problem to be certain it is right, rewriting awkward phrases, or redoing incorrect problems.

This is *not* the way to help children with school work. The children learn to depend upon their parents for good grades, rather than assuming the responsibility themselves. Children may even do careless work, realizing that their parents will correct their mistakes. Children don't try to remember to do assignments; they depend upon their parents to remind them. They develop the habit of turning to parents for assistance whenever they run up against any problem rather than trying to figure it out for themselves.

What should parents do? Teach their children that homework is their responsibility and that, if they get good grades, they can have the satisfaction and rewards that go along with them, but that, if they get bad grades, they have to accept the criticism and penalties.

Parents can assist by making some rules about study times and hours, these depending on the age and needs of their children, or about nights and times allowed out. Parents can enforce study hours, but some children will stay in their rooms during those times, frittering their time away and accomplishing nothing. No matter what parents do, they can't force children to study. It's still up to them. However, establishing general guidelines assists children who are not yet mature enough to assume the complete responsibility of disciplining themselves.

Parents can give direct help with homework (if they are scholastically able) by explaining how to do problems, by discussing assignments when requested, or by asking test questions as needs arise—but without actually doing what the children should be doing for themselves. If children are having difficulty with certain subjects, and if parents can't explain the problems, they can try to arrange for extra help from the teacher or even, if possible, from a tutor. The right individual help at the right time may increase the children's understanding to the point where they are motivated and capable of doing much better on their own from that time on. The parents' role is to encourage maximum learning and to create the necessary conditions so that such learning can take place.

7

Socialization, Moral Development, and Moral Behavior

SOCIALIZATION

Meaning

Socialization is the process by which children acquire the dominant values and behavior patterns of the group of which they are a part (Kagan, 1971, p. 41). It is the process by which they learn the ways of a given society or social group so that they can function within it. The dictionary defines *socialization* as "to make fit for life in companionship with others." Thus, children are socialized when they acquire desirable behavior and socially approved values and when they suppress undesirable behavior and values.

Cultural Variations

But what is desirable or undesirable varies from culture to culture and group to group. A Chinese boy is taught to be polite, shy, and quiet, in contrast to a boy in the United States, who is usually boisterous and exuberant. A Mayan Indian peasant boy in Guatemala is taught that he must learn to help his father work the coffee plantations, remain close to his family, and contribute to their financial stability. The son of a Chicago lawyer is taught to do well in school and become independent of his parents as soon as possible (Kagan, 1971, p. 42).

Even in one country, such as the United States, there are wide variations in socially approved behavior. The American Indian girl is taught to put family and tribal welfare before her own and to cooperate in a society that emphasizes group living. A child of English lineage is taught the importance of individual freedom and independence and that the value of the individual is more important than the value of the group. A child of the streets in an urban ghetto learns to be tough and aggressive. A child in a middle-class suburban family may learn to be sensitive and dependent. What children are taught will depend upon the values and mores of the group of which they are a part. Thus, a child socialized to live in one culture may be ill prepared to get along with those of another group, if a change in residence or membership is necessary.

Agents of Socialization

Who exerts the greatest influence on the child: parents, peers, or other persons?

Generally speaking, parents exert the greatest influence, followed by siblings, peers, teachers, and public media (television, films, books, and so on), in that order (Kagan, 1971, p. 155). There is a hierarchy of influences according to the age of the children, however. Parents and siblings exert the greatest effect during the preschool years when the life of the children centers primarily around their home. Peers and teachers exert their maximum effect after the children are old enough to go to school and spend much time out of the house with their friends. Public media exert the greatest effect after early adolescence, at a time when children receive maximum exposure to them.

There is also another hierarchy of influences, one related to different areas of children's lives. Adolescents, for example, are usually willing to follow parental suggestions in such matters as religious or political affiliation or educational or vocational plans, but they soundly reject parental control over such matters as style of dress, tastes in music, dating customs and practices, or choice of friends. In these latter matters, adolescents are far more likely to accept the influence of their peers (Rice, 1978a, p. 285). Thus, parents are effective agents of socialization in some matters, but not in others.

The attitude toward smoking marijuana is one example of any area of life where parental values have had very little influence on adolescent behavior. In a recent year, only 7 percent of adults age 35 to 49 had ever smoked marijuana, in contrast to 53 percent of youths age 18 to 25 (Rice, 1978a, p. 286). This wide difference in behavior between adults and youths indicates that socialization as related to marijuana smoking came from peers not parents. In this case, the parents had failed in teaching their own values to their children. In contrast to this, however, another study showed that 68 percent of college youths identified with their family in political views (Yankelovich, 1974, p. 126). In this case, parental influence was significant.

Family Factors and Social Learning

There are a number of different factors that determine parental influence. One variable is the degree of emotional closeness between parents and their children. Children who have a close emotional attachment to parents are more likely to be parent-oriented than will those who are distant from them, hostile toward them, or rejected by them (Larson, 1972). One researcher found that mothers who were most successful in socializing their children were those who were most likely to have frequent verbal and physical contacts with them, and these contacts were often positive, supportive, and warm (Pollitt et al, 1975). Mothers who were least successful in socializing their children were more distant and less affectionate, used verbal instructions less often, and were more prone to use physical punishment (Pollitt et al., 1975, pp. 534, 535).

Socialization and moral learning take place when children have strong emotional attachments to their parents, since it is this type of bond that enhances the development of a sensitive conscience. One investigation of delinquent 15- and 16-year-old boys on parole showed that their violence and destruction was indicative of a lack of conscience, a low capacity to resist temptation, and little evidence of guilt. When young, these boys showed an almost pathological independence, having been punished often for requests for attention and affection (Bandura & Walters, 1959). One cross-cultural comparison of American and Italian boys showed that those whose fathers were not sufficiently affectionate were less socially oriented and less well adjusted socially than those who received adequate parental affection (Lasseigne, 1975).

I've found that, as a group, working mothers are very concerned about the influence that they have on their children, since they have to be away from them for many hours a day. Such mothers can be the primary socializing influence, provided that they and their children are close emotionally.

THE DEVELOPMENT OF MORAL JUDGMENT

Moral judgment means the capacity to make moral decisions: to know and understand what is right from what is wrong, or what is good from what is not quite so good. Here is a dilemma that has been used to stimulate children to use reason in making moral judgments.

In Europe, a woman was near death from cancer. One drug might save her, a form of radium that a druggist in the same town had recently discovered. The druggist was charging $2,000, ten times what the drug cost him to make. The sick woman's husband, Heinz, went to everyone he knew to borrow the money, but he could only get together about half what it cost. He told the druggist that his wife was dying and asked him to sell it cheaper or let him pay later. But the druggist said, "No." The husband got desperate and broke into the man's store to steal the drug for his wife. Should the husband have done that? Why? [Kohlberg, 1969].

The purpose in presenting this dilemma is not to try to get children to come up with a right or wrong decision, but to encourage them to think about the reasons for their answers. By analyzing children's responses, it is possible to determine at what stage they are in the development of their capacity to make moral judgments.

Stages of Development

In general, there are three different levels at which children and adults make moral decisions.

Level I may be identified as a *premoral level*, since little thinking actually takes place. Children who are at this level are considered well behaved in a stereotyped way, since they give unquestioning obedience to superiors and since they respond without thinking to what is considered good or bad, as defined by their social reference group. Response at this level is motivated by a desire to avoid punishment or by the need to gain rewards for others. Children at this stage judge the morality of an act by the physical consequences, regardless of the meaning or value of these consequences to an individual.

Level II is best described as a *morality of convention* where goal is conformity—to live up to the expectations, rules, and laws of one's own family, group, or nation in order to avoid the disapproval and censure of others and to avoid guilt feelings. This level is less egocentric than Level I and is more sociocentric, since it is based upon a desire to maintain and support the social order.

Level III is morality that emphasizes *universally applicable principles*, such as individual rights, human dignity, or equality. These universal principles of justice are considered valid beyond existing laws, social conditions, or peer mores. Therefore individuals governed by these ethical principles may, under some circumstances, break unjust civil laws because they recognize a morality higher than existing law. In the case of the husband Heinz, this level of morality might say that he was justified in stealing the drug to save the life of his wife when all other attempts to obtain it failed, not because it was right to steal, but because the need to save a human life was a moral obligation that took precedent over obedience to the civil laws that protect property. The United States soldier who refused orders to participate in the massacre at the Vietnamese village of My Lai in 1968 was identified as being at this level (Fraenkel, 1977, p. 56).

Generally speaking, progression from one of these stages of moral thinking to another cannot be equated with the specific age of a child, although the chances of being at an advanced level of moral thought are greater as one grows older. However, with any one age group, individuals are at different levels of development in their moral thinking. Some are retarded;

others are advanced. Much of this is because the ability to make moral judgments is partially related to basic intelligence. The great majority of adults in the United States never reach Level III (Rice, 1978a, p. 518). Most are at Level II—and live at a conventional, conformist level of morality.

Implications for Parents

These principles of development of moral judgment have important implications for parents, which may be summarized as follows.

All young children need rules to follow if they are to behave properly. The younger the children are, the more they need the constraint and guidance of parents in doing what is right. Since young children do not have either the knowledge of right and wrong or the capacity to make proper judgments, the parents' role is to make these decisions for them by establishing rules and principles to govern their behavior. These rules can be enforced by establishing a system of rewards and punishments.

As children get older, they are governed less by hard and fast rules and more by a sensitized conscience that reflects group feelings and desires. They begin to want to conform to group expectations in order to avoid the disapproval of others and the censure of their own guilt feelings. But conscience development takes place primarily by interaction with others. It depends on positive parental attitudes and on a family environment that emphasizes warmth and acceptance. It depends also on extensive peer-group participation, on involvement in groups that evidence a high level of morally responsible behavior. Children can learn acceptable principles of moral conduct from such groups. This is why it is wise to expose school-age children to organized groups that exert a positive influence.

Children also learn by having a wide variety of positive experiences, by having an opportunity to discuss alternative forms of behavior, and by discussing the various options that are open to them in making decisions. Ultimately, parents have to allow older children more and more opportunities to make moral decisions, and to place more and more responsibilities upon them for the decisions that they have made. The goal is to help children to accept moral principles for themselves, principles which are arrived at in reciprocal relationships with other people, where, out of mutual respect, they begin to desire to treat others as they themselves would wish to be treated. Thus, they pass from a *morality of constraint*, which depends upon external restraints, to a *morality of cooperation*, where they desire to do the right thing out of concern for the feelings and welfare of others (Piaget, 1932).

THE DEVELOPMENT OF MORAL BEHAVIOR

Character and Behavior

Unfortunately, the ability to make moral decisions does not guarantee that such decisions will be made. One can identify the moral thing to do but still not do it. Moral behavior is partially an outgrowth of moral character. From this point of view, personality type controls actions. People act lovingly as opposed to hatefully because they are loving people. They act trusting rather than doubting because they are trusting persons. They act unselfishly as opposed to self-centeredly because they are unselfish people. "I am, therefore I do." This is the same philosophy as the one which emphasizes that "by their fruits you shall know them." Goodness begins inside and is expressed by persons in their everyday lives. Whatever parents do, therefore, which helps children to grow to be loving, trusting, caring persons is, in a very real sense, moral education.

Teaching Moral Behavior

But moral behavior may also be encouraged by efforts on the part of parents to teach their children how to behave in moral ways. This involves imparting the knowledge and understanding of what is right and wrong. It involves motivating children to do what they know is right. It involves sensitizing the conscience to act as a guide when parents are not present. It involves developing moral habits of thought and conduct. It involves training in self-discipline and impulse control and in resisting temptation. It involves the development of specific virtues, such as honesty, kindness, or industry. But the important question is: How? There are primarily five methods by which parents teach moral behavior (Kagan, 1971, p. 156).

Instruction

One is through verbal instruction: telling children what is right and what is wrong, describing what they should do and not do, explaining to them the reasons why certain behavior is desirable or undesirable. Here also, verbal instruction is more effective within the context of a warm, loving parent-child relationship. Children are more likely to want to follow their parents when they love and admire them than when the opposite relationship exists.

Verbal instruction is also most effective when it is clearly given, readily understood, and accepted. As every parent knows, just telling children how to behave does not ensure compliance. The message may be completely misunderstood, either because the parent has not made it clear or because the child is distracted and not listening. Or, if understood, the message may be rejected as undesirable, unnecessary, or impossible to follow. Any one of these may be the reason why children don't follow what parents say.

Rewards

The second way parents teach is by using rewards: giving verbal praise and recognition, bestowing attention and love, or offering physical or monetary remuneration. Suppose, for example, that a girl finds a purse with some money in it. She decides to return it, and, in exchange, the owner compliments her: "You are a wonderful girl to be so honest and return my purse." The girl feels pride in herself and experiences a warm feeling inside. If the owner gives her a reward, she feels doubly blessed. Then when she gets home and her parents learn of what she has done, she becomes the object of their special attention and love. "We're very pleased at what you've done. Here's a big hug and kiss. Mother is going to cook your favorite supper to show you how proud we are of you." All of these things together: praise, recognition, the monetary reward, the special attention and love her parents give her, plus the favorite dinner which her mother cooks, make the girl very glad that she returned the purse and act as a stimulus for performing subsequent acts of honesty.

Most children need some incentives for doing what is considered "right" or "good." Verbal recognition and praise are certainly two of the most effective. Eventually, as "right" actions become habitual, the self-satisfaction gained becomes the reward.

What about giving children money or gifts for doing what is expected or for being good?

I don't object to paying children for doing work, but I do object to rewarding them in this way for proper conduct or behavior. A child who is paid for being good soon expects to be paid on all such occasions, or he or she develops the habit of not doing good unless he or she is paid. I would rather give verbal praise or special privileges as a direct result of responsible, moral behavior. These rewards build self-confidence and self-esteem and stimulate proper behavior for its own sake.

Punishment

The third way parents teach is by using punishment. "Whether the punishment be spanking, threat of rejection, or deprivation of goals, the anxiety generated by anticipated punishment usually leads to inhibition of the undesirable response and, in some cases, to substitution of an acceptable act" (Kagan, 1971, p. 156).

Suppose that a boy tells a lie. His parents find out about it, give him a mild spanking, a severe scolding and reprimand, and send him to his room for the afternoon. His bottom hurts a little, he feel anxious and guilty because he had done wrong and his parents are mad at him, he misses their presence and approval, and he regrets his actions because he can't get out of his room. All of these factors make him regret his action and build his resolve not to lie to his parents again.

Guilt, such as the boy experienced in the above example, is necessary in order to prevent subsequent wrongdoing. The guilt was stimulated by a combination of punishments, the most important of which was the verbal scolding, and the subsequent loss of the love and approval of the parents. Since all normal children seek love and approval, they will ordinarily try to adjust their behavior to win such approval. If they do wrong, they lose approval, and they will be unhappy and will be stimulated to modify their actions the next time.

Scolding or disapproval has a real advantage over a physical punishment, such as spanking. Disapproval is not a quick and tangible punishment. The feelings of regret remain, leaving a child with unhappy feelings that can only be removed through attempting to get back into the good graces of parents by trying to please them. Isolation in his or her room also gives the child a chance to think about his or her wrongdoing, and he or she is stimulated to do better in the future.

Of course, disapproval can be counterproductive and destructive to the child's ego if parents never forgive, never feel the child has offered sufficient atonement, and never approve. In this case, the child's anxiety and guilt are continuous, and he develops a feeling of constant failure and rejection. He may even give up trying to please and may become completely antisocial or incorrigible. This is why disapproval needs to be followed by acceptance and reconciliation.

A spanking is a quick and tangible punishment that rights the balance, since it is payment for wrongdoing. However, since payment has been made, there may be no cause for guilt, so there is not as much stimulus to do right the next time. Another disadvantage to physical punishment is that unless it is accompanied by verbal explanation, a particularly young child may not connect it to the wrongdoing. Parents who ask: "Why are you being punished?" often learn that their children don't really know why, so the spanking has accomplished nothing. Of course, if physical punishment is harsh and cruel, especially if it is accompanied by parental rejection, it develops immature, hostile, rebellious, cruel persons, just the opposite of what truly socialized, moral persons ought to be.

The most effective teaching uses both rewards and appropriate punishments. The parents assist moral development by consistently emphasizing what they consider to be right or wrong as they guide their children's behavior. Eventually, children internalize (believe and accept both intellectually and emotionally) these messages from their parents. After that, the children's own inner standards will reward them by allowing them to feel good when they do right and punish them by causing them to feel bad when they do wrong.

Example

The fourth way parents teach is through example. Parents live and behave in certain ways. As their children *identify* with their parents, they *imitate* them and *model* their lives and behavior after them. One parent said: "Figure out what kind of a person you want your child to become, be that yourself, and he will be like you when he grows up." This is most likely to happen if children are in close contact with their parents and if they admire their parents and want to be like them. Sometimes, parents evidence the kind of character and behavior that children dislike, so that the children reject the parental image and resolve *not* to be like them. Even then, it is hard for the children to break away completely from the parents' influence and not to adopt some parental characteristics, even though these may be negative. One thirty-year study of adults who had been referred as children to a clinic because of antisocial behavior showed that the father's antisocial behavior was the most significant factor in predicting the antisocial behavior of these individuals (Robbins, 1966).

Most often, children identify with their own parent of the same sex. Boys imitate their fathers. Girls imitate their mothers. One author describes his observation of a father and son out for a walk.

One afternoon I was amusing myself by watching a four-year-old child and his father out for a walk. The father had his hands in his jacket pockets and walked with his head down. Occasionally he kicked at a stone on the sidewalk. Similarly, his four-year-old son had his hands in his pockets, walked with his head down, and occasionally kicked at a stone. It was as if the same person was being represented in two sizes: full size and miniature. . . .

Watching the two was both heartwarming and very instructive. It was heartwarming to see that the child wanted to be like his father. The father and his son probably had a very positive relationship. It was instructive in that the child's imitation of his father's actions showed how very important parents are for providing cues which influence their children's behavior. Our children observe what we do and, if the situation is right, they often repeat our actions. Like it or not, whenever we are around our children, they are learning from us. What our children learn might not be intentionally taught, but they are certainly learning [Norton, 1977, p. 130].

Much of what children learn is acquired by imitating their parents. Children mimic their parents' speech, and they even develop speech habits and accents similar to those of their parents. They dress up to look like their parents and play house, repeating the same words and actions that they have observed in their parents. They absorb parental attitudes and values about almost everything. Often their recreational interests and even their hobbies are a reflection of parental concerns. Whether parents realize it or not, they are teaching their children by what they do as well as by what they say.

If I get a baby sitter a great deal so that I can work while my daughter is young, won't the sitter become her model rather than me?

The sitter will act as a model for the child but will not ordinarily replace the modeling role of the mother. Rather, the modeling role of the sitter is supplementary to that of the mother. If the mother loves her daughter, cares for her, and spends time with her when she is at home, she will always be the primary attachment figure and exert the greatest influence. The only time this does not happen is when the mother abrogates almost all responsibility and never allows her daughter to develop a close, caring relationship with her.

The mother will discover, however, that the sitter exerts an important influence (Murray, 1975). Many speech habits, mannerisms, attitudes, values, and behavior patterns will be learned from the sitter. This is why it is important that the mother employ the type of person for a sitter that she feels is a good influence on her child. Otherwise, negative teachings may have to be unlearned.

Experience

The fifth way that parents teach is by providing experiences, opportunities for doing, for practice. Children learn many things through experience. When parents want to teach their child to ride a bicycle, they can give a certain amount of verbal instructions, but they then sit their child on the bike and encourage him or her to ride. Eventually, the only way the child can learn to ride is by riding.

Many moral virtues and habits can be taught through practice. The way to teach children to share is to give them opportunities to practice sharing with others. When I was a boy, my parents encouraged me to decide how much of my weekly allowance I was going to set aside to put in the collection at Sunday School. I was asked to sign a pledge card, even if it was only five cents a week. I was given a package of envelopes, one for each week, in which to put my money. My mother made it clear that I was responsible for keeping my pledge, for putting in my own money. By encouraging such a practice over the years, my mother was teaching me to share a part of what I had.

Some parents make the mistake of doing such things for their children. By so doing, they prevent their children from having a chance to learn for themselves. Most virtues can be taught best by parents encouraging children to practice them from the time they are young.

8

Some Questions of Discipline

MEANING AND PURPOSE

Teaching

The word *discipline* comes from the same root as does the word disciple, which means a "learner." Discipline, therefore, is a process of teaching, of education, a means by which socialization takes place. Its purpose is to instruct in proper conduct or action. Its ultimate goal is to sensitize the conscience and to develop inner controls so that individuals live according to the standards of behavior established by their groups (Rice, 1979a, p. 568).

From one point of view, discipline is one means by which parents show that they love their children and are concerned about them (Salk, 1975, p. 176). This sounds strange to some parents. They feel that to show love means to express affection or to give things to their children. But it also means to share one's ideas, attitudes, habits, and expectations. It includes guidance, preparing children to live with others in the world, and teaching them how to act in a socially acceptable fashion.

Control

Discipline may mean control. Without control, babies creep and toddle into danger, whether it be under a moving car or into a nearby swimming pool. Little fingers get into electric sockets or touch hot stoves. Without control, older children get into trouble. Just yesterday, a teen-age boy, a friend of our daughter, was taxied home, safe but quite drunk, from a New Year's Eve party. Unfortunately, the boy got into an argument with his father upon arriving home. He became angry, jumped into his car, and sped away at 100 miles an hour. The father tried to dissuade him from driving, and later he tried to go after him. But it was too late. The boy wrapped the car around a tree and was killed instantly.

Without control, life itself may be impossible. Discipline teaches children that living imposes limitations, that freedom is impossible without responsibility. It defines, sets, teaches, and controls the limits of behavior, and it encourages a cooperative responsible use of free will.

Punishment

Some persons confuse discipline with punishment, especially with physical punishment. Parents may use various methods of punishment, such as spanking, grounding, isolation, sending the child to his or her room, or denial of privileges. But it is possible to discipline without using any punishment at all. As one mother said: "I accomplish far more by just talking to my children than by using any form of punishment."

Actually, first asking children to do something and then seeing that they do it is discipline—and very effective discipline, too, because it achieves results.

STRICTNESS VERSUS PERMISSIVENESS

Parental Differences

One of the questions parents face is how strict to be in disciplining their children. Some parents have been brought up very strictly and strive to raise their own children the same way. Other parents are quite permissive. They seldom place any restrictions at all upon their children's actions or freedom, either because they aren't able to, because they are afraid to, because they don't want to, or because they don't see the need to, for one reason or another. The various types of parents, as related to discipline, may be divided into three groups, as follows (Norton, 1977, p. 3).

Authoritarian. These parents attempt to shape, control, and evaluate the behavior and attitudes of children according to an absolute standard. They value obedience and favor punitive, forceful measures to curb their children's self-will when it conflicts with what the parents think is right conduct. These parents believe that children should accept their word for what is right, without verbal discussion (Baumrind, 1971).

Permissive. These parents attempt to accept their children's impulses, desires, and actions in a nonpunitive way. They allow their children to regulate themselves as much as possible, using discussion and reason in explaining family rules, without overpowering the children's desires or demanding household responsibilities or orderly behavior (Baumrind, 1971).

Authoritative. These parents attempt to direct their children's activities in a rational, issue-oriented manner, encouraging verbal discussion in explaining policies to them. They exert firm control but do not hem children in with restrictions. They recognize children's rights and interests, but they also set standards for future conduct (Baumrind, 1971).

Which Type?

Research on the effects of each style of parenting on the behavior of children has shown that the parents of children who are the most self-reliant, self-controlled, explorative, and content are the parents who are authoritative (Barton et al., 1977). Permissive parents have children who are the least explorative, self-reliant, and self-controlled. Authoritarian parents have children who are the most discontented, withdrawn, and distrustful (Norton, 1977, p. 4). These findings indicate that firm but fair enforcement of parental policies most facilitates the development of socially responsible behavior.

Other investigations reveal this same fact: that firm but fair discipline seems to produce the best results. One study of over 500 teenagers showed that parents who accepted their children and who used firm but not hostile control, tended to have children with superior academic motivation who were ambitious, who worked hard and effectively, and who were obedient and law-abiding (Nuttall & Nuttall, 1976).

Authoritarian Discipline

Interestingly enough, both authoritarian discipline and overpermissiveness on the part of parents produce negative results. Parents who try to overcontrol their children, especially those who use harsh, unfair measures that are administered coldly, without love and affection, produce hostile, disturbed, angry, unhappy children (Medinnus & Johnson, 1969, p. 386). Punitive and severe parental discipline builds up a store of hostility which stimulates aggressive impulses that are directed toward others. Furthermore, children imitate the behavior which they observe in parents, so that hostile parents produce aggressive children (Grotberg, 1971, p. 117). Parents who use cruel punishment have succeeded only in providing an example of cruelty for their children to follow.

Permissiveness

Overpermissiveness also produces negative results. Children who are not guided and who are spoiled and pampered are ill prepared to accept frustrations or responsibility, or to show proper regard for others. They become domineering, self-centered, and selfish. They get in trouble with others who won't pamper them the way their parents have. Without guidance, they often feel insecure and confused. They often interpret their parents' lack of control as disinterest, and they end up blaming their parents for not preparing them for life (Rice, 1979a, p. 417). Lax discipline, rejection, and lack of parental affection have also been associated with delinquency (McCord & McCord, 1964).

CAUSES OF BEHAVIOR

The methods of discipline which parents use are not the whole issue. Discipline itself, by whatever method, does not always produce positive results. One of the reasons for this is that discipline may treat the symptoms but not get at the causes of behavior. If the causes are not found and corrected, parents may find that no method of discipline produces permanent results, so they need to dig deeper in order to eliminate the reasons for the misbehavior in the first place.

Causes of misbehavior may be grouped into two categories, according to whether the reasons are major or minor. The major causes of misbehavior include fear, resentment or hostility, and tension in the home. The minor causes of misbehavior are boredom, fatigue, curiosity, and the desire for independence.

Major Causes

These reasons are considered major because they are very influential in affecting children's misbehavior and because they are sometimes difficult to overcome. *Fear* can result in misbehavior in children. The fear may be of loss of love, of strangers, of new situations, of punishment, of being hurt, or of natural phenomena, such as the dark.

I'll never forget 5-year-old Susie's first day in kindergarten. In spite of her young age, Susie was a big, husky girl, with straight, bobbed hair, a round face, and a very square, determined chin. Upon arrival on her first day, Susie announced that her mother told her she didn't really have to go to kindergarten. Whenever I asked her to do something, she would stamp her foot, grit her teeth, and exclaim: "No, my mother says I don't have to." This behavior continued for the first several days of school. What was wrong? Actully, Susie was frightened—of her new surroundings, of her teacher, and of the other children. Her defense was to withdraw, to remain quite uncooperative, and to blame her mother for her behavior.

Children who are insecurely attached to their mothers may fear loss of love when the mother goes to work, and they may act horribly to try to keep their mother at home. Contrary to popular concepts of them, these children are not spoiled. They are just the opposite: They are very much in need of mother's attention and affection. Small children who get up repeatedly after being put to bed may be afraid of being alone or afraid of the dark. They can't be considered "bad." They are motivated not by a desire to be rebellious and to disobey their parents, but by anxiety and fear.

Resentment or hostility may arise from any number of incidences and result in antisocial behavior. One mother brought her 9-year-old son, Hank, to see me because he was always getting into fights at Vacation Bible School. But there was a significant pattern to his behavior. Hank usually got into fights while trying to protect younger children. In talking to the boy, I discovered that his parents were very critical of him and that they constantly belittled him at home, a fact which he resented. He was made to feel very "naughty" and guilty. But in church school, he was considered a big shot because he was older and stronger than many other children, who looked up to him. Whenever they got into any kind of trouble, they would report: "That other boy (girl) hit me," and Hank would go to his or her aid and punish the offending child. This was his way of feeling important to himself and in the eyes of his friends, even if it got him into trouble.

In another instance, a mother was concerned because her 2-year-old daughter had not yet begun to walk. The girl would crawl all over the house but would not stand up. Investigation of the total family situation revealed that a 4-year-old son in the same family was jealous of his baby sister and resented her terribly. Just by chance, while the mother was out of the room, I watched while the 2-year-old pulled herself up by holding to the top rail of the playpen. The 4-year-old ran over to the play pen, pounded his sister's hands, and forced her to let go and to fall. This incident proved to be the key to why baby sister wouldn't walk. Every time she tried, she was hit by her jealous older brother! Resentment because of jealousy of a sibling is often the reason for very antisocial behavior. If parents punish children for jealousy, the resentment increases, and the wrong behavior often gets worse. The only way to solve the problem is to try to eliminate the cause, and the behavior will usually improve.

Children will become very resentful if they feel their parents are unfair to them. I remember one 10-year-old whose grades in school dropped very sharply when her parents did not give her a new bicycle for her birthday, as had been promised. The parents had not bothered to explain the reason: that the family income had been sharply reduced and that they couldn't buy the bike but that they would at a later date, as income improved. As a result, the girl's bitterness resulted in her poorer school work.

Tension in the family is another major cause of antisocial behavior. I remember one mother who would get so upset when she and her husband quarreled that she would run to her 5-year-old son and scream: "Your father is trying to kill me!" It wasn't true at all. The mother was obviously mentally disturbed, but is it any wonder that the boy was nervous and did not get along very well with other children in school? Whatever upsets parents affects the behavior of their children. It is no accident that calm, relaxed, happy parents usually have the calmest, best-behaved children.

Parents have to remember that behavior is caused. Whenever ordinary methods of discipline seem ineffective, parents should suspect deeper reasons for their children's behavior and try to uncover and correct the causes. The behavior will usually improve.

Minor Causes

Not all causes of antisocial behavior are as important as those in the examples just given. Some causes are minor but are nevertheless quite common. Most can be corrected fairly easily. One common cause is *boredom*. Children get into trouble because they have nothing better to do. The solution is to find worthwhile activities. This doesn't mean that parents have to entertain their children whenever they get bored, but it does help if parents provide supplies and opportunities for children to entertain themselves. One couple always takes a bag of crayons, paper, and several new toys along whenever they go to visit grandmother. Their children become so occupied with their playthings that they don't have time to get into trouble. Older children who are bored need more group activities and more work and responsibility. One important reason why some adolescents get into trouble is the lack of job opportunities for them. If they were busy working, they wouldn't have so much free time to get into mischief.

Fatigue is a frequent cause of misbehavior. Tired, hungry chldren are not "bad" children, but they are very difficult to control. There's no point in punishing them. Feed them and/or put them to bed.

Natural *curiosity* stimulates children to get into things that they shouldn't. Left unsupervised, an active toddler may pull every book off low-lying shelves, remove the pans from the kitchen cabinet, or make utter chaos out of mother's jewelry box or cold cream. Some children have a passion for removing knobs from television sets and stereos. One mother is presently complaining that her 4-year-old is driving her crazy because he wants to take everything apart with his screwdriver. The other day he crawled under the kitchen table and removed the screws from the table legs. The table collapsed. Is the boy a "bad" child? No, but he certainly needs a lot of socially acceptable ways of satisfying his almost insatiable curiosity!

Much rebellious behavior is due to a *desire for independence*. This is certainly true of adolescents, but it is also true of children who are 2 years of age, which is the age when many children start stamping their feet and saying "No. Me do." The only way in which children can become persons in their own right is to exert their own will, to try to express their own desires, and to achieve some degree of autonomy. Obviously, no 2-year-olds and few adolescents are old enough to use freedom responsibly without some control by parents. But adolescents need some freedom, along with guidance. If they are restricted too closely, as already described under the section on authoritarian discipline, they become very resentful, hostile, and rebellious, so whenever parents aren't around, they express their negative feelings in very antisocial ways, which may get them into serious trouble.

SOME APPROACHES TO DISCIPLINE

Deciding What Is Important

Before parents can be effective disciplinarians, they have to decide what they consider most important for their children to learn. Some parents discipline their children severely for trivial things and completeley overlook important things. One mother told me that the only time her husband takes any interest in the children is when they're noisy and bother him while he's watching TV. He explodes, takes off his belt, and gives them a severe beating. "One of these days, I'm afraid he's going to injure them seriously," the mother explained. Yet this same father took no interest in his children's schoolwork or in their friends.

It is certainly possible to overlook important goals, so parents should spend considerable time discussing their objectives in child rearing and deciding what they expect of their children as they grow up. Writing down overall goals and expectations and outlining important household rules clarifies expectations so that both parents and children remember them.

Older children and teen-agers can be included in the discussion, and some consideration can be given to their opinions in arriving at decisions.

Assuming Joint Responsibility

In the household where there are two parents, it is helpful if both share in disciplining the children. For one thing, it is not fair to expect that one person be the "executioner" and carry out all decrees of punishment. One boy remarked: "I was always afraid of my father because he was the one who disciplined us." For another thing, it is unwise to delay discipline by telling children: "Wait until your mother comes home". The parent who is baby-sitting the children when incidents arise is the one who ought to take corrective action—and the sooner the better. In particular, young children may not remember what they are being disciplined for if daddy "waits until mother comes home."

Considering the Ages of Children

The particular methods employed will partially depend on the ages of the children. Distraction may work for infants, but it is useless as children get older. Moving breakables is possible for toddlers, but it is futile for older children who climb all over the house. Preschoolers can be disciplined by environmental manipulation: by removing the situation from the child or the child from the situation. The older children are, the more they can be guided by reasonable discussion and verbal communications. Parents should strive to give simple, clear directions to explain and defend their own points of view when challenged by their children, and to keep the channels of communication open by listening to their children's explanations and reasons.

Controlling Voice and Facial Expressions

Tone of voice and facial expressions are also helpful ways of getting a message across. It is confusing to children if parents say "no" while smiling. Most schoolteachers learn that expressions and voice tones should match the content of the message they are trying to communicate. One teacher explained: "When I'm trying to impress the children, I never crack a smile. I look serious and stern. If I don't, the children think I don't mean it."

This does not mean that parents need to shout. Some parents get so used to shouting at their children that the children learn to tune them out and to ignore what is being said. A simple message delivered in a firm manner at a reasonable level of sound is more often received and understood by children than one delivered at the top of one's lungs. I remember that I was always impressed by teachers who got the attention of their classes by whispering. Instead of shouting over the children's noise, they began lowering their voices and letting the children quiet down so that they could be heard. The system worked. The soft tones had a soothing effect and also conveyed readily understood directions.

Frowning or looks of displeasure can also be effective means of discipline. One study of methods of discipline used by teachers compared the effectiveness of isolating a child for a few minutes versus using an exaggerated show of displeasure (frowning, leaning forward, and looking right at a child for ten seconds without saying a word). The results showed that the latter method was every bit as effective as punishing children by using isolation (Norton, 1977, p. 120).

Avoiding Re-enforcement of Negative Behavior

I have already discussed, in Chapter 7, the importance of using positive re-enforcement: praise, recognition, encouragement, and rewards of various kinds as ways of stimulating desirable behavior. At the same time, parents need to avoid giving re-enforcement to undesirable behavior.

Let us suppose that children use words that parents find offensive. Every time they do, the parents make a big fuss over it, a fact that doesn't go unnoticed by the children. Henceforth, the children discover that whenever they feel rejected and ignored and want to get their parent's attention, they only have to repeat the bad language, and the parents are right there, paying attention. This kind of parental behavior is unwittingly stimulating and encourages undesirable behavior in children. Sometimes it is best for parents to ignore bad language and to give special attention to proper language, so that children will be encouraged to use it instead.

The following anecdote illustrates both an unwise and a wise use of re-enforcement.

Danny, ten, kept Mother in a constant state of uneasiness. He frequently failed to obey her order to come home directly from school. One day it was five thirty and Danny still had not come home. Mother was frantic. Since the boy rode his bicycle to school she was absolutely sure that he had been struck by a car. She had just decided to call the local hospital when Danny came in, his pants and shoes soaked and muddy. He carried a jar of filthy-looking water. "Danny! Where in the world have you been? It's five thirty! I've been absolutely frantic. Where were you?" "I went down to that pond we saw on the highway. Look, I got some tadpoles." "How many times have I told you to come home after school and to let me know where you are?" Mother demanded angrily. "You have no right to worry me like this!" Danny's face remained passive as Mother continued her tirade.

> The following day Mother attended a Guidance Center with a friend. A similar problem came up in the discussion. Mother received an idea. She was cheerful whenever Danny came home. But once, when he was late, she was gone! (Dreikurs, 1964, p. 271).

Mother had learned that making a fuss over Danny's tardiness reinforced his negative behavior. By being cheerful and giving attention only when he arrived on time, she gave positive reinforcement to proper behavior.

Avoiding a Power Struggle

Parents can get themselves in a real bind if their efforts to discipline result in a continuing power struggle or a battle of wills between themselves and their children (Ginott, 1969). One of the emphases in the Parent Effectiveness Training program (P.E.T. program) is the "No-Lose" method of solving conflicts (Gordon, 1975, p. 194). This approach emphasizes resolving conflicts with children through discussion in efforts to arrive at a joint decision through mutual agreement. Parents aren't required to sell the solution to their children or to use power to force compliance, because the children have had a part in the decision and have already accepted it. Such an approach treats children as equals, develops their thinking skills, encourages more love, and minimizes hostility. Furthermore, children are more likely to be motivated to carry out the decision because they have participated in making it (Gordon, 1975, p. 201). The following conversation (Gordon, 1975, p. 229) is given as an illustration of how the method can be used even with young children.

> Cathy: *I don't want to go to my baby sitter's anymore.*
> Mother: *You don't like going to Mrs. Crockett's house when I go to work.*

Cathy: No, I don't want to go.
Mother: I need to go to work and you can't stay at home, but you are sure unhappy about staying there. Is there something we could do to make it easier for you to stay there?
Cathy: (silence): I could stay on the sidewalk until you drive away.
Mother: But Mrs. Crockett needs you to be inside with the other children so she knows where you are.
Cathy: I could watch from the window when you drive away.
Mother: Will that make you feel better?
Cathy: Yes.
Mother: Okay. Let's try that next time.

But what if your kid runs into the street in front of a car? Don't you have to use power methods in preventing a tragedy?

Yes, of course. Crisis situations demand immediate and firm parental action: bodily removal of the child from the street. But I emphasize that, prior to such a crisis, parents can use nonpower methods of trying to prevent children from going into the street in the first place: talking about the danger, showing a picture of a child hit by a car, watching the children play in the front yard for a couple of days, and reminding them each time they go beyond the limits (Gordon, 1975, p. 232).

Some Do's and Don'ts

If discipline is to accomplish its purpose of developing inner controls, there are a number of principles that will enhance this development.

Discipline is more effective when it is consistent rather than erratic. Variable rules or erratic enforcement of them confuse children, since the children are never really certain what is expected of them. Here is a good example of discipline that is ineffective because enforcement is inconsistent.

> Mother was completely fed up with the struggle to get Alex and Harry out of bed in the morning. She had attended a Guidance Center where she received an idea that she decided to put into practice. She bought an alarm clock and told the boys that it would be up to them to set their alarm and get themselves up. The next morning she heard the alarm go off and then stop ringing. She listened and waited. Nothing further happened. Finally, a half-hour later, she realized that the boys had fallen asleep again. She wakened them. "I told you that you would have to get yourselves up and I meant it. Your alarm went off a half-hour ago. No, come on. Get up!" (Dreikurs, 1964, p. 255)

In this example, the mother didn't really mean it when she said that the boys would have to get themselves up. She still took the responsibility. She should have left them alone after they shut off the alarm. If they didn't get up for school, they should have suffered the consequences.

Parents should never make threats that they can't or won't keep. Suppose, for example, that children want a pet dog. They are told that they can have one if they promise to feed it, clean up after it, and take care of it. They do keep their promise for several weeks, but as the newness wears off, they gradually neglect their pet. Mother finds herself assuming more and more responsibility. She prods and reminds the children, but they still forget. Finally, one day she threatens to get rid of the dog if the children don't take care of it. They respond by caring for the dog for two more days. By the end of the week, the mother has resigned herself to caring for the animal because she can't bring herself to getting rid of it.

In this case, the discipline was completely useless because the mother didn't follow through with her threats. The children ended up learning that it was all right to be irresponsible and to break a promise. The moral is: Before threatening, parents should think about whether or not they can, or should, follow through with their threat. If they aren't able to, or shouldn't, they should never threaten in the first place.

Parents also need to back one another up. Children are experts at playing one parent against the other. They check first with one parent, then the other. Suppose the first parent says "No," but the second parent says "Yes." Naturally, the child will feel that permission has been granted by the "Yes." But in saying "Yes," the second parent has completely undermined the discipline of the first. For this reason, parents need to check with each other before giving a quick answer. If one parent has already made a decision, the other should back it up, even if the second disagrees. Their differences can be worked out later in private discussion. Better still, parents and children can discuss the issue together so that whatever decision is made is known to all.

Discipline is more effective if parental requests are sparse, but reasonable. Some parents make so many requests in rapid-fire succession that the children don't have a chance to carry out the first before they are given others. Parents can't follow through on so many requests. They may even forget what they have asked their children to do or not to do. In such cases, the requests are futile. Whatever is requested ought to be made with the expectation of compliance. Children will soon learn that parents mean what they say.

Parents need to make use of logical, natural consequences as an aid in discipline. Suppose children get a certain amount of money for their allowance but spend it all before the week is over. They should have to wait until the next week for more. I know a number of parents who always make excuses for their children when they do wrong or always bail them out or cover up for them when they get into trouble. Suppose a child doesn't do assignments in school and receives a failing grade as a result. The parent reports the teacher to the principal and makes such a fuss that the teacher hesitates to give a failing grade again, even though the child deserves it. Such parents prevent children from learning by having to suffer the consequences of their actions.

Parents need to learn not to take sides when siblings fight. In fact, unless the children are in danger of hurting one another, it's better to stay out of their fights completely. Parents can never really find out who started what and who's to blame. If they take sides, this creates further resentment and trouble. Children usually forgive and forget very quickly if parents don't interfere. If fighting continues, it's always more effective to discipline all of the children who are involved. This way, the children know that they will all suffer the consequences, and they won't be able to tell tales on one another and get one another in trouble.

Parents should avoid using methods that threaten children's self-esteem. Belittling, repeated criticism, or sarcastic remarks are examples of disciplinary measures that undermine children's egos and are harmful because they destroy self-confidence. Parents should also avoid measures that undermine children's security:

> "If you don't mind, I'm going away and never come back."
> "You better be good or I'll call the policeman and he'll put you in jail."

Such measures may be temporarily effective in controlling behavior, but they are devastating to children's senses of security and well-being, so they should never be used.

DISCIPLINE AND THE WORKING MOTHER

Very typically, children of working mothers present some special disciplinary problems because their mothers are at

work so much. The following are typical examples of problems that children present.
1. They may demand much special attention and care from their mothers as soon as mother comes home. This is why I suggest that a mother devote the first hour or so after arriving home exclusively to the children. The more the mother tries to ignore her children or push them away, the more demanding they become.
2. Children are often tired, irritable, and fussy after they have been in a day-care center or nursery school or after they have been cared for by another person. The sooner the children can be fed, the better. Snacks in the afternoon help to prevent fatigue and irritability. Or the sitter can feed the children before the mother comes home; that way, they usually aren't as tired and fussy if she arrives home late.
3. The children may be rebellious and uncooperative and won't do what the parents say. This is especially true if the children are anxious about the mother being gone. Parents have to be more patient and understanding than usual, and they should be careful not to punish children for separation anxiety or for feelings of rejection. Children often get into fights with siblings after the mother has gone, and they may show increased tendencies to be jealous of one another. Parents have to be especially careful not to show partiality. Parents may have to resort to punishing all the children if any one fights with another.
4. Sometimes, children refuse to mind the sitter. Mother has to leave strict orders to obey the sitter and to acknowledge her authority.
5. Children often call the mother at work whenever

they are having problems and want her to settle things then and there. If calling becomes excessive, mother may have to lay down some strong rules about children not calling except in cases of emergencies or of calling only certain persons or at particular hours.

6. Children are often dirty and disorderly and leave a mess for the mother to clean up when she gets home. She should expect, from the beginning, that the children will do their share of the household chores and that they will keep things as neat as she has left them. Older children ought to be asked to take over part of the total responsibilities, such as cleaning, doing the laundry, or preparing the dinner before the mother gets home.

7. Most children want to have friends over while the mother is away. Most parents object, either because it's not fair to the sitter or because they are afraid the children will get into mischief when not supervised. Policies need to be carefully discussed and clarified so that children know what is acceptable.

8. Children who consider themselves too old for sitters but who are not old enough to care for themselves present special problems. Will a child be allowed to go to another's house or to have a friend over to stay with him or her? In some cases, special arrangements can be made with neighbors, or others, so that the children know whom to call if there is trouble. One good solution is to hire a sitter old enough to be completely responsible but young enough to provide good companionship to the children. An example

might be to hire a high school student to keep a sixth grader company. Many problems can be avoided by working things out ahead of time and by leaving clear instructions.

9

Sex Education

SOURCES OF INFORMATION

Where do children get their information about sex?

A survey of nearly a thousand college students from twelve different major universities in the United States revealed that the student's initial sources of sex information were the following: 37.8 percent of the total information came from peers, 20.9 percent from literature, 19.5 percent from school, 15.5 percent from parents (primarily from the mother), 5 percent from experiences, and the remainder from physicians and ministers (Thornburg, 1975, p. 316). When students were asked what kinds of information were provided by each source, the following results were obtained.

Mothers provided information primarily to their daughters, and this was on menstruation and the origin of babies, with little information given on other subjects.

Fathers were a fairly insignificant source of all types of information for both boys and girls.

Peer groups were the primary sources of information about such subjects as sexual intercourse, contraception, ejaculation, homosexuality, masturbation, and prostitution. Boys were more dependent on peers for this information than girls were.

The schools preferred to stick to health and hygiene subjects, such as venereal disease, menstruation, and abortion, offering very little information on petting and intercourse.

Increasing amounts of information were obtained by both boys and girls from literature (Thornburg, 1975, p. 319).

The significant thing about this study is the small percentage of initial sex information (15.5 percent) which came from parents. Only 2.1 percent of all information came from the father. Apparently, parents only pay lip service to the philosophy that sex education belongs in the home. If it does, it certainly isn't taking place there, except by default.

GOALS

Since sex education is such a controversial subject, it might be well to look at some important reasons why it is needed and at what it attempts to accomplish.

Attitudes

One of the important purposes of sex education is to help children to develop healthy attitudes about the body and its functions. All children are curious about their own bodies. Infants will spend hours looking at their own hands. They will learn that they can move their hands as well as open and close them. They try to put their hands into their mouths and suck on them. They also discover other body parts. Babies may spend long periods of time examining their navels or playing with their toes.

In the process of exploration, children also discover their genitals. They are curious about them, and they touch them and play with them, but no more so than in relation to other body parts. However, if a mother says: "That's nasty, don't do that" and spanks her daughter's hand when she scratches her itchy vagina, or if a mother reprimands her son for playing with his penis, the children begin to learn that some parts of the body are not to be examined, that they are somehow different than other parts, that they are nasty and dirty, and that "nice boys and girls" shouldn't be interested in these body parts. Consequently, as children grow up, they learn that anything having to do with their organs of reproduction is somehow "evil" and "bad."

The same negative attitudes may develop with respect to other normal body functions. Human feces becomes "shit." Menstruation becomes the "curse". Sexual intercourse becomes "fuck." Children learn to be embarrassed about their bodies. They learn to repress sexual interests, and they grow up with the attitude that anything having to do with human reproduction is a forbidden subject.

Both boys and girls are interested in each other's bodies. Their interest is a naive innocence. Little girls look with intense interest, certainly not with lust, at baby brother's penis, or they are amazed when they discover that daddy can urinate standing up. They may even try to imitate him next time they go to the bathroom.

The parent's role is to accept children's curiosity as quite normal and to be very matter of fact about the body, nudity, and bodily functions. Certainly there is no harm in preschoolers seeing one another or their parents nude. If parents find their children touching themselves, the best thing to do is nothing. It should be of no concern at all. It is quite normal and harmless.

Then, as children grow older and want privacy, they

should have it. Reasonable modesty is a good thing, but excessive modesty can be quite harmful. There are adult women who won't go to a physician until the final stages of pregnancy because of their excessive modesty. Yet adequate prenatal care is vital to the health of the mother and the baby during the early stages of pregnancy. Excessive modesty, then, can be quite harmful. How many men and women never make a happy sexual adjustment in marriage because of negative conditioning about sexual matters? I've known married couples who've never seen one another undressing or undressed. Any sexual activity always took place in total darkness. Such attitudes are detrimental to loving, uninhibited, pleasurable sexual relations in marriage. How important it is, therefore, for parents to develop healthy attitudes and feelings in their child.

Physical Development

Sex education can also help children to understand the process of the physical development of their own bodies and to prepare for the bodily changes at puberty. Parents need to explain such things as menstruation and nocturnal emissions. A girl who has not been prepared for menstruation ahead of time may become very frightened or embarrassed. She's afraid that she's bleeding to death or that she has been injured. She's embarrassed that she has stained her clothes, and she is too fearful to tell the teacher. One girl was sent home by the school nurse, and when the girl told her mother what had happened, the mother slapped her soundly across the face and warned: "Don't you dare ever talk about that again." The girl was devastated. One teen-age boy thought he had wet the bed when he had a nocturnal emission. His father whipped him severely and told him not to let that happen again. Years later, this same boy, now married, was not able to ejaculate during intercourse.

Parents should try to explain bodily changes *before* such changes take place. Children need information and need to have fears and anxieties minimized. Preteens who mature earlier or later than their peers worry that they are abnormal. Parents can help their children to understand the variations in maturation rates and can counsel them so they are not anxious.

Young people are also very worried about their builds. Girls worry about being flat-chested, but they are also embarrassed if they develop overly large breasts. Boys worry about being slimmer, shorter, taller, or weaker than others. Both sexes worry about such health problems as acne or obesity. It's terribly hard to go through high school being called "Fatso." So another important parental role is to see that adequate medical and health care are provided those adolescents who need it; otherwise, they develop all sorts of psychological and social problems because of physical difficulties.

Friendships

As children mature, they become more and more concerned about being accepted by friends and by social groups; they are especially concerned about getting acquainted with the opposite sex. During the elementary years, children are interested primarily in friendships with those of the same sex. But at puberty, all of this changes. The girl who was looked down on by the fifth-grade boy as a sissie now takes on a new charm and fascination. Most boys are gradually able to overcome their own embarrassment and to dare to talk to girls and to get to know them as persons. Unfortunately, some older adolescents are never able to make satisfactory heterosexual adjustments. However, most who do not are unhappy, lonesome persons. One major goal of parents is to assist their children in learning how to make many friends of both sexes.

Sex Roles

Sex education also seeks to help children accept their own sexuality: their maleness or femaleness and their appropriate sex roles in the society in which they are growing up. These roles are changing so rapidly that the old standards of what a man or a woman is and what each should be and do in life are no longer valid. Parents teach their children these things primarily by the example they set, the roles they themselves play. If parents believe in equality between the sexes, in equal opportunities regardless of gender, and in flexible sex roles in the family, they best teach their children if they become living examples of these ideas themselves. Sex education does include teaching boys that it is not unmanly to change a diaper or to baby-sit and teaching girls that it is all right to prepare for a career in a traditionally masculine profession.

Reproduction

One more usual purpose of sex education is to help children understand the great miracle of life: where babies come from; how they are conceived, grow, and are born; and how life is passed on from generation to generation. Children are interested in all kinds of babies, both animal and human—chickens, birds, dogs, and people. Children need to know that all babies grow from tiny eggs but that some creatures (birds, turtles, and others) lay their eggs outside the body, where the babies hatch out. Other creatures (people, whales, cats, and others) keep their eggs inside their bodies where the babies grow until they are born.

There is a great need for factual, truthful answers about all phases of human reproduction. If parents are honest and truthful, they can maintain the confidence and trust of their children and build better relationships with them as they grow up.

Behavior

Another major goal of sex education is to encourage knowledgeable, mature, responsible, sexual conduct. Parents need to discuss behavior and morals along with the facts of life. The day is past when parental silence, which tries to keep children ignorant, is the way to keep children from sexual experimentation. Children are being taught from movies, television, magazines, books, street corners, in public rest rooms. Not all such information is factual, and much is associated with negative attitudes and feelings and with an irresponsible use of sex. The mass media seldom presents sex within the context of marriage, as an intimate expression of two people who love one another. It often portrays nonmarital (either premarital or extramarital) sex, sadistic sex, perverted sex, or meaningless, physical sex without emotional involvement. There is need, therefore, for parents to present a more mature point of view and to help their children not only to grow to be sexually responsive but also to be sexually responsible. Such things as venereal disease and premarital pregnancies are preventable—with the right sex education and with parental and medical help.

Marriage

One of the most important goals of sex education is to prepare young people for sexual adjustments in marriage. A number of years ago, a mother came to see me with her 22-year-old daughter, who was to be married. The mother wanted me to counsel her daughter, but only if I never mentioned anything about sex. And this was a week before the wedding!

Most parents today are quite surprised to learn that many young people are still quite ignorant of the basic facts about making love. Parents assume that, because their children seem so socially sophisticated, they know all about sexual relations. They don't. They need to be taught, and parents can be a big help. Parental efforts should be positive, factual, honest, and personal, dealing with the intimacies of love play, the basic facts about sexual intercourse, male-female anatomy and responses, and the typical adjustments that many couples have to make. Parents might also remember that just because a couple have already had sexual relations before marriage does not mean that their sexual life is completely satisfying. Why not be just as concerned about helping one's daughter achieve orgasm as about helping her select a wedding dress? Why not be just as anxious to help one's son control premature ejaculation as to help him get a good job? (For additional information, see Rice, *Sexual Problems in Marriage*, 1978b.)

METHODS

But the real question is: How is the best way to go about sex education? What can parents do and say? What methods or techniques work best at home?

Begin Early

The first step is to begin early. Sex education begins almost from the time a child is born. When a father says to his young daughter: "Come sit on my lap and give Daddy a big hug," he is helping his daughter to learn the meaning and expression of love. Learning to express feelings physically begins with physical demonstrations of affection between family members. Attitudinal development takes place gradually, from birth on, as babies are diapered, toilet trained, bathed, dressed and undressed, and as they absorb the attitudes and feelings of their parents.

The first questions usually arise at around three years of age. I would start off by using correct words for the various parts of the body. It's just as easy to use the words "penis," "vagina," "testicles," "breasts" and "urine" as it is to use their slang counterparts. I'm always very amused at the words parents make up to disguise normal functions such as toileting. One mother came to see me after I had given a talk on sex education and was very upset that I had suggested using the word "penis." "What do you call it?" I asked. "Tinklebell," was her reply. I'm not really sure that "tinklebell" was an improvement, or that such words as "tinkle," "pee," or "wee-wee" sound better than "urinate." Slang words have a negative connotation, whereas the correct words do not.

Generally speaking, parents should answer all questions as they arise, as simply and honestly as they know how. If children are old enough to ask, they are old enough to get an answer. Parents can take advantage of natural opportunities to initiate discussion and impart information: the mother's pregnancy, a neighbor's pregnancy, the birth of animals or human babies, or bathing a baby. I don't object to a birds and bees approach to telling all about how animal babies are born, but parents eventually have to get around to talking about human babies. Children can learn all about the birth of kittens but still not realize where human babies come from.

One of the chief obstacles to discussions about sex between parents and children is the parents' own embarrassment. One mother admitted: "I know I should talk to my children, but I get so tense and nervous that I'm never able to get started." Another real problem is the parents' own lack of knowledge. As one mother admitted: "I don't really understand menstruation myself, so how can I explain it to my daughter?"

There are several things parents can do. One, they should read all the good books and literature they can, which will help them to understand the subject of human sexuality. Two, parents should discuss the subject between themselves. The more they talk about sex and use the words and phrases that they will employ in teaching their children, the easier it will be to talk to the children. They can ask one another sample questions and practice answering them. Three, if parents begin when children are young, they will become more experienced as children grow and as the questions become more difficult to answer.

Most parents worry about sex play. Some amount of peeking or looking at one another, or sex play, such as playing doctor, should be considered quite normal. I feel that the best time to satisfy children's curiosity is when they are young and can see one another, as well as their parents, naked. As children grow older, diagrams and pictures from good books help as valuable teaching aids. I would not leave young children unsupervised, especially with older children who are known to instigate sex play. If such children are discovered in the neighborhood, one answer is simply to keep one's own children away from them. Generally, the less fuss parents make about incidents, the less upset children become. Teaching children not to take their clothes off if other children ask them to and to tell parents if such requests are made, and not to accept favors or rides from strangers are basic to preventing child molestation.

Gradeschool Children

School-age children are filled with questions, and they are quite uninhibited about asking them and discussing them unless parents have reprimanded or punished them for doing so. Generally speaking, children should have all of the basic facts about conception, fertilization, the growth and birth of babies, physical maturation at puberty, the names and functions of the male and female reproductive organs, and sex as a means of expressing love in marriage *before* they reach puberty. In fact, the younger children are told, within the level of their understanding, the less embarrassed they are and the easier it is to discuss such matters with them. Unless parents have laid a good foundation of years of honesty and matter-of-factness, adolescents will be too embarrassed to ask their parents the things they most want to know.

But if I tell too much, won't this encourage sexual experimentation? Aren't children more likely to get into trouble?

No one has ever been able to show that too much knowledge gets children into trouble. The opposite is usually true: Ignorance and the desire to know and satisfy curiosity lead to experimentation and difficulties. Many parents tell too little too late. One teen-age boy complained: "For years, every time I asked my parents a question, they replied: 'Wait 'til you're older.' Now that I'm 18 and ask, they say to me: 'What, you're 18, and you don't know that! They still won't tell me."

The hardest questions for parents to deal with concern those relating to fertilization and sexual relations. Here are some sample questions and answers.

Q: What starts the egg growing into a baby?
A: Before it can start to grow, it has to be fertilized, or joined, by a sperm from the father. (It's helpful to show diagrams of a sperm, an ovum, and the sperm entering the egg. See your local library for children's books on sex education.)
Q: Where do the sperm come from?
A: They grow in the father's testicles. (A diagram helps here, too.)
Q: How does the sperm get out of the father into the mother?
A: When the mother and father make love, or have sexual intercourse, as it's called, they hug and kiss one

another. They lie next to one another. The father puts his penis into his wife's vagina and releases millions of sperm inside her.

Q: How do the sperm find the egg?

A: They have long tails and swim up the vagina, through the opening of the womb or uterus, through the uterus and then into the Fallopian tubes, where the egg is. There, one sperm joins with the egg, or fertilizes it, to start the egg growing into a baby. (Show diagram.)

Q: Why do people want to make love even though they already have all the children they want?

A: Because they love one another, and this is one way they show their love. Besides, they like to have sexual intercourse because it feels good and because it gives them a lot of satisfaction and pleasure.

Such answers are honest, are factual, and are explained simply, without overburdening children with too much information until they are interested. When they are, then more detail can be given.

Teen-agers

If they have been given all of the basic facts by the time they reach adolescence, teen-agers want to know about sexual feelings and sexual behavior, about such things as petting and necking, and about whether or not they should engage in premarital sexual relations. They also worry about masturbation, venereal disease, contraception, and abortions. Many parents find it very hard to discuss sexual behavior except in the most general terms—"Don't get into trouble"—which isn't very helpful. What adolescents need is frank discussion about their own sexual feelings and responses, about how these feelings and responses are stimulated and aroused, and about the need and the means to gain some control over their own emotions.

Today's young people are under tremendous pressure to express their sexual needs by "going all the way." Several surveys among high school students have revealed that at least one-third of boys and girls have had premarital sexual intercourse by age 17 (Vener & Stewart, 1974; Sorensen, 1973). Unfortunately, about half of all teen-agers who have sexual relations use no method of contraception (Rice, 1978a, p. 376). One survey showed that only 19 percent of 15- to 19-year-old girls or their boy friends always used some method of contraception whenever they had intercourse (Zelnick & Kantner, 1972). The result has been large numbers of out of wedlock teen-age pregnancies: over a million a year, leading to over 350,000 abortions.

What can parents do about this situation?

The first defense against out of wedlock pregnancies is moral teaching against premarital sexual intercourse. If parents do not approve of premarital sex, then they ought to make every effort to bring up their children with the same point of view. We do know that religious prohibitions against intercourse before marriage are more influential in influencing sexual behavior than any other factors. Parents who agree with these teachings have an obligation to explain them and the reasons for them to their children.

However, parents have to teach their adolescents that not everyone agrees or accepts these values. In fact, some young people are quite exploitative in their sexual behavior and will use others for their own pleasure without regard for reputation or consequences. Therefore, parents should also emphasize that making decisions about sexual behavior is a personal matter and that all persons must decide for themselves and be willing to bear the consequences of their decisions. The thing that parents can do is to create an atmosphere of honesty so that various feelings and ideas can be discussed frankly and thoughtful decisions can be made. If one's teen-agers decide to have premarital intercourse, then this is their choice and their responsibility. Parents can let children know that they don't approve, but they can still be willing to let their young people decide for themselves.

The second line of defense against premarital pregnancy is using the best contraceptives available. If parents know that their son or daughter is having sexual intercourse or that he or she plans to, the most immediate need is to take him or her to a doctor and/or family planning clinic to obtain contraceptives. Once teen-agers start having intercourse, the chances are that they will continue to do so. Parents should also tell their teen-age son to use condoms himself rather than relying on any method a girl uses—unless he knows her very well and can completely rely on her word.

Isn't giving contraceptives to teen-agers an admission of defeat, and won't it encourage promiscuity?

Yes, it is an admission that teen-agers need contraceptives because they are sexually active. No, it won't encourage promiscuity. The only teen-ager who needs contraceptives is one having intercourse already or one who intends on having intercourse. The one important consideration is that contraception prevents pregnancy and should always be used when needed.

10

Sex-Role Development

THE PROCESS OF DEVELOPMENT

Meaning

Sex-role identification is the process of learning to feel and behave like a member of one sex (Smart & Smart, 1972, p. 331). It has occurred when masculine or feminine behavior, as defined by a particular culture, is no longer deliberate or imitative but is automatic and generalized to all areas of the self, from the style of thinking and walking to the style of sexual behavior (McCandless, 1967, p. 449).

Assignment

Adopting a masculine or feminine sex role is a process that takes place over a period of time. But it is a process that begins at birth when a male or female gender is assigned, according to the visible genitalia of the newborn child. Once this assignment has been made, from that point on the child is considered a boy or girl. This assignment, henceforth, becomes the foundation upon which the structure of the child's personality is built.

Social Learning

After assignment of gender takes place society expects the child to begin thinking and acting like a boy or like a girl. If the child is a girl, she is often dressed in pink. She is given fancy, frilly dresses to wear. The older she gets, the more she is expected to wear girls' underwear, girls' shoes and stockings, girls' blouses, and girls' coats. Her hair is fixed the way a girl's hair should look. She is allowed to wear a ribbon or a bow.

She is given dolls and other toys appropriate for little girls. She is encouraged to play house, or nurse, or school, and to keep herself neat and clean. She is taught to be a "little lady": quiet, submissive, and well mannered. She is allowed to be sensitive and to cry if her feelings are hurt, but she is reprimanded or punished if she gets too loud, boisterous, or aggressive. She is allowed to play only girls' games, such as jacks, jump rope, or hop scotch. Rough games like football are reserved only for little boys. Even around the house, she is given only "women's work" to do, such as washing the dishes, cleaning the house, or washing or ironing clothes. Outside chores, such as mowing the lawn, sawing wood, or shoveling snow, are reserved for her older brother.

As she grows up, she is encouraged to enter occupations that are typically feminine: school teaching, nursing, secretarial or clerical work, library work, or certain types of factory work requiring delicate dexterity and coordination. She is also pressured to get married. If she does marry, all of her family and friends keep asking her when she is going to become a mother.

Thus, we see that what society expects a girl to be and do becomes the basic influence in molding her into a woman. Also, once a child knows that she is a girl, she begins to value femaleness and to act consistently in accord with gender expectations. She observes her older sister, her mother, and other females acting like women, so she begins to identify with them, to imitate them, and to model her behavior after theirs. The more she is rewarded and praised for being a girl, the more she values her "femaleness." The more she is punished and condemned for any actions or traits that are masculine, the more she tries to eliminate these from her life. Thus, once gender is assigned and accepted by the girl and by others, she is programmed to become a woman.

Ages

It has been found that sex-role stereotypes are developed quite early. Children can correctly apply gender labels by age 3. They have already developed differential toy preferences and have learned that there are activities and duties appropriate for each sex. Furthermore, there is evidence that 3-year-olds can correctly associate sex-typed articles, such as clothing, with the appropriate sex, and that by age 5 children prefer these same-sex objects to opposite-sex ones (Flerx, et al., 1976). By this age, also, children begin to associate personality differences and social roles with each sex. Males are viewed as "physically more powerful and invulnerable." Mother's roles are seen as housekeeping and child care, and the father's role is seen as earning a living. By early elementary age, boys are already described as object-oriented; more competent in physical activities; more aggressive; and more achievement oriented, independent and dominant. Girls are characterized as person-oriented; more competent in verbal communication; and more nurturant, submissive, passive, dependent, emotional, polite, tactful, and neat (Grotberg, 1971, p. 121).

EFFECTS ON FEMALES

Limitations of Stereotypes

The problem with sex-role stereotypes is that they severely limit the opportunities and roles that are open to children as they grow up. And prescribed personality traits, if adopted, may place serious limitations on what children are able to achieve or on the relationships they are capable of forming.

Female Personality Traits

Let us look first at the effect of stereotyped female personality traits on women. In the past, according to Rice (1979a, p. 199) women were supposed to be:

Unaggressive	Sentimental
Submissive	Softhearted
Weak	Sensitive
Dependent	Aware of feelings of others
Gentle and tender	Emotional and excitable
Kind	Frivolous and fickle
Tactful	Illogical
Warm and affectionate	Talkative

But the fact remains that many of these traits are disadvantageous to the woman who has to be out in the world supporting herself and sometimes supporting her children and a husband or a parent. The unaggressive, submissive, weak female is not able to achieve as much as the more assertive, stronger person. Even at home, her husband and children walk all over her because she hasn't learned to stand up for herself. If she is considered emotional, excitable, frivolous, and illogical, she is thought to be unworthy to assume positions of leadership in government or in business. Because she is talkative, she can't be entrusted with important secrets. If these traits have been cultivated in women, then these characteristics become means of keeping them subservient and inferior.

What about the gentler female traits: tenderness, kindness, sentimentality, softheartedness, sensitivity, and awareness of the feelings of others? These traits have always been much needed in all types of human relationships, a fact which has qualified women to play the nurturant role as wives and mothers. But because women possess these traits, whereas men are not supposed to exhibit them, women have been more vulnerable to the hurts and upsets of intimate living. As a result, more women than men are dissatisfied with marriage, and greater numbers of women attempt suicide or suffer from mental illness than is true of men. The very sensitivity that helps them in their nurturant role also makes them more exposed to the hurts and injustices of life. I'm not suggesting here that we give up trying to raise our daughters to be kind and sensitive, but what is needed are greater efforts to raise our sons in a similar manner, so that they too can better fulfill the companionship roles that are required of them in intimate relationships.

I would suggest, however, that if we expect our daughters to be breadwinners, and apparently this is the direction in which we are headed, or if many women remain single or are required to raise their children alone, as is now expected of some, that we need to develop in them the same assertiveness, independence, and rational thinking that we seek to develop in our sons. New roles require different traits if women are to succeed.

Employment Opportunities

At the present time, some of the sex-role stereotypes that are labeled "feminine" also mark women as "inferior." Western culture gives lip service to equal status, rights, and opportunities for women, but it doesn't really live up to its ideals. Discrimination is rampant. Even the Civil Rights Act of 1964, which sought to guarantee equal employment and pay opportunities for women, was not enough to eliminate the wide discrepancies in wages between males and females. At the present time, women still earn only 60 percent of the amount of income that men receive for the same job, assuming an identical level of education, experience, and the same number of hours of work (Rice, 1979, p. 221). In addition, even though the median number of years of schooling completed is now identical for men and women (12.4 years), women continue to be in the minority in managerial, professional, technical, and skilled occupations, with the majority in office, clerical, or service occupations. Large numbers of employed women are in five occupations—secretary-stenographers, household workers, bookkeepers, elementary school teachers, and waitresses (Rice, 1979a, p. 220). Such discrimination will remain as long as chauvinistic views label whatever is feminine as inferior.

Opportunities for Choice

What women seek are opportunities to develop their talents to the full, to achieve whatever they are capable of achieving, and to be able to decide for themselves the directions in which they want their lives to move. At the present time, the majority of women indicate that they want marriage, children, and a career. One nationwide survey of women of all ages revealed the following:
52 percent—wanted marriage, children, and a career
38 percent—wanted marriage and children without a career

4 percent—wanted marriage and a career without children
2 percent—wanted a career only
3 percent—couldn't decide (Roper Organization, 1974)
These findings are comparable to others which indicate that U.S. women still place marriage and children high on their list of priorities and that the majority want a career in addition to family life. But the important thing is that women have options, that they have a choice.

Remedies

The key to changing the situation lies in the way that children are socialized. Much has been done to eliminate discrimination and stereotypes in children's books and literature, but much still needs to be done. One study focused on the annotated catalog of children's books, distributed by the National Council of Teachers of English to thousands of teachers and used for ordering books with federal funds. It showed that titles were listed under headings: "Especially for Girls" and "Especially for Boys." It was found that boys "decipher and discover," "earn and train," or "foil someone." Girls "struggle," "overcome difficulties," "feel lost," "help solve," or "help out." One boy's story moves from "truancy to triumph." A girl "learns to face the real world" and to make "a difficult adjustment" (Howe, 1971).

Much has been done to change school courses and programs that promote sex-typed roles. Traditionally, home economics was for girls, shop courses for boys. Now, in some schools, both programs are offered to both boys and girls. Guidance counselors used to urge girls to become teachers, secretaries, or nurses. Now, girls are being urged to enter all professions, as is indicated by the rapidly increasing percentages of females in all kinds of professional schools.

One of the biggest perpetuators of sex-role stereotypes is the mass media, especially the ads. Women are still responsible for "ring around the collar"; they go into ecstacies over their lemon-smelling furniture polish or their no scrubbing floor shine. It's always the wife who is awakened in the middle of the night by the husband who has a scratchy throat, and stuffed nose or who has a headache and can't sleep. The wife dutifully gets up and gets the appropriate remedy for her husband, who goes to sleep promptly. Just once, it would be a relief to see the roles reversed. Until the mass media shows fathers advertising Pampers or using Cheer, it's doubtful that some fathers will ever feel obligated to or comfortable about changing the baby or laundering the clothes.

One result of this kind of advertising has been that women are now assuming a disproportionate share of the burden in their families. They are going out to work, but they are also coming home and doing almost as much work as they did before they were gainfully employed. In other words, most husbands are not assuming their fair share of the total burden, even though their wives are earning a larger share of the family income. This has led many feminist writers to insist that housework is still women's enemy and that men as well as women ought to participate in all of the domestic chores (Rice, 1979a, p. 225).

One of the most important things parents can do is set the right examples for their children to follow. If sex roles in the individual family are flexible and interchangeable, with family members doing "our work" rather than designating "women's work" or "men's work," the children will learn by experience and by example.

EFFECTS ON MALES

Male Personality Traits

Stereotyped male traits have also had negative effects on men. In the past, men were supposed to be:

Aggressive   Adventurous
Dominant   Courageous
Strong   Independent
Forceful   Ambitious
Self-confident   Direct
Rugged   Logical
Virile   Unemotional
Instrumental

Certainly, some of the above traits were needed in frontier days when men had to battle against nature and wage war against their enemies. Men had to be adventurous, courageous, and forceful just to survive. When most work required strength and physical stamina, to be strong and rugged was a distinct advantage. But today, when machines can do everything, physical prowess is no longer needed. William Whyte pointed out a number of years ago, in *The Organization Man*, that a man can live his whole life and never have a chance to find out whether or not he is a coward (Whyte, 1956). And as far as family life is concerned, to be overly aggressive, dominant, independent, and unemotional are distinct disadvantages. Some measure of aggressiveness does help in business, in furthering oneself and one's ideas in relationship to others, but the overaggressive male gets in trouble with friends, family, and society and to have a whole earth full of aggressive males results in wars and destruction. Modern men need to be less aggressive and more cooperative (Rice, 1978a, p. 351).

The Inexpressive Male

One of the tragedies of the stereotyped masculine personality is the resultant inability of males to express honest, tender emotions (Balswick & Peek, 1971). Men are not supposed to show feelings; they aren't supposed to cry; they are supposed to be impervious to sorrow, pain, and tragedy and to be able to "take it like a man." As a result, some men think that it's unmanly to tell their wives, "I love you" or to give their children (especially their sons) a big hug and a kiss. Men are supposed to be interested in sex because "real men" are virile. But they are encouraged to be quite indifferent to love. The all-American hero is the rugged cowboy who defends the weak. He loves his horse and is intrigued by a girl, but he usually spurns the girl and rides off on his horse. To fall for the woman and to let his emotions get the better of him would be to betray his masculinity.

The other type of masculine hero is the playboy, the male who has dozens of girl friends to give him sexual pleasure. The more "playgirls" he has, the more manly he is considered to be. But he is never to become emotionally involved or to fall for any of them. To do so is to show weakness and a lack of strength.

Modern male children are well indoctrinated in both the "cowboy syndrome" and the "playboy philosophy" (Balswick & Peek, 1971). As a result, these boys grow up trying to gauge their masculinity by their sexual prowess, by their ability to seduce, arouse, and satisfy numerous sexual partners without emotional involvement. One result has been sexual exploitation; another has been the inability of some males to provide deep, intimate, emotionally tender companionship in relation to their wives and children. And because some men are denied the privilege of expressing honest emotions, they suffer from internal tensions and from psychological problems that interfere with peace of mind and creative living.

Vocational and Family Roles

Another of the measures of masculinity in American culture has been the size of a man's paycheck. If he is a good provider, he is a "real man." But it has become harder and harder for him to make a living for his family, no matter how hard he works. The uneducated and unskilled male can never hope to keep up. One result has been a sense of failure and inadequacy as a male. The more capable work very long hours, devoting less and less time to their wives and children. If they do succeed in earning a superior income, they have usually been rejecting, absentee husbands and fathers.

As a result, many women are emphasizing that as more and more women go back to work and earn greater amounts of money, they are also "liberating" their husbands from the total burden and freeing them to spend time at something else besides just earning money. I do feel that the present trend is in the right direction. As more and more husbands and wives share wage-earning responsibilities, more can share in family recreation and maintenance. Highly segregated sex roles result in a lack of companionship and intimacy in the family. Cooperative sharing of roles results in more companionship among all family members and in greater opportunities for meaningful relationships.

SOME IMPORTANT QUESTIONS

Should husbands and wives strive to produce a unisex, to bring up their sons and daughters in an identical fashion?
There are some radicals who have advocated dressing all children alike, interchanging boys' and girls' names, and raising them identically in every way. I don't feel it's necessary to go to these extremes. To emphasize identical physical appearances is a superficial way of looking at a deeper problem. The real problem is a matter of attitude. Girls are treated as second-class citizens, because children are reared to feel that females are inferior. The solution is to teach children that there are two sexes and that each is equally important, intelligent, and capable. As long as children are taught to feel that

the two sexes are equal but not identical, then discrimination against women will be minimal. There is a need to help boys and girls know and understand one another and to help them develop deep admiration and respect for one another. If there is respect, equal rights and opportunities will follow.

Should there be any differentiation in family chores and responsibilities for boys and girls?

Not if parents expect that all of their children will learn to do everything as they are growing up. I feel that both sexes should be exposed to both inside work and outside work, without regard to sex. It's a real advantage to teach girls how to do carpentry work, how to fix electrical appliances, and how to mow the lawn or paint the house. And it's also helpful to boys to learn how to care for younger children, how to cook, or how to do the laundry. If husbands and wives are to share responsibilities after marriage, then parents need to bring up their children to share responsibilities in their families.

Our daughter says that she wants to become a civil engineer. We've been trying to discourage her, since we don't feel that it's any kind of work for a woman. What do you think?

I think that being a civil engineer is a marvelous profession for a woman if she has an aptitude for it and if she's well trained in it. A girl today in a traditionally male profession can demand a top salary. In fact, she will have an easier time finding a job than would a man. My own philosophy is that all occupations today ought to be open to both sexes and that whoever is most qualified ought to be allowed to do them. I'd like to see more men trained to teach young children, since I feel the children will benefit, just as I'd like to see more women physicians or scientists. The important thing is for maximum opportunities to be open to all people, regardless of their gender. In the long run, society will benefit, since we would be making maximum use of the skills and talents that are available.

11

Friends and Peer Relationships

PRESCHOOL CHILDREN

Infants and Toddlers

Babies and toddlers in the United States are not often put together in groups. But what observations have been made indicate that babies do interact with one another from about 5 months onward (Smart & Smart, 1972, p. 160). Their first social response is simply to notice one another and to smile at one another. When they are able to move around, they crawl all over one another. When they can stand up, they occasionally knock one another down. By 9 months of age, they offer a toy to others and oppose toys being taken away (Crow & Crow, 1968, p. 272). They also comfort others in distress and pick up the ones who get pushed over. Conflict over toys seems to be at a peak between 9 and 14 months, with personal aggression increasing with age. But cooperation also increases as children become more experienced in relating to one another. Observation of children in infant centers indicates that helpfulness is more apparent than efforts to dominate. By the time children are toddlers, they have learned much about fending for themselves in a group and about how to find satisfaction there. "They have made a strong beginning in establishing group relations that are a main source of emotional security and orientation" (Smart & Smart, 1972, p. 161).

Two-Year-Olds

Children of this age enjoy playing alongside one another rather than with one another, since cooperative play is not very evident, at least in the beginning (Spock, 1977, p. 386). Nevertheless, children benefit from being together. They need to get used to one another's company. Social interchange becomes more frequent; friendly behavior gradually replaces negative behavior. Sex preferences are not yet evident.

Two-year-olds do a lot of grabbing, hitting, and pushing, not usually with an intent to hurt, but for the purpose of getting a toy someone has. Since they are egocentric, they are not aware of the effect that their own actions have upon others, nor of the moods and feelings of others (Medinnus & Johnson, 1969, p. 401). They think in terms of "my ball" or "my book," and they protest when denied what they want. As a result, they inevitably run into conflict from their social interactions. They need supervision, training, and experience in considering the needs and interests of others.

Three-Year-Olds

As children grow older, they engage in fewer solitary activities, do less passive watching of other children, and become less inclined toward isolated play. Friendly contacts occur with increasing frequency, and cooperative behavior also increases (*Developmental Psychology Today*, 1971, p. 241). Children may select one friend, sometimes two, with whom they identify for short periods of time.

We see the beginning of group play and activity. The development of language makes communication possible, so that when two children play together they talk about what they are making in the sand, about dressing up their dolls, or about pretending to be a mother or a baby. Group membership, however, is constantly changing, with children moving in and out of a group.

Three-year-olds are likely to be victims of aggression by other children in nursery school, so teachers have to provide supervision and be careful to re-enforce socially acceptable acts. The teacher who says, "Yes, that's right," and smiles, nods, and shows interest when children help or show friendliness and concern for others, or when they share ideas or toys, is encouraging positive behavior. When the teacher turns attention away from children who are threatening or disrupting others, she is discouraging antisocial acts and avoiding re-enforcement of them (Smart & Smart, 1972, p. 280).

Four- and Five-Year-Olds

Four- and five-year-old children begin to depend less on parents and more and more on peers for companionship and social interaction. They now share affection and tangible objects. They offer approval and make demands on one another. Best friends in a group will pair off. Groups of three children are quite common. Occasionally, up to five or six children will form a group and spend most of their play time with one another.

Their behavior varies. One moment they are aggressive, the

next moment cooperative. Their behavior is affected a lot by the attitude of others at home or in school. If cooperation is stressed, children become less competitive. If competition is encouraged, rivalry becomes a strong motivator of behavior, and jealousy is quite common. For this reason, most experts try to discourage competitive activities for this age group.

Children of this age develop definite preferences in playmates. Some children in a group become leaders and are quite popular with nearly everyone. Other children are content to be followers. Although there is still much intermingling between the sexes, the children begin to show preferences to be with others of their own sex. There is, however, little prejudice in evidence. Children choose friends without regard for race, color, ethnic origin, or social class.

As preschool children interact with other children of the same age, they gradually discover that they come from a variety of family situations. Some have siblings, others none. Some have young parents, others have old parents, and some have only one parent at home. They have different mealtimes, different toys, and different parental rules and regulations governing behavior. These initial engagements with peers are a tremendously broadening experience, and most children besiege their parents with endless questions about how and why life is different in other families. "How come I don't have any brothers or sisters?" "Why can't I have a big bike like Mary has?" "Why doesn't Johnny have any Daddy?" (Weiner & Elkind, 1972a, p. 80).

Play is vitally important to personality and social growth during the preschool years. Weiner and Elkind (1972a, p. 80) write:

> *It is primarily through activities involving toys and games that youngsters learn about each other as people and about their own capacities to handle stresses and strains of interpersonal relationships. A child who for one reason or another lacks*

opportunities to play with age-mates misses out on a vital social learning experience, and there is considerable risk that he will become the kind of person who is uncomfortable, inept, and uncertain of himself in interpersonal situations.

The parents' role is to see that their preschool children have the opportunity for a wide variety of social experiences. Such experiences are vital to their children's total development as social creatures.

ELEMENTARY AGE CHILDREN

Friendships

By the time children start first grade, they are no longer interested in being alone so much of the time (*Your Child from 1 to 6*, 1962). They want to be with friends. They still seek out a special companion, but their circle of friends is widening. During the preschool period, most of their friends were confined to the immediate neighborhood, but now children meet many friends from other areas served by the school (Garrison et al., 1967, p. 293). Some of these persons are different from others the children are used to playing with. This makes it harder for children to get acquainted and to learn to get along, but it is a broadening experience and helps them to mature.

Parents become concerned about the kinds of friends their children want to bring home or want to visit. They worry, and with justification, about the influence of these friends upon their children. Parents want to know: "Where do these children live?" "Are their parents at home?" "What kind of persons are these children?" "How do they get along in school or in the neighborhood?" "Are they problem children?" Parents are wise to be concerned, because peer-group influence over children becomes more and more important. However, parents can't tell the type of children individuals are by what the father does, by whether or not the parents are divorced, or by the size of the house the family lives in. And parents can't believe all the stories they hear from neighbors. How, then, can they check up on their children's friends? First, by getting acquainted with the children themselves, by inviting them over, observing them, and talking with them. Parents who take the time to get acquainted can make better judgments than if they accept the gossip of others.

Second, parents should listen to what their own children say about their prospective friends. Usually, children will defend one another, but they also know better than anyone else the kinds of reputations other children have at school. What kinds of students are they? How do they behave?

Third, parents need to get acquainted with other parents. They should invite these parents over for coffee, or go to visit them, or talk to them over the phone. Parents are wise to get to know the families of the children their offspring play with.

Of course, children want to select their own friends, but parents can exert an important influence by talking things over with their children. Certainly, parents need to spell out some ground rules about how far away and where children are allowed to play, about what time to come in, and about the types of activities that are permitted. Grade-school children need some supervision, so it is helpful if there are concerned parents nearby. Parents who welcome other children to their home and make things as pleasant as possible will always be assured that they know where their children are, what they are doing, and with whom. Some parents become such nags, or are always so upset, or are so worried about spoiling the house, that children never feel comfortable coming over. This is really too bad, since their own children will be brought up at neighbors' houses.

Our daughter is very shy. We've just moved to a new neigh-

borhood and school, and she has a lot of trouble making new friends. What can we do?

The most important thing is for parents to try to ascertain the reasons for their daughter's shyness and to correct the reasons. Children are not born shy. They develop it over a period of years. Sometimes, unwittingly, parents are the chief cause of their children's shyness. Here are some things parents do that may create problems of shyness.

They are overprotective and won't allow their children to do what others do or allow them to play with other children in the usual way. This is especially likely to happen if children are frail or sickly. The parents try to protect their children from germs, noise, and rough and tumble play, but as a result, they keep their children from making friends or from learning how to do what others do (Ross, 1965, p. 2).

They expect too much of their children, try to push them too fast, and are very critical of them when their children don't measure up. Such attitudes and feelings undermine their children's self-confidence, so they become afraid of failure, of rejection, of ridicule, and of criticism, and they react by trying to avoid social groups where they are embarrassed.

They show partiality to older or younger children at home, ignoring, criticizing, and rejecting one child, so that the child feels inferior, unwanted, and unloved. If the one child is also compared unfavorably with others, he or she grows up afraid that others won't like him or her and consequently becomes very reticent in social groups.

Suppose that parents live in areas where there are no other children for theirs to play with. As a result, their children never have a chance to make friends, so shyness results from a lack of experience in being with others. This is likely to happen to children who live in remote, rural areas where there are no other families close by. I know of another case where an Air Force family moved seventeen times in three years. Their son became very shy and introverted, not because he didn't meet others but because every time he started to make friends, the family moved. The constant effort to readjust became too much, and he became more and more a loner.

Sometimes children become shy because of things over which parents have little or no control. Children from racial or ethnic minority groups, who are visible because they are different, may have great difficulty in feeling a part of a total group. Children from impoverished families are often shy among those from the middle classes. Children with physical handicaps are often shy. Ross (1965, p. 15) writes:

> *The crippled child, the hard of hearing, the one with defective eyesight has to build up some defenses against conditions he cannot cope with. The spastic child fears falling, the blind child is shy about unfamiliar places, the deaf one is anxious lest something come up suddenly behind him. Shyness in these instances is a kind of safeguard. These children need special help in learning how to use their environment safely. They need special care and patience from all members of the family.*

Whatever the reason for shyness, once parents recognize the causes, they can best help their children overcome their fears by eliminating the reasons.

Popularity

Popularity means to be liked or accepted by others. Children differ in the degrees to which they strive for popularity or achieve it. If a group of children are asked individually to name other children whom they most like or with whom they would most like to be associated, it is possible to discover which children are most and least popular. Usually, such surveys show that even those children who are rated most popular have a few acquaintances who are indifferent to them or dislike them and that those who are least popular are rarely unpopular with everyone (Northway, 1961, p. 5).

Nevertheless, since children place such emphasis on being popular, it is helpful to sort out those qualities of personality and character that make for popularity or unpopularity. What types of children are most popular? Generally speaking, popular children:

- Are socially aggressive and outgoing.
- Have a high energy level that they use in activities approved by the group.
- Have a high need for approval.
- Actively participate in social events enthusiastically.
- Are friendly and sociable in relation to others.
- Accept others, are sympathetic, protective, and comforting toward them.
- Are cheerful, good natured, have a good sense of humor.
- Are above average in intelligence and school performance, but not too high above others.
- Are likely to come from middle or upper social classes.

There are some social and sex differences in the qualities considered important to popularity. Boys need to show physical prowess, athletic ability, skill in competitive games, and daring. In fact, in some antisocial groups, the most popular boys show superior fighting ability. In the upper elementary grades, girls are rated most popular who are considered physically attractive and socially sophisticated and mature. Middle-class children put greater emphasis on scholastic achievement than do lower-class children. "A lower-class boy who excels in school work risks alienation from his peers. . . . A lower-class girl can be a good student without alienating her friends [Kagan, 1971, p. 143]."

What types of children are considered least popular? Gen-

erally speaking, the least popular children (Northway, 1961, p. 18):
- Are shy, introverted, self-centered, and withdrawn.
- Are anxious, fearful, and moody.
- Are impulsive, with poor emotional control.
- Show a lack of sensitivity to others and to social situations.
- Are hostile and overaggressive.
- Behave considerably younger or older than their age groups.
- Are different looking or unconventional in behavior.
- Are more likely to be of low intelligence.
- Are more likely to come from low socioeconomic groups.

There is a difference between children who are unliked and those who are disliked. Unliked children are socially invisible. They are loners (U.S. Dept. of Health, Education, and Welfare, 1966, p. 51). No one knows they are around, because they tend to be shy, withdrawn, or uninterested in social contacts. Disliked children are quite visible, but they behave in obnoxious, socially unacceptable ways.

Ken was a short, stocky, redheaded child with a great big smile. He wiggled a lot, and while the rest of the class was having a lesson, he might be engaged in such activity as fiddling under his desk with an elastic and two sticks. Although he was bright, he was a noisy and clumsy child. He rushed in where others tried to tiptoe. At a party, he broke his hostess' crystal chandelier through a little mishap with his catapult. He frequently went home with someone else's bicycle because he was in too big a hurry to seek out his own. He loved pushing, shoving, and tripping people. He could break up games or plans as easily as he did the chandelier, and he was always interrupting the flow of activity. His schoolwork was as messy as his desk was untidy, although in personal appearance he was remarkably neat. He could say the wrong thing as easily as he could do the wrong thing. In brief, he seemed to have no perception of what a social situation was or what the group wanted. He pushed himself and his own wants instead [Northway, 1961, p. 18].

There are several ways of helping unpopular children, depending on the reasons for their problem. Shy, introverted children can't be pushed into popularity, but parents can help by inviting individual children over as playmates or by inviting them to go on trips or picnics with the family (Spock, 1977, p. 434). Often, the very shy feel quite adequate on a person-to-person basis or in small groups. Anxious, fearful children need an improved self-concept and self-esteem. One way to achieve this is to encourage hobbies, interests, and activities in which these children are interested and can excel. Another way is to see that they have opportunities to take lessons in activities in which they can become skilled. If they can gain recognition for their superior knowledge of some hobbies or for their skills in some activities, they can feel better about themselves. Some children need to be taught how to dress and act, so they don't feel like misfits. Acting-out, overaggressive children who are disliked because of obnoxious behavior may need counseling to work through negative attitudes and feelings that prevent them from being more friendly and sociable. Suggesting socially acceptable ways for them to gain recognition may help them to redirect their efforts in the right direction.

Gangs and Clubs

Ages 10 to 11 are the ages for the beginning of clubs and gangs. These groups arise out of the need for children to be with others rather than to be alone. Children form play clubs, neighborhood gangs, fan clubs, and secret societies with special rules, observances, passwords, and initiation rites. They make plans to build a fort or club house, to go to the movies, to take a hike, or to have a picnic. Members are obliged to participate in the group's activities, and outsiders are excluded (Weiner & Elkind, 1972a, p. 135).

Gangs are usually organized along sex lines. The boys will have their gangs and the girls their social clubs. Whether groups are helpful or harmful depends upon their nature, purpose, and membership. Gangs of delinquents in tough neighborhoods provide some semblance of protection for individual members, but the members themselves may engage in fighting, stealing, gambling, drinking, or in pushing and using drugs (Crow & Crow, 1968, p. 279).

This same drive that impels children into gang activities can be channeled into well-organized, supervised clubs where individuals can give acceptable expression to their social needs. This is the age for Cub Scouts, Brownies, Boy Scouts and Girl Scouts, 4-H Clubs, YMCA and YWCA groups, Police Athletic League, Little League, or Boys Clubs. Parents would be wise to encourage their children to join and participate in worthwhile groups.

Competition

One of the problems of some groups is that they place undue emphasis on competition. Children of this age are naturally competitive. As individuals, they are competing with one another to see who can be the strongest or fastest or who can collect the most baseball cards or win a game. But some groups, such as Little League, emphasize winning the game, regardless of the effect of this competition upon individuals. Many authorities, including the American Academy of Pediatrics, feel that it is unwise to push preadolescents into highly competitive sports (Garrison, et al., 1967, p. 282). Young school-age children are not ready socially or psychologically for highly competitive games. The urge to win is so strong that the experience stimulates too much tension and anxiety, and defeat becomes a real blow to self-esteem.

Children ought to be encouraged to compete with themselves. Thus, a Cub Scout or Brownie can be encouraged to work for the next achievement rather than to become involved in stiff competition with other youngsters or groups. Those who are physically inept, unathletic, or unskilled at competitive games suffer terribly if they are excluded from teams or group activities. The purpose of such activities should be enjoyment, recreation, and the enhancement of self-esteem and self-worth, not the destruction of these (English & Pearson, 1945, p. 142).

Cruelty and Aggression

Children of this age can be very cruel. They callously exclude one another from their groups, say things that shame or belittle others, or pick on those who are younger or weaker than they. They hate their rivals, verbally castigating them because they want to feel important themselves. For this reason, children need to learn to stand up for themselves and, especially, to protect themselves from bullies.

I remember counseling with one mother who—because of her religious upbringing—strongly objected to fighting. She had taught her 9-year-old son never to fight; in fact, she had literally taught him to turn the other cheek and never to hit back if someone hit him. Unfortunately, one bully at school found this out and would daily hit, abuse, and taunt this boy each afternoon on the way home from school. The youngster came home battered, bruised, and crying, but he obeyed his mother and would not fight back. Of course, the more he refused to fight, the more the bully called him a "sissie" and picked on him. After several sessions of counseling, the mother became convinced that she could not let her son take any more punishment, so she told him never to start a fight or to hit first but that, if the bully hit him, to hit him back. The next day her son came home triumphant: "I really hit him, Mom. I knocked him down and made him cry. He won't pick on me again." And he didn't.

Of course, the best way to deal with bullies is not to have anything to do with them, but if they insist on trouble, children have to be prepared to deal with the situation. I encourage younger children to enlist the aid of older, stronger friends if they cannot handle the situation themselves. Occasionally, parents may have to step in and threaten retaliation if the bully will not leave their child alone.

TEEN-AGERS

Heterosexual Adjustments

The greatest challenge to the teen-ager is to learn to make friends with those of the opposite sex. Those who are most successful are usually those who have made satisfying social adjustments earlier and those whose self-esteem is intact. Children who arrive at puberty with an inadequate self-concept and with deep-seated feelings of inadequacy have the most trouble getting acquainted with those of the opposite sex. However, most adolescents find that feeling at ease with the opposite sex takes time and experience. Teen-agers ask such questions (Rice, 1978a, p. 325) as:

> "How do you go about talking to a girl?"
> "Why are we so self-conscious when we meet boys?"
> "How can you get a boy to notice you and like you?"
> "Why is it that boys shy away from being introduced?"

Parental Mistakes

The reactions of parents are often crucial to adolescents in their efforts to achieve heterosexual friendships. Parents make several common mistakes.

One is to tease the teen-ager who expresses any interest in the opposite sex. Parents need to accept such interest as normal and to encourage their teen-agers in their interest.

Another error is to try to push teen-agers into social activities in which they are not interested. Parents who can't stand their children being unpopular, who are afraid their daughter will be a "wallflower" or their son "gay," only increase their children's self-consciousness and their sense of social failure.

Some parents are just the opposite. They try to discourage or even forbid social activities for which their teen-agers are ready. One mother forbids her ninth-grade daughter from going to school dances because the mother is afraid her daughter will become "involved with boys." Another mother remarked: "My Alice is a Junior and doesn't have any dates yet. I'm just as glad. This way I don't have to worry about her." Such attitudes are cruel and unrealistic, and they really don't solve the problem with which the parents are concerned.

Parental Assistance

What can and should parents do?

Parents can accept the fact that the desire for boy-girl friendship is a normal part of growing up.

Parents can welcome their teen-ager's friends—of both sexes—to their home. If having guests becomes excessive, some limitations can be placed on the number and frequency of visits, but without making teen-agers feel unwelcome.

Parents should encourage young teen-agers to participate in group activities and group dates. Shy children who are tongue-tied on a one-to-one dating basis often fit very well into a small group in which they feel comfortable.

Parents can encourage informal get-togethers and activities for young adolescents rather than formal affairs, such as dances, that involve pairing off. I know one PTA that planned a formal dinner and dance for sixth graders! The affair included corsages and formal dresses and suits! I'm sure that many of the youngsters would rather have had a coke party, with a variety of games and activities.

If teen-agers feel self-conscious because of health problems, such as obesity or acne, parents can get adequate medical assistance to help them with their problems.

Parents need to accept the fact that their teen-agers want to dress and look like others of their own age, since this is one way of gaining acceptance. Even if parents do object to certain hair or clothes styles, they can learn to live with them, realizing how important appearance is to their adolescents. Certainly, parents should not force unacceptable fashions upon their teen-agers.

Parents need not panic when their teen-ager starts dating or starts going steady. It's not the end of the world. In fact, parents can be thankful if the partner is a suitable one. If he or she is not suitable, I feel that parents have a right to discuss their feelings and the reasons why they feel as they do with their children. Teen-agers will listen if parents don't try to force their own wishes on them. If parents object, they should say so, but they should let their teen-agers know that the choice is up to them. If the partner is unsuitable, most thoughtful adolescents discover this for themselves and drop the relationship. But the important thing is for parents to establish an atmosphere of honest discussion in which they and their children can feel free to discuss their points of view.

12

Adolescents and Working Mothers

It is not easy to bring up teen-agers in today's world. And it is even more difficult if both parents work, since they have less time and energy to devote to their children and since there are fewer opportunities for family members to be together. Yet millions of mothers are working and are also quite successful in raising their adolescents to be mature adults.

REALIGNMENT OF FAMILY RESPONSIBILITIES

Overwork

One of the problems of all working mothers is an overload of work. One survey by the United States Department of Agriculture showed that women who were full-time job holders still spent an additional 4½ hours daily on homemaking tasks, or three times the amount of time spent by the husbands ("How Much Does He Do Around the House?", 1971). The husbands averaged a total of 1½ hours a day on yard and home care, car upkeep, food preparation and/or cleanup, taking care of children, and on all home tasks combined. Another survey showed that business and professional fathers of grade-school and teen-age children devoted only 4 percent of their total time each week to household tasks and child care (Smith, 1969, p. 109). Although a democratic philosophy of marriage emphasizes that the husband and wife share everything fifty-fifty, in actual practice, even the wife who works full time outside the home still takes the primary responsibility for housekeeping and child care. Many wives are exhausted from the overwork and deeply resent having so much to do.

Sharing the Work

One possibility, in addition to expecting the husband to assume part of the responsibility, is to expect adolescents to help out. Certainly, a minimum requirement ought to be to ask them to care for their own room, bathroom, personal belongings, and clothes. I feel that everyone ought to help out with the rest of the work of caring for joint living spaces, such as a den, kitchen, family room, or living room, plus doing such things as lawn mowing, gardening, and snow shoveling. Chores in conjunction with meal preparation and clean-up are also needed if the total family is to function.

One system is to list various responsibilities on a sign-up sheet, with mutually agreed upon requirements to sign up for a certain proportion of chores, depending upon the number of jobs that need to be done and the number of persons in the family. Chores may be rotated so that no one person is stuck with the same jobs all the time.

Another system is for family members to decide orally who does what, according to interests, desires, and talents, and then to keep these jobs over a long period of time. One person may enjoy gardening or lawn mowing; another may prefer vacuuming; another may like washing dishes or windows. Individual interests and abilities may be taken into consideration. One wife remarked:

> I'm glad we don't have to decide each week on who does what. It's too much of a hassle. We each have our responsibilities which everyone knows about and accepts. This is much easier for us than changing jobs all the time.

Enforcement

The problem is getting everyone to do what he or she says he or she are going to do. What do you do when people don't do their chores or when they always have excuses as to why they didn't do them?

Each family needs to decide as a group how they want to enforce the rules. Those persons who have to be absent should still have the responsibility of trading off their chores or getting a substitute. Some families make those who don't do their chores do extra work as a penalty; others have to pay a fine into a common "kitty" (which is used for family outings or get togethers) in addition to doing their chores. Whatever system works for the individual family may be all right. The family can't be run like the army, but each group has to have a few basic rules and requirements for its members. If there are no rules, chaos results, and the burden falls too heavily on some, while others never learn to be responsible. I do feel that it's important that the father, mother, and children all share the burden. I also object to the splitting of chores along sex lines, with the females doing all of the inside work and the males doing the outside work. It's important for boys to learn home management and baby tending and for girls to learn carpentry, lawn maintenance, and other traditionally masculine responsibilities. Of course, those with fewer obligations outside the home ought to be expected to bear more responsibilities in and around the house. There is no reason that a woman who is employed outside the home should be expected to come home and perform all of the traditional feminine chores, nor is there any reason why a man shouldn't be expected to assume his fair share of those chores. We need to teach our daughters some of the traditional male responsibilities also, and the time to begin is when the children are growing up. Hopefully, a family can develop a philosophy that doesn't emphasize man's work and woman's work but that refers to "our work."

SUPERVISION

Leaving Teen-agers Alone

Another thing working mothers worry about is leaving their teen-agers home alone. Mothers complain that their adolescents mess up the house; that they invite friends over to drink, smoke pot, and have parties; and that they entertain members of the opposite sex without parents around to chaperone. Teen-agers insist that they are old enough to take care of themselves and that they certainly don't need anyone to babysit them. They are highly insulted at the idea that their mothers want someone at home to look after them.

During the school year, the most that teen-agers are home alone is from after school until mother and father get home from work: at most three to four hours Monday through Friday, plus perhaps one half-day on Saturday, although it is seldom that both the father and mother have to work even half-days on Saturdays.

Possible Arrangements

There are several possibilities. One is to try to get teen-agers involved in after-school pursuits, so that they won't be coming home so early. One of the best possibilities is for the teen-ager to get an after-school job, which is excellent experience. Another is to participate in school clubs and extracurricular activities, although some of these end by four o'clock. Another arrangement is to have adolescents stay over at someone else's house or to let them bring home one friend to be with them. Parents can insist that home chores be performed after school, which, if done regularly, can keep teen-agers so busy that they won't have time to get into mischief. Or parents can insist that after-school time is when homework assignments should be done.

I do feel that parents have a perfect right to work out definite rules about having a group of friends or a girl friend or boy friend over when adults are not at home. Most parents don't think it's a good idea.

However, one mistake parents make is to treat all children alike. Some teen-agers are quite neat and clean, even in mother's absence; are not interested in having groups of friends over to have fun parties; and will not get into mischief with a boy friend or girl friend. Other adolescents can make a shambles of a house, invite their friends over and turn up the stereo so loud that the neighbors call the police, and do try to make out with their steadies when parents are away. (Adolescents have premarital sexual relations more frequently at home than in automobiles, outdoors, motels, or other places.) I don't feel that parents should close their eyes to what happens when they're away, but neither should they look for trouble when their teen-agers are quite trustworthy. Do teen-agers abide by their parents' wishes? Can they be trusted when parents are gone?

Trust

Parents have no choice but to trust their teen-agers unless the children have demonstrated that they can't be trusted. In fact, one of the most frequent complaints of teen-agers is that their parents don't trust them: "Why are our parents always so afraid we are going to do the wrong thing?" "Why can't they trust us more" (Rice, 1978a, p. 412).

Some parents have more difficulty trusting their adolescents than others do. Some parents tend to project their own anxieties, fears, and guilts onto their children. The most fearful parents are those who are most insecure or who were problem children themselves while growing up. For example, mothers who were the most sexually promiscuous when they were young are the ones who are most suspicious of their daughter's behavior with a boy friend. Basically, most adolescents feel that parents should trust them completely unless they have given the adult reason for distrust (Rice, 1978a, p. 413). The wisest course is to talk very frankly with adolescents about these concerns and to work out some general agreements that adolescents will follow. Working mothers can save themselves a lot of worry if they can be honest with their teen-agers, especially about talking over anxieties. Most teen-agers won't deliberately defy their parents if they feel that their expectations are reasonable.

TIME TOGETHER

Strangers in the House

One mother complained:

Ever since I started to work, I don't get much time to spend with the family. I hardly ever get to see the kids. I'm gone all day and am not home until 5:30. Weekends they spend most of their time with their friends. We used to be so close, but now I feel like we're a group of strangers living in the same house.

This is a common complaint in families with teen-agers, and not just in those where the mother works. In some instances, mothers are so busy with their social lives that they have a minimum of time available to spend with the children. In other families, adolescents are so involved with their activities and friends that they are seldom with their parents. Actually, many teen-agers don't spend much time with the family. They go through a period of years where activities with friends become so all-engrossing that their parents hardly ever see them.

Yet teen-agers also want parents to take an interest in them and to be available to offer help and companionship when it is needed. One boy complained:

> I'm the star player on the school basketball team, but never once has either parent come to see me play. They're either too busy or too tired or can't get a baby sitter for my younger sister. The crowds cheer me, the girls hang around my locker, some kids even ask for my autograph. But it doesn't mean much if the two most important people in my life don't care [Daly, 1963, p. 86].

Working mothers do find that they have far less time available either to attend PTA meetings and functions that involve their children or for a social life for themselves.

Scheduled Opportunities

What's the answer? Time together usually has to be scheduled. Some families schedule a "family time" where everyone is expected to be together. This can be an evening, an afternoon, or even a whole day. One woman physician with four children explains:

[The] children . . . know that Sunday is going to be the day for everybody. We don't always go off and do something. . . . We're all here together. We all have dinner together. That sort of thing. With the boys, and I think with the girls, during the four years when I was in practice, I used to set an afternoon aside for each one, just that child and me to do whatever he or she wanted to do [Callahan, 1971, p. 211].

Most couples find that they have to cut down on their separate social life, otherwise they never have any opportunities to be with their children.

Communication

Here again, it's not the amount of time that parents and children spend together, but it's what they do with the time available that counts. Families shouldn't feel that they always have to be involved in recreational pursuits. Just spending time talking is one of the most important things they can do. Teenagers have so many anxieties; there are so many daily happenings that they want to talk about; there are so many questions that come up. Some of the things seem trivial, such as: "Why didn't Mary want to go to the movies with me?" or "How come Chuck got to play on the first string and I didn't?", but these are the concerns that make up the lives of teen-agers. Then, out of the blue—without warning—they will bring up quite serious matters such as: "I don't know what I want to be when I get out of school" or "Bob wants me to sleep with him. Should I?" Parents can't force serious discussions, but such conversations do arise if parents provide informal, relaxed opportunities when no one else is around, and if they will use such occasions to listen and not to lecture. One mother related her experiences:

Most kids in grade school will gab on and on. . . . But starting in junior high, things change. They're thinking about things in a

> much more serious way and it's not easy to pull it out. . . . But, boy, I've learned this: They need to talk. They've got a lot sitting inside them. . . . What's really bothering them may not come out at the dinner table. And you can't just sit down and say, "Let's have a talk" and expect the kid to loosen up [Curtis, 1976, p. 51].

This mother went on to say that when she began to sense that something was going on that needed to come out or that her teen-ager was worried about something, she prolonged what she was doing in the kitchen in order to give her child an opportunity to stay in the kitchen with her to talk about it.

One of the complaints of adolescents is that parents do not listen to their ideas, don't accept their opinions as valid, or don't try to understand their feelings and points of view. Adolescents want parents who will talk with them, not at them. They say:

> We want parents we can take our troubles to and be sure they'll understand. Some parents won't listen or let their children explain. They should try to see things a little more from our point of view [Rice, 1978a, p. 411].

The most important thing parents can do to help troubled adolescents is to listen. That is the beginning of communication. Psychiatric social worker Virginia Satir reports that the average family dinner lasts ten to twenty minutes and that some families spend as little as ten minutes a week together (Rice, 1978a, p. 411). If families are to communicate, they have to be together long enough to do so.

PART II

Child Care

13

Baby Sitters and Substitute Care

FINDING A SITTER

The question every working mother asks is: "Where can I find a sitter?" After a mother has lived in a community or neighborhood for some time, she begins to discover primary sources of supply and to get acquainted with individual sitters. The usual procedure is to make inquiries of relatives, neighbors, and friends, or to get suggestions from older teen-agers. Sometimes such tactics don't work, especially if a mother has just recently moved to a community. In such cases, the mother has to broaden her search.

Baby-sitting Agencies

One source of supply is the agencies that are listed in the yellow pages of the phone book. Look under Baby Sitters, Sitting Services, Child Care, or other similar categories. Phone and ask to speak to the head of the agency to find out all the particulars. What type of people does the agency employ? How are sitters selected and what screening procedures are used? Are any particular qualifications required? Can a number of sitters be sent out from whom the mother can choose? What is the fee? Can special arrangements be made on a full-time, regular but part-time, or long-term basis? What areas of the community do the sitters come from? Are any close to where you live? What arrangements are usually made for transportation? It is also helpful to describe what one has in mind, the services that will be required, the type of sitter one prefers, the nature and hours of the employment, where one lives, and as much other information as you deem appropriate. If the mother is lucky, and if the agency is a reliable one, she will be able to discover several worthy applicants for the position that she has in mind.

Employment Agencies

Both public and private agencies list child-care workers and baby sitters who are seeking employment. The major public agency run by the state is the Employment Security Commission. Its services are available to all. It usually lists persons who are looking for full-time work or for part-time work on a fairly permanent basis. The numerous private agencies place persons on a full- or part-time basis. Different agencies specialize in different types of jobs. Some only place persons who are looking for part-time positions. A phone call to the different agencies will reveal to you how much help you can expect to receive from them.

Newspaper Advertising

No matter what you've been told, advertise your position in the help wanted section of the local newspapers. You'll have to screen all applicants very carefully, but if you're peristent, you may discover just the person you want.

One growing source of supply is young men and women who have graduated from high school and haven't found other employment, or college-age youths who, for one reason or another, have dropped out of school. College towns are full of college drop-outs who want to stay in the area. Many are "into children" and are looking for small wages plus board and room or for just enough money to live communally with other young people. These youths know how to get around a city and will take children to a museum or play monopoly on a rainy afternoon. One young mother in the Cambridge, Massachusetts area put an ad in the *Phoenix* and got over fifty applicants. She comments:

> The young woman I chose is fantastic. She comes when the children are home. . . . She wouldn't think of using a car when a bike or bus is available, and she gets around better than I do. My kids, whom I used to have watched in a fenced-in backyard, make it to the local stores now and through her have met other kids in the area. Television is a bad word in our house now [Curtis, 1976, p. 114].

Schools and Colleges

Call the guidance office, the dean's office, and the employment offices of local high schools, junior colleges, and colleges and tell them your needs. They may be able to help you. The one real difficulty in using students who are in school is scheduling: dovetailing their classroom hours into your baby sitting needs. If you need full-time help of students, it may be available only in the summer or from those who have already graduated or dropped out. Some high school departments of home economics have special training programs to prepare students to be baby sitters, child-care workers, or aides. Inquire to see if your local schools have such programs. If so, they are a rich source of trained help. Similarly, some colleges offer associate degrees or diploma courses for those not seeking full four-year degrees. Inquire to see if local schools have such programs and if any graduates are available.

Clergymen

Sometimes clergymen know of young people or older women who are looking for part-time or full-time child-care positions. Phone calls to those close by may reveal some readily available sources of help.

Senior Citizens' Organizations

Similarly, senior citizens' clubs and organizations often know of older persons who are willing to baby-sit on a regular basis, sometimes to live in, if needed.

Friends and Neighbors

Many working mothers are able to make arrangements for child care with a friend or neighbor. One common arrangement for women who are employed part time is to trade off baby sitters: "You sit for me on Tuesday, Thursday, and Saturday, and I'll sit for you on Monday, Wednesday, and Friday." Another arrangement is simply to take one's child over to the neighbor's house so she can watch him or her there. (See Chapter 14 for a complete discussion of Group Home Care.) Some mothers form neighborhood play groups of two or three children, hire a "teacher," and split the cost among the parents

(Curtis, 1976, p. 115). Such arrangements can be a real bonus for children who are at the age when they need to play with others.

Relatives

Some couples are fortunate enough to have relatives who are competent sitters and who are willing to help. Parents, grandparents, aunts, uncles, cousins, or others may be able to share in the child rearing. In these days of the nuclear family, however, when couples live apart from their relatives, none may be available to help. Or, even if they live close by, relatives may not be able to help for economic reasons (they need to work themselves), or they may be unwilling to help. Many parents or grandparents are leading productive lives of their own, or they feel that they have raised their family and don't want to be saddled with young children once more. Actually, one can't blame them. Many spend twenty-five to thirty years raising their own children. Now they feel they need a vacation. In such cases, couples will have to hire help outside the family.

SELECTING A SITTER

Age

Which makes the better sitter, an older person or a young person of high school or college age?

I would go more by the qualification of the individual than by the age (Fromme, 1977). However, there are advantages and disadvantages to older and younger persons. In comparison to those of college age and below, older persons are usually more steady and dependable, and there is less turnover in personnel. They are usually neater, will pay more attention to the physical care of the house and the children, and will do more housework and cooking. Most older women love to care for babies, especially before the babies begin walking. College-age persons or young marrieds are more flexible and cheerful and are better companions to active children; they will play games, take them places, and do many more things with them. Children are usually happier with them than with older persons. The turnover of teen-age sitters is very great. They are usually messier and less responsible than older people. Some are so busy using the telephone, watching television, entertaining friends, or eating that they don't have time to watch the children. Children usually have a lot of fun with them, but I would worry about teen-agers who don't seem very mature.

Ideally, young adults in their twenties or early thirties combine the best characteristics of both groups, but there are exceptions. Some teen-agers are fabulous with children and are very handy around the house as well. Some older persons are messy and lazy. It all depends upon the individual.

Personality Qualifications

I prefer sitters who are emotionally mature, well-adjusted individuals, free from excessive fears, anxieties, jealousies, hostilities, and other neurotic tendencies. I look for those who are self-assured, cheerful persons; who are emotionally stable; who are calm, easygoing types, free from moodiness and outbursts of temper; who can stand a reasonable amount of pressure or frustration without getting upset. They should be loving, kind, warm-hearted persons who are able to give and to receive genuine affection.

It helps to have persons who are socially well adjusted; who get along well with others; who like other people, especially children; and who are liked in turn. They need to be responsible, trustworthy, punctual persons whom one can completely depend on, who will follow through with what they say they will do, who will accept directions and instructions without resentment, and who have a desire to please. They should be flexible and adaptable to new situations and requests.

They should be reasonably intelligent persons who can stimulate cognitive growth in children. This means persons who like books, stories, and music; who use correct English; who are able to carry on an intelligent conversation; and who can stimulate creative curiosity and self-expression.

They should be in good health, with good health habits, which they can teach to children. They need to have a lot of physical stamina and energy to keep up with the rigors of their job. It helps if they know something about foods and nutrition and know how to select a balanced diet. I prefer persons who don't smoke, but this is a personal prejudice, since I try to keep children from starting. I insist that they not smoke pot or drink on the job.

I realize that the ideal sitter, whom I have outlined according to my own preferences, just doesn't exist. Besides, individual requirements may differ some from my concepts. Sometimes, it's helpful to try to match the sitter to the children, since different children need different handling and care. For example, some children need more firmness, so that a particular sitter can be too easygoing and indulgent. Some children need a lot of love and affection from a warm, kind, outgoing "maternal" type. Children who tend to be overactive, nervous, and easily overstimulated thrive best with sitters who are extremely calm, even-tempered and patient. Also, some sitters and children get along well together, whereas others just don't, so it's unwise to force people together who get on one another's nerves (Inoff & Halverson, 1977).

Professional Qualifications, Experience, and References

One of the most important considerations is to find out if the person is qualified by way of training and experience to perform the duties that one has in mind. Will the job entail only child care, or does it include such things as housekeeping, shopping, cooking, or laundry as well? Is the person willing to do all that is required? If so, does the person have sufficient practice and experience to perform well the duties required?

It is very important, particularly in employing persons one does not know, to ask for references. If the person has a variety of experiences, ask for three references from the most recent employers. But the references are no good unless one follows up on them, so phone them, if possible, or write them to find out as much as possible about your prospective sitter.

Health Certificate

Also, I feel it's important to require a certificate of good health from a physician. I know of one mother who employed a sitter who had tuberculosis. Both of her preschool children caught it. I certainly don't want a sitter who has infectious diseases of any kind to feed or bathe a baby. So, to be on the safe side, ask your sitter to get a health exam and to bring a certificate from the doctor. If she can't afford it, and if you feel that you like her otherwise, pay for it yourself—as a final precaution. It's worth it.

Expected Tenure

One of the most important requirements is to provide stability of care for young children (Murray, 1975). This means hiring a sitter who will stay with you over a long period of time. The more often you have to change sitters, the harder it is for children to adjust (See Chapters 2 and 3 for a complete discussion of this problem.) And the more often sitters are changed, the harder it is for the sitters themselves to adjust. After all, it takes time for them to get acquainted with you and your children and to learn to respond sensitively to their needs. The longer a sitter has cared for a particular child, the more responsive the sitter becomes and the more the sitter can provide care that is equivalent to that which the mother can provide (Rubenstein 1977). Therefore, I would emphasize that, with any prospective sitter, you consider only those persons who will be with you over as long a period of time as possible. One mother says that she has used the same baby sitter for fourteen years and that the sitter has never missed a day during that time (Callahan, 1971, p. 214). Obviously, this is too much to expect or hope for, but it is helpful, for example, if one can have the same sitter during those critical years when your child is less than three years of age. Even nursery school and kindergarten children are upset by a frequent turnover of personnel, so in your interview find out all the particulars that might influence how long your sitter can be with you. How long will she (or he) be in the area? Is the person in school and will he or she be graduating soon? Is marriage contemplated? Is the person married and, if so, are the husband and/or wife permanently settled in this geographical region? Is the woman planning on having a child? What other vocational plans does the person have? What are the financial needs of the prospective sitter? Where are other family members or relatives located? Ask any and all questions that will have any bearing on the tenure of your sitter.

If changes in sitters are necessary, don't leave your children with strangers. Rather, have the new sitter come and get acquainted ahead of time—when you are home or while your other sitter is still there. It's important that your child form attachments and get acquainted with the new sitter before he or she starts working for you (See Chapters 2 and 3 for a complete discussion).

Residence, Transportation

Another important consideration is where the prospective baby sitter lives. How far away will the sitter be living? How long will it take to travel to work? (This may be important when emergencies arise and you need the sitter quickly.) Will the sitter be driving? Will the sitter be using public transportation? How much will it cost? Will you be expected to pay for commuting costs? Will the sitter require transportation to and from work?

Sometimes, of course, the parents want a live-in baby sitter whose living quarters are in their own house or in servants' quarters. There are advantages and disadvantages to such an arrangement. The advantage is the ready availability of the sitter, especially if parents have evening meetings or have to be out of town for days at a time. Another advantage is that such a person may also double as housekeeper, especially when the children are asleep or in school. Some mothers find that the person who is organized, neat and tidy, and good at housekeeping is not the same kind of person who is good with children, so such parents prefer splitting the responsibility. They hire a live-in governess who is a nursemaid, teacher, and superivisor for the children and also hire a special person to come in several days a week as housekeeper. Obviously, such arrangements are expensive.

The Interview and Questionnaire

I thoroughly believe in selecting baby sitters from a number of applicants, not just hiring the first one who comes along. This means that all prospective applicants should be

interviewed in person, preferably by both parents (if both are home), so that two opinions are obtained. The purposes of the interview are several:
- To evaluate the personality and personal qualifications of the applicants.
- To evaluate such factors as age, references, experience, competence, possible tenure, and availability.
- To evaluate the applicants' philosophies of child rearing.
- To describe the job responsibilities and the terms of the employment.

The couple can save time by making up a job application form, asking for age, marital status, dependents, sex, place of residence, availability, education, wages expected, and other factual information, as well as experience and references. One psychologist has suggested that children be present during the interview, so that the parents can observe how the prospective sitter interacts with them (Salk, 1977, p. 88). The parents can also ask their children how they like the different applicants. Even 3- or 4-year-olds can tell if someone really likes them or not, and it's certainly unwise to hire someone the children don't like or someone who doesn't like the children.

One of the most important purposes of the interview is to find out as much as possible about the child-rearing philosophies of the applicants. Parents should try to hire someone who most nearly reflects their own views. If parents are interested in meeting children's total needs, the parents need someone who believes in need fulfillment rather than deprivation. For example, if they believe infants should be fed when hungry, picked up when distressed, diapered when wet, talked to, rocked, or cuddled, then it's important to have a sitter who will do these things—not because she has to, but because she feels it's the right thing to do for the children and because she wants to. Or, some parents are very firm about such matters as eating a balanced diet, avoiding too many sweets, taking baths, brushing one's teeth and hair, and going to bed on time. Certainly, they have a perfect right to expect that the sitter will follow through with these things, too. Some parents are concerned about their children's cognitive growth and development and like to have their children hear stories and have opportunities for art work, for crafts, or for creative activities. They need a sitter who will offer these opportunities for children. Some parents try to control the T.V. programs their children are allowed to watch. Yet some sitters will let children watch forbidden adult programs "as special treats" or simply because they make no effort to offer any guidance. It's very maddening to employ sitters who repeatedly ignore parents' wishes or who feel that they know better than the parents and are going to do what they want to do regardless of the parents' feelings. Some sitters will even argue with the parents: "Oh, three cookies won't hurt him." They go ahead and give the child cookies, even though the parents have forbidden it. If parents can't trust the sitter to do as she or he is told, then probably they should not hire that person in the first place.

One young mother decided before she interviewed prospective sitters to make up a whole list of questions that would acquaint her with the child-rearing philosophies of the applicants. Here are just a few of the questions she asked:

- Is it better to put toddlers in a playpen or to let them crawl free?
- Do you believe in saying "no" when children touch knickknacks, or would you rather put them out of reach?
- Do you pick up an infant when he or she cries?
- How do you feel about taking children on errands, or on trips?
- What are the ways in which you would discipline a 3-year-old?

- What are your views on children watching television? How much do you watch T.V.?
- How do you feel about developing children's eating habits? About giving sweets?

These questions are offered only as samples, and they are far from complete. Couples should make up a list of their own questions, the ones that they feel are important to ask.

SUPERVISING THE SITTER

Probation

I prefer hiring a sitter and putting that person on probation for several weeks or a month. That way, you have an out if you decide that the individual will not work out.

Written Instructions

No matter how competent, every sitter needs to know what parents expect and how and what things parents want done. One way to avoid misunderstandings is for parents to think carefully about and work out what they will require and then to write out instructions for the sitter. How much housework is the sitter expected to do? Will she have responsibilities for cleaning; giving the children their baths; fixing the baby's formula; cooking meals for the children, herself, and/or the couple? Is she expected to have a meal prepared when the working couple arrive home? Is she expected to keep the house neat and clean, to see that the older children pick up after themselves? Will she have any responsibilities for laundry, diaper washing, bed changing? Will she have to take the children on trips, outdoors to play, to the circus? Will she have to get them ready in time to meet the school bus? Will she have to drive Mary to her piano lesson? What time are the children expected to be home from school? Are they allowed to go over to a friend's house? Are older children and teen-agers allowed to have friends over when parents are not home? There are really dozens of things that need to be spelled out, and the best way to avoid misunderstandings is to put everything in writing: schedules, basic rules, general duties—everything.

Emergencies

Parents ought to leave full information about where they are and about where and how they can be reached in case of illness, accidents, or emergencies of various kinds. It is also wise to write down:

> *The name and telephone number of your doctor, as well as the telephone numbers of the fire department, police, medical emergency service.*
>
> *The name and telephone number of a responsible relative or friend who can be called if you can't be reached.*
>
> *Details about the house—how to regulate the heat, where to locate the fuse or relay box, how to lock doors and windows, what to do if the heat or lights go off* [Infant Care, 1977, p. 53].

It's important that at least one parent be available in case of an emergency. This is one reason why it helps a lot if one's job is not too far from home. Salk writes:

> *My children have always been proud of the fact that I've been at their school within 12 minutes of getting a call that there's been an accident or an illness. It's essential for working parents to make their whereabouts known to the school authorities or the housekeeper, and it's crucial to respond immediately to an emergency. Even if you're in the middle of a board of directors meeting, I think your colleagues will respect you more if you put your child's needs first than if you let the school or the babysitter handle it. If you freely give your child time at a*

moment of crisis, he won't find reasons to steal it from you on other occasions. He'll feel secure and know that he can count on you [Salk, 1977, p. 154].

Illnesses

Parents will have to decide under what circumstances they will come home or stay home because of illness. Some mothers will take a child's temperature, and if the child has a fever and has to stay home, the mother also stays home. Others go to work unless the children are quite ill. Each mother has to play it by ear. Even if the child is only mildly sick in bed with a slight fever, both sitters and children appreciate the mother calling home frequently or the mother allowing the child to call her at work (Salk, 1977, p. 154).

Of course, some children discover that the only way they can get their mother's attention is to be sick, so they may even pretend illness. The answer is to give enough time and attention at other times so that illness seldom becomes an attention-getting technique.

One of the toughest situations is the child who is chronically ill or who suffers from a long-term illness. The mother feels guilty about leaving her sick child, but she is also very apprehensive at missing so much work. Under such circumstances, she is fortunate if she has a sitter who can provide practical nursing care for her children so that she can remain at work. Some bosses are very understanding, at least for a while, but others aren't and may fully expect that the mother make adequate arrangements to handle such emergencies. "If you have sick kids and have to be home with them, then you're obviously not producing as much as the men and women without families are," one mother said. "It's just an attitude, and you can sense it. It's a cold silence when you say you can't make it in to work" (Scott, 1977, p. 143). Some mothers volunteer to take work home, to work nights, or to make it up when they return. In other situations, the husband is able to take time off for a while so the total burden won't fall on the wife. Some wives have to quit work entirely because they don't feel right about leaving their child and neglecting their job. Certainly, one solution, if feasible, is to get a temporary leave of absence until the child is better.

14

Family Day-care Homes, Group Day-care Homes, Infant-care Centers, and Day-care Centers

FAMILY DAY-CARE HOME

Description

A family day-care home is an arrangement whereby a day-care mother (care-giver) takes care of children in her own home (*Day Care for Young Children*, 1974). This is the most common arrangement for children under three, although the arrangement may include other children. The 1972 Federal Day Care standards require that there be one care-giver per six children (including the mother's own children under 14 years of age), provided that at least half the group is over three, but in no case may one adult care for more than two infants or three toddlers (Cohen & Zigler, 1977, p. 461). The need for regulations as to the number of children that one care-giver may care for becomes evident in the following description of a home where no limitations were imposed:

> When Mrs. _____ opened the door for us, we felt there were probably very few, if any, children in the house, because of the quiet. It was quite a shock, therefore, to discover about seven or eight children, one year old or under, in the kitchen; a few of them were in high-chairs, but most were strapped to kitchen chairs, all seemingly in a stupor.
>
> It wasn't until we were in the kitchen that we heard the noise coming from the basement. There we found over twenty children huddled in a too small, poorly ventilated, cement floor area. A TV with an apparently bad picture tube was their only source of entertainment or stimulation.
>
> When we went to look at the back yard, we passed through a porch, where we discovered, again, children, children and more children. The children were literally under our feet [Keyserling, 1972, pp. 135, 136].

Most states provide licensing arrangements to care for other people's children in family day-care homes. The license tells you that the home has been inspected and that it meets health, safety, and other conditions. Parents should ask to see the license or should call the agency that issues the license (usually the department of social services) to find out if the license has ever been revoked and, if so, for what reason. Unfortunately, a license is not obligatory in many states, and only a fraction of the day-care homes that are in operation have applied for a license. This is why parents have to be extremely careful about their selection of a home.

What to Look for in a Day-care Home

Parents should try to find a home near their own or near the place where they work in order to avoid excessive travel time to and from the home. The day-care home should be large enough to take care of the children comfortably. It should be well lighted, well heated and ventilated, safe, in good repair, and, usually, above basement level. If there are stairs, they should have a handrail. Upstairs windows should be securely screened or barred, and all heaters should be ventilated and screened. It is helpful to have an outdoor fenced-in play yard with gates that cannot be opened by small children. Outdoor play equipment should be safe and suitable for the ages of the children. Meals should be prepared in a clean kitchen and served in a clean dining area, with proper utensils for the children. There should be a toilet(s) in good repair, a washbasin with hot and cold running water, and a footstool so that small children can reach it. There should be separate towels, washcloths, and sheets for each child, as well as a place in which each child can keep his or her own things. There should be a separate room where a sick child can be placed while he or she is waiting to be called for.

Unfortunately, many unlicensed homes do not even begin to approach these standards. Here is a description of an unacceptable home:

> *The condition of the home and surroundings . . . was appalling. . . . There was not one toy or article with which the children could amuse themselves or be amused. There was no TV in evidence. The outside of the home looked as if it were about to be condemned, and the inside wasn't much better. I arrived in 80 degree heat, and there was no ventilation evident. The rooms were extremely cluttered and dirty. . . . The backyard was not fenced in and was in weeds* [Keyserling, 1972, p. 134].

Here is another description:

> *This interviewer can still recall quite vividly one particular home she visited where she counted a total of eleven children — five infants and six other small children from about one to four years old of both sexes and almost naked, running and scream-*

ing in the four-room house. The strong urine smell, the stale odor of uneaten food everywhere, and the bugs crawling around made one nauseous. There was one very obese, sullen, unpleasant woman in charge . . . [Keyserling, 1972, p. 135].

It is evident that no parents should leave their children in a day-care home without visiting and inspecting the place for themselves.

What to Look for in a Day-care Mother

Even if your state does not require a license for a day-care mother, parents should meet her and talk with her about such things as discipline, food, toilet training, sleep, play, and hygiene and find out how she feels about these things. Parents may also want to visit the day-care home to observe the caregiver "in action." What is her attitude and relationship to the children? Does she seem warm and affectionate, and, does she like the children? Is she kind but calm and firm with them? Does she seem interested in teaching them to care for themselves, for their belongings, and for other children? Does she provide interesting materials to use and activities to do? Does she seem to be in good health, and is she energetic enough to be able to keep up with the children? Are the children happy? Do they seem to like her? Would your child be happy with her? Has the care-giver had any special training to prepare her for her role? (*Day Care for Young Children*, 1974).

At the present time, state licensing requirements are often very vague as to what they require of a day-care mother. The regulations may merely specify that the woman be of "good character and reputation" or that she be in good health, as indicated by a doctor's certificate. Some states specify some further qualifications, such as the following (Keyserling, 1972, p. 147):

- Should have an affectionate attitude toward children and must be able to deal with them firmly and consistently.
- Should be a mature and relaxed person who likes and understands children.
- Must be able to read and write.
- Must have patience, endurance, and sound judgment and love children.
- Be neat, clean, cheerful, friendly.
- Have a harmonious family life.
- Not be elsewhere employed.

One of the sources of controversy is whether or not states should require any formal training of these care-givers or whether it is enough that they be "warm, understanding" women (Collins & Watson, 1977, p. 115). Certainly, the best care-givers realize the importance of providing an intellectually stimulating environment. The following is a description of an adequate caregiver:

> Mrs. _____ has great understanding . . . love and warmth, and her personality is very well suited for what she is doing. Very clean home, adequate to the needs of the children. Takes children out for play, to parks, local excursions. She shows tremendous interest in children . . . keeps a good supply of books, toys and games. Through reading and using encyclopedias has educated herself [Keyserling, 1972, p. 135].

Evaluation

When it is well managed, provides a suitable environment, and is run by a qualified caregiver, family day care is often the best group care for young children. It is usually available close to home. The hours can be flexible, depending on the needs of the parents. Children usually adjust more easily when they go from their home to another home similar to theirs. A good family day-care mother can supply the mothering young children need. This arrangement has the added advantage of being able to serve several children of varying ages from the same family. The youngest children adjust more readily when older siblings are around (Host & Heller, 1971, p. 121). If done well, family day care is my second choice among the types of care that are suitable for children 3 years of age or under. (Care in the child's own home is my first choice.)

GROUP DAY-CARE HOME

Description

The group day-care home offers family-care for older children, usually ages 3 through 14, with a maximum of twelve children allowed in the group, including the mother's own children, and a child-staff ratio not to exceed six to one. This type of arrangement is suitable for children who need before and/or after school care and where a great deal of mothering or individual care is not needed. This is also an appropriate arrangement for school-age children who are out of school for the summer or holidays.

A Good Example

Here is a brief description of one very fine group day-care home run by a care-giver whom we shall call Debbie (Galinsky & Hooks, 1977, p. 193).

Debbie applied for licensing and, in order to comply to standards, had to fence in her yard, put knives and detergents safely away, provide space for ten children (including her two preschoolers), and have tuberculosis tests for herself and her family. She interviewed parents to find out what they were looking for in a day-care home and selected those children she felt would fit into the kind of family she had to offer. She accepted eight children varying in age from 3 to 8 years, and employed another person as her assistant (making a child-staff ratio of 5:1). During the summer, Debbie had her full complement of ten children every day, but during the winter she had about half the group in the morning and the rest—the older ones—after school.

Debbie uses her front and back yards and the bottom floor of her house. Upstairs is off limits, except to her own children. the fenced-in back yard includes a picnic table, a tire swing, a treehouse, a sandbox, wheel toys, a bright yellow slippery slide, and—in the summer—a plastic wading pool. Debbie takes the children on frequent trips to the local zoo, the firehouse, museums, libraries, pony rides, and even a tour to McDonalds. During the school year, people in the community come in to teach specific things, such as tumbling, or to provide a story hour.

The schedule begins at breakfast. The morning usually includes a combination of free play and planned activities in the back yard. The children usually lunch in the yard or, on cold or rainy days, have a picnic in front of the indoor fireplace. After lunch, the children are divided into "nappers" and "nonnappers," with the nappers sleeping on floor mats in the large dining room. The nonnappers choose "quiet time" activities from the toy or materials shelf. All children join in activities after nap time. The parents arrive between 5:00 to 5:30 and Debbie requires them to stay for a few minutes while their children show off things they have made. Debbie insists on communication with parents and on developing an openness with them about the children.

Debbie handles the food details a little differently than some centers. She asks the children to bring their own lunch, but she provides morning and afternoon snacks. She insists on individual drinking glasses with names and colors to identify the one for each child. She has made special arrangements for medical care in case of emergencies, with parents' permission, and she keeps a close watch for colds, fevers, swollen tonsils, and so on. If a child is sick during the day, the child is put in a special room until the parents arrive to take him or her home. Debbie has low-cost liability insurance that covers accidents while the children are in school or on trips.

The above description is that of a superior home (Galinsky & Hooks, 1977, p. 193). One of the secrets of Debbie's success is that she continues her own education by enrolling in child development classes, schools, and conferences. Details may vary, but parents should try to select homes that are equally as well managed.

INFANT-CARE CENTERS

Philosophy

Much of the controversy over day care has focused around infant-care centers—those for children under three years of age (Chandler et al., 1968). In spite of general government opposition in the past to day care for children under age three, infant-care centers continue to multiply, so federal and state agencies have had to take a new look at such programs. In fact, a separate government bulletin has been issued that describes day care for infants (Huntington et al., 1971). This bulletin says in part:

> *Day care programs for infants and toddlers, organized with great care and operated with vigilance,* reflect a blending of the conviction of the importance of experiences during the first few years of life; concern about possible harmful consequences if these programs are not well carried out; and satisfaction that such programs meet an acute family need and serve a major function in strengthening family life.

If there is any consensus about infant care programs, it is that we must keep an open mind about them. For many years professional, health and welfare organizations concerned with standards for day care and with organized programs for children have urged that children younger than three years not be in group care. Family day care, in which a small number of children are cared for in a private home, has always been the preferred method of care for the very young. Even with this as a model, in actual fact large numbers of babies have been cared for in inadequate, unsupervised settings since this was almost all that was readily available.

Controversy existed concerning the effects on babies of being away from their mothers for part of the day. Some felt that the separation itself would have detrimental effects. Research has now shown that it is the inadequacy of the care frequently suffered in such settings that harms the child and probably not the fact of the brief separation itself. Now being rethought are the ways to ensure the quality of mothering care the baby receives for the hours he is away from home as well as at home and the ways in which day care programs may most effectively meet the needs of babies and their families [Huntington et al., 1971, p. 5].

The philosophy has now developed that good day-care services, even for infants, help parents to meet the needs of children, help enrich children's lives for periods of time during the day, and can be family-strengthening rather than parent-and-child separating (Macrae & Jackson, 1976). The key lies in the quality of the service that is provided (Gutelius & Kirsch, 1975).

Quality Care

In general, an adequate program in a center for infants meets the following needs in the lives of these children:
   1. *Adequate nourishment.* Children need not be fed

on a rigid schedule, but rather according to when they are hungry. Keeping a record of feeding times shows each child's pattern.
2. *Protection from and care of physical disorders and disease.* The health of children must be given primary consideration (North, 1971).
3. *Increasing control over body systems and development of regulatory mechanisms.* Infants need to be diapered as required, with toilet training beginning at about 18 months of age, in cooperation with similar efforts on the part of parents.
4. *Rest, solitude, and peaceful moments.* This means rest periods in the schedule, providing opportunities for nap time or at least quiet times for children to spend as they choose.
5. *Opportunities for both indoor and outdoor play and recreation.* This means an outdoor play area, preferably adjacent to an indoor area so that children can get to it themselves.
6. *A relatively small number of adults having continuous, focused, and affectively meaningful relationships with children.* Child-staff ratios should be 3:1 for infants 0-1½-years old and 4:1 for toddlers 1½-3 years old. Every effort should be made to ensure stability of personnel.
7. *Frequent contacts with adults and other children who are expressive and warm.* This means care-givers who like children, who show their appreciation to them, who can give of themselves, and who are patient and affectionate.
8. *Verbal interaction.* This means care-givers who talk to infants; who enjoy picking up babies, looking directly at them, and smiling and speaking directly to them; and who will make exten-

sive use of pictures, story books, and music as children get older.
9. *Adults who help children learn controls.* This means care-givers who teach what is permissible and what is not permissible, but they should be persons who are not excessively punitive in controlling behavior and who are not given to outbursts of anger. This means that adults need to respond sensitively to children's behavior and to reward and re-enforce desirable conduct.
10. *Adults who are models for the children to imitate and who are examples of relative success.* This means care-givers who show the children what it is like to be proud and to have high self-esteem.
11. *Adults who respect children as individuals and who respect their family and ethnic identities.* Care-givers must be acquainted with, accept, and appreciate the children's cultures, customs, and languages and help children to develop pride in their own uniqueness.
12. *Consistency, regularity, and order in the physical environment.* This means regularity of mealtimes, bedtimes, and daily schedule, as well as the stability of personnel involved with the children.
13. *Maximum opportunities for learning and acquiring mental and motor skills.* This means freedom to explore, to be interested, and to be challenged. Toys and creative activities appropriate to the children's age levels, an environment rich enough in appropriate stimuli, and support and encouragement in developing their own abilities should be provided.
14. *Protection from negative emotional states.* Children should be protected from anxiety and terror

and should have freedom to express their feelings and attitudes. Care-givers should be sensitive to children's feelings and be able to help them to handle fear, sadness, and anger as well as to experience love, joy, and satisfaction. Introductions to the home should be gradual, with parents staying until children feel more secure and until they will not be upset by parents leaving (Huntington et al., 1971).

DAY-CARE CENTER

Varieties of Programs

The general term *day-care center* applies to a variety of types of child-care centers, located in different places: in community centers, places of business, or neighborhood buildings. Centers may be open all day long, from 6 A.M. to 6 P.M., or only during certain hours or seasons. They may serve a variety of ages, from infancy through age 14. At the present time, Federal Day Care standards distinguish seven age groups and child-staff ratios: 0-$1\frac{1}{2}$ years (3 children per care-giver): $1\frac{1}{2}$-3 years (4 children per care-giver); 3-$4\frac{1}{2}$ years (7 children per care-giver); $4\frac{1}{2}$-6 years (10 children per care-giver); 6-8 years (13 children per care-giver); 9-11 years (16 children per care-giver); and 12-14 years (20 children per care-giver) (*Day Care for Young Children*, 1974).

Qualities of a Good Center

The following questions should prove helpful in selecting a high quality center:

Arrival: *How do children act when they arrive? Do they come* in eagerly or hesitantly? How do parents and caregivers interact during this time? How are children greeted by the caregivers? Activities: Are there ample opportunities for the children to work and play? Is there a choice of activities? Are they appropriate for the children's ages and stages of development? Do the activities foster the children's physical, social, intellectual, and emotional growth? Do adults allow children to explore and discover for themselves?

Transitions: How are shifts from one activity to another handled? Are transitions smooth? Is there a minimum of waiting time between activities? Do the children know what to do?

Lunch and Snacks: Are these relaxed, social times, when caregivers and children enjoy sharing food and conversation? Are children encouraged to eat nutritious and balanced meals?

Naptime: Is it a restful period? How do adults help children who have trouble relaxing?

Departure: What is the quality of interaction between caregivers, parents, and children at departure time?

Materials: Does the program provide a good variety of stimulating materials? Are they attractively displayed and readily accessible to the children?

Space: Is the space aesthetically pleasing and comfortable? Does it reflect respect for the child; that is, are children's art work and other projects prominently displayed? Is the space as accident-proof as it can be? Does it allow for freedom of movement? Does it provide for both group and individual activities?

Support Services: What health services are provided for the children? For families? What social-support services are offered? Are there opportunities for staff training?

Caregiver-child Relationships: Is there a caring and individual relationship between teacher and child? Is there genuine respect for each other's racial, socioeconomic, and cultural background? Are boys and girls treated equally? Do children feel free to express their questions and feelings to caregivers? How are behavior problems handled? Do caregivers help children understand problems and seek solutions? Do they respect children's needs to let off steam and show emotions? Do they help children develop their own self-control? *Do they console and comfort unhappy children?*

Child-child: *Do children respect each other? Do they have fun together? Do they learn from each other? Do they console and comfort each other? Do they help each other?*

Caregiver-caregiver: *How do the caregivers interact with each other? Do they seem to be working together?*

Relations with Parents: *Do parents have any say in the setting of goals? How is the parent kept informed of his or her child's experiences in the program? Do parents have ready access to teachers? How do parents and teachers communicate? Is the relationship friendly and accepting? In what ways does the program respect and reflect the values and goals of parents?* [Galinsky & Hooks, 1977, pp. 9-11].

The last question is the key criterion. When parents find the right program, they are able to say: "It felt right. It clicked. You know when it's the right place."

15

Child Care in Other Countries

As the need and demand for more group child-care services increases, experts have found it helpful to find out what other countries are doing. Two different countries, Israel and Russia, have been selected for discussion in this chapter, since they represent two different approaches to the problem.

ISRAEL

The Kibbutzim

Actually, there are several different forms of child care in Israel. There are *residential institutions*, which serve mostly as placement for children from broken families. There are *day-care centers* for children of working mothers, and there is the collective form of child rearing in the communal settlement

—the Kibbutzim (Grotberg, 1971). Much of the interest in child-care arrangements in Israel has focused on the Kibbutz as a possible model for child-care arrangements elsewhere in the world.

The Kibbutz is a voluntary, predominantly agricultural collective settlement of between 100-400 members. All property is owned collectively. All earnings go to the central commune, which distributes "to each according to his need." Work assignments of menial tasks are determined daily by a work committee, with the more skilled jobs assigned for long periods. Both men and women work eight to nine hours daily and attend numerous meetings in the evenings. Each couple occupies a one- or two-room residence that serves as living and sleeping quarters. Meals are eaten collectively in a central dining hall. Other family functions, such as laundry, are performed communally (Grotberg, 1971, p. 40). About four percent of the Israeli population live on the Kibbutzim.

CHILDREN

The children live from birth on with their age group, not with parents. These groups reside in separate children's houses, with each group moved from the infants' house to the toddlers' house to the kindergarten to the older children's houses at appointed times, changing adult caretakers each time. In some of the Kibbutzim, the children sleep alone at night, with only a circulating night watchman and an intercom system as a means of communication (Callahan, 1971, p. 51). The children's houses have kitchens, laundries, play yards and equipment, and animal farms, so that the children eat, sleep, play, and study in their respective houses with their age mates. A typical preschool group includes six to eight children, cared for by a trained caretaker and her assistant, who are also responsible for the physical care of the quarters.

CONTACT WITH PARENTS

Kibbutz parents have a great deal of personal contact with their children. Most of the actual caretaking of infants, especially during the first six months, is performed by the mother. Mothers visit many times during the entire day (as many as six times per morning) and are permitted to take time off from work to do so. In fact, a higher percentage of Kibbutz mothers nurse their babies than do city mothers. By the time the child is 8 months old, the caretaker performs about half of the feeding and caretaking acts. She gradually takes over until, by the child's second year, she handles all caretaking routines, while the mother's diminishing visits to the children's houses become purely social (Grotberg, 1971, p. 44).

The most important parent-child contact is during the "children's hour," a daily late afternoon period when the parents spend one or two hours of "togetherness" with their children. The children are taken away from their houses to the parent's quarters or to various outdoor areas of the Kibbutz. Infants may be given supper and put to bed briefly in the parents' room. Older children often come to their parents' room on their own. The period of family interaction is an integrated part of life in the Kibbutz, and the fact that parents are unfettered with the usual responsibilities of discipline and training allows them to give undivided attention to their children. Thus, the children are not denied the opportunity to develop emotional attachments to their parents. In fact, some may be closer to their parents than are children in some nuclear families (Murray, 1975, p. 775).

CARETAKERS

The caretakers in the Kibbutz are well trained. Their roles are those of professional educators, and they may actually instruct the mothers in infant care. They train children in basic habits of cleanliness, eating, and cooperating within the group. They are accountable to the education committees of the Kibbutz and are elected by and represent the total community.

THE PEER GROUP

The peer group becomes all-important to the children, since associations may be life-long. The child visits his parents but returns "home" to his companions. The group provides emotional support, companionship, and a feeling of belonging.

EFFECTS ON CHILDREN

A number of studies have been undertaken to establish the effects on children of growing up in the Kibbutz (Rabin, 1965). In general, none of the dreadful consequences predicted by Western psychoanalysts for such a system seem to have come true. Two observers report:

> ... *We can sum up the Kibbutznik: he is healthy, intelligent, generous, somewhat shy but warm human being, rooted in his community and in the larger Israeli society. He shows no signs of the emotional disturbance we would expect from a violation of our ideal mother-child relationship* [Rabkin & Rabkin, 1969, p. 46].

Careful analysis reveals both strengths and weaknesses. Comparison of Kibbutz infants, 10-year-olds, adolescents, and young men were made with other Israeli children who were reared by their families. The results seem to show that Kibbutz babies were behind the family-reared children in a personal-social scale and in speech but that the 10-year-olds had more than caught up, and the adolescents and young men were able to function normally, both in Israeli society and in the army. Infants did show some personality disturbances from multiple mothering, especially from repeated changes of caretakers.

Children 7 to 12 years old were considered ahead on all measures. This was attributed primarily to the excellent noncompetitive educational methods. Some observers feel that Kibbutz adolescents lack the inner emotional richness that characterizes the middle-class child who grows up having to cope with an ever-changing environment (Bettelheim, 1969). At the same time, the Kibbutz system does not produce homosexuality, drug addiction, abused children, or crime (Callahan, 1971, p. 52, 53).

COMMENTS

The Kibbutz system, as a collective arrangement serving both parents and children, has worked well for those who have been attracted to it. Parents are free to engage in a meaningful adult life of their own, while at the same time bearing children and maintaining close family relationships. Kibbutz members are proud of their system and are willing to pay its price. The great majority growing up in it prefer raising their children the same way (Grotberg, 1971, p. 41).

RUSSIA

Types of Programs

In 1956, the Soviet Union instituted a program to shift a major part of child care from the family to day nurseries. The program includes children from three months to seven years of age. *Day care* comprises 85 percent of the care outside the family and consists of five to ten hours of care daily. *Boarding care*, the next most common type, cares for the children five days each week and returns them to their parents on weekends. *Residential care* involves the total care of children who cannot be cared for in families (Nye & Berardo, 1973, p. 394).

Philosophy

Basic Soviet philosophy holds that it is the duty of the government to assist parents in creating "the Soviet man"; that is, citizens who are devoted and loyal to the state and who are trained to serve it. Since mothers as well as fathers are expected to work for the state, children are sent to day-care centers by three months of age. This frees the mother to go to work and allows the state to hire professional, state-supervised teachers and child-care workers. Policies are dictated by the state, and all programs are standardized to produce good Soviet citizens. Individuality, questioning, and rebellion are not tolerated (Callahan, 1971, p. 48). Thus, all teachers or "upbringers" are the purveyors of the new culture, and they are selected and trained to teach the political ideas of the state. From the Soviet point of view, every advantage that an industrial nation can provide is given to the children, and part of this claim is merited by the extraordinary priorities and investments that sustain the child-care program (Grotberg, 1971, p. 8).

Care of Infants

Babies are cared for in the state nurseries, with one "upbringer" and an assistant in charge of each seven or eight children. Babies are on a "regime," which is a schedule of programmed re-enforcement to develop motor and language skills and to promote group cooperation. Infants are put in groups in large playppens at heights that permit adults to interact face to face with them. Gradually, the children are taught to share toys, to help each other, and to play together. Nurse-teachers try to prevent conflicts and to encourage the children to help one another. The following description emphasizes the positive role that the "nyanya" or nurse-teacher plays in the lives of the infants:

Accompanying the description of every task of the nurse or "*nyanya*" is the instruction to be happy, tender, gentle, and encouraging. Nowhere is there mention of stern measures to be taken, no negative responses, no punishment. The role of the worker in the child-care facility is to set an example for the behavior of her charges, to take a positive approach to the learning of appropriate skills at each stage of development. A positive emotional state is seen as important for the physical well-being of the child, as well as providing a better atmosphere for learning. When a child cries or is unhappy, it is seen as a failure of the upbringer [Meers & Marans, 1968, p. 245].

Older Nursery Children

Obedience and self-control are taught early, since a proper attitude toward work is a major goal. Children learn to supervise one another and to accept supervision. Small groups are urged to compete in work and character building with other groups. The children themselves are given the responsibility for enforcing the desired values and responses. They are encouraged to denunciate deviant members and to punish laggards and dissenters with ostracism. Thus, children who most conform to adult values and to the state party line are rewarded with control of their peers. Adult teachers are all women who have been conformists, and hence they are trusted to be in charge of maintaining collective values. This produces docile children who are dependent on adults and on collective security (Bronfenbrenner, 1970).

Family Values

The values taught by the schools are also taught by parents. Mothers are restrictive, protective, and very loving, but they also demand obedience and conformity. Actually, Russian society is very child-centered and very much involved with raising children. Teachers and child-care workers are given much respect and are supported by the parents and by the larger society. Generally, Soviet parents spend more time playing and talking with their children than most American parents do, even though the chldren are in schools and child-care centers for long hours. Russian babies and children have a great deal of physical affection and attention launched upon them, which usually produces warm, friendly people.

All women receive state-provided prenatal medical care, as well as care for their babies following birth. Collective child care does enable mothers to go to work, although many are overburdened by the long hours of employment combined with the responsibilities for care of their families after they come home. Women do not have an idyllic existence. They work very hard, have little freedom of choice or movement, and are expected to work and conform for the greater good of the state. Certainly, the system, as is, is more appropriate for a totalitarian government than for a democratic society, but Americans could, without sacrificing important freedoms, adopt some features that do provide aid and security to mothers and their children (Callahan, 1971, p. 50).

PART III

The Family

16

Working and Pregnancy

PLANNED PARENTHOOD

Goal

The overall goal of planned parenthood is to enable couples to have their children by choice, not by chance. This means having the number of children they want when they want them—and having no more.

Benefit to Working Women

Family planning is of tremendous help to all couples, but it is even more important to the working woman who is trying to combine successfully her roles as a wage earner, wife, and mother. Theoretically, without birth control, the average woman would bear over twenty children during her fertile years. Obviously, such a high fertility rate would be disastrous to the mother's health, would create financial chaos for all but the most affluent couples, would make any kind of husband-wife companionship and intimacy difficult, and would almost totally prevent any significant outside employment of the mother. How could any woman hold down a continuous job and bear one child after another? She couldn't.

Benefit to Children

Also, it is vitally important to the children's well-being that they be wanted children. The mother who becomes pregnant accidentally, who has to interrupt, even temporarily, a job she enjoys, may take out her resentment on her child. In fact, it has been found that mothers who do not develop close and intense attachments to their infants in the first few months after birth often neglect them because they did not want them in the first place (Robson & Moss, 1970). Certainly, every child born into the world has a right to be wanted and loved.

Benefit to Employment

Also, from the standpoint of her work, excessive fertility is a real handicap. If the woman withdraws from the labor force periodically to have a baby, she is limiting herself to lower-paying, less responsible positions, and she misses out on many opportunities for advancement because her employer never knows if he will be able to count on her or not. If she quits work periodically for long periods of time so that she can care for young children she risks substantial depreciation of her skills through disuse and obsolescence (Waite & Stolzenberg, 1976, p. 249).

Lower Fertility

Most working mothers realize these things very well and, in fact, limit the number of children they have because of their work. Numerous research studies substantiate this fact: that the women who have the longest work records and the highest status jobs are those who (1) wait the longest after marriage before the birth of the first child, (2) have the lowest fertility rate, and (3) have the longest interval between births (Groat, et al., 1976; Clifford & Tobin, 1977). Sipila elaborates on these findings, which apply especially to women in industrialized countries:

Women who are employed full time in developed countries tend to have smaller families (or to remain childless) more often than those who are employed part time or not at all. Women who have worked for a major part of their married lives have smaller families than those who work only sporadically. Women in professional occupations, which require higher education and provide greater social and economic rewards, have smaller families than those in blue collar and service occupations. Women with a high degree of work commitment are more likely to know about and practice modern and effective methods of birth planning [Sipila, 1975].

And from all indications, it is women who want to work, and it is especially those who want full-time employment in superior occupations or careers who are most motivated to limit the numbers of children they have (Waite & Stolzenberg, 1976).

TIMING PREGNANCY

Maternal Age

At the present time, the median age of women in the United States when first married is 21.2 years of age. On the average, they have their first baby one and one-half years later, or when they are 22.7 years old (Glick, 1977). Ideally, from many standpoints, this is too young. For one thing, the most stable marriages are those where the couples wait until they are at least 25 years of age or older to get married. The younger couples are below age 25, the greater their chances that their marriage will not succeed. For another thing, it is helpful if couples have several years to adjust to one another and to work out difficulties in their marriage before contemplating having a baby. The happier their marital relationship, the better for their child.

From the standpoint of the health of the mother and the baby, isn't it unwise to wait too long before having one's first child?

Strictly from a health standpoint, women should try to have their first child before they are 30 years of age (Guttmacher, 1973, p. 196). The risk of having premature babies is lowest when the mother is 25-29 years of age but highest when the mother is younger than age 20 (Rice, 1978a, p. 440). The risk of bearing a mongoloid child or a child with some other type of birth defect is lowest when the mother is less than 30 years of age and rises rapidly with each increase in age over 30 (Kennedy, 1971, p. 26). Both infant and maternal mortality rates are lowest when the mother is betwen 20 and 30 years of age. Of course, improved medical care has made childbearing at both younger and older ages much safer than it was years ago, but the safest ages are still between 20 and 30. If a couple marry at about 25 years of age, wait two years to have their first child, and have two children two or more years apart, I feel that they have selected the optimum ages for both marriage and parenthood, considering marital factors, health considerations, and various personal and social considerations.

Time of Year

Some mothers may want to try to time their pregnancies so that their babies are born during certain times of the year. For example, a woman who teaches school nine months out of the year may, if given a choice, want to time her pregnancy so she gives birth during the summer months when she is on vacation from work. This way she will have a period of time off before her baby arrives, and she will have additional time off after the baby is born. Other women try to time their pregnancies and the date of birth of their babies to coincide with periods when they are not ordinarily too busy at work or when they know they can get time off. One woman commented:

> *I make calculated guesses of when I can get time off. I calculate on time off before I get pregnant—I mention that in ten months or so there may be a child coming and see what can be arranged* [Holmstrom, 1973, p. 22].

Of course, the best laid plans may fail, primarily because a woman doesn't get pregnant at the time she expects. Overall, only about one-third of couples are able to achieve pregnancy the first month they try. About half are able to do so within three months. The remainder require four months or longer. Over 14 percent require over one or more years (Guttmacher, 1973, p. 345).

The Birth Date

The simplest method for calculating the expected birth date is by using Naegele's formula, as follows: Subtract three months from the first day of the last menstrual period, and then add seven days. Thus, if the date of the first day of the last period was December 16, subtracting three months gives the date, September 16, and adding seven days gives the birth date as September 23. This is really a shortcut for counting 280 days. In other words, a woman ordinarily delivers nine months and seven days from the beginning date of her last menstrual period (Guttmacher, 1973, p. 62).

Another problem with trying to figure out the exact date of the child's birth is that babies don't always arrive on schedule.

Forty-six percent arrive the week before or the week after the calculated date, and 74 percent arrive within a two-week period before or after the anticipated date of birth (Guttmacher, 1973, p. 63).

Induced Labor

One way of assuring that a baby will arrive when scheduled and when it is convenient for the mother is to induce labor at the appropriate time. In fact, some doctors regularly induce labor at their own convenience.

There are many convincing arguments for and against such a practice. Induction is often used when it is needed to save the mother or child from death or damage. For example, if the birth is overdue longer than three weeks beyond full term, in some cases the placenta is inadequate to supply the necessary nutrition and oxygen to the baby. The baby suffers from postmaturity and may cease to grow altogether. Or, if the placenta is adequate and the baby continues to grow, it becomes so large that delivery becomes more difficult (Seidman & Albert, 1963, p. 166). In either case, induced labor may be needed.

What about using induction for reasons of convenience? Certainly, it is a great convenience to the mother and to the doctor to induce labor at a time appropriate for them. This is especially helpful to the career woman who must carefully schedule her work around her expected date of confinement.

But there are other factors that must be taken into consideraton before the doctor decides whether to induce labor as a matter of convenience. Unless there are medical reasons why the baby ought to be delivered early, most doctors insist that the baby be fullterm. Just before the due date, the cervix becomes soft and easily dilated. Unless this condition is present, labor may be longer than usual. Sometimes, medication stimulates excessively vigorous contractions, so that labor is shortened and abnormally painful. If additional analgesia or anesthesia is given to compensate for the discomfort, the additional amounts may have a depressive effect on the baby. Intensified contractions can also decrease blood flow to the baby by placental or cord compression (Sugarman, 1977, p. 410). In other words, it sounds wonderful to be able to induce labor at the most convenient time, but it's not as uncomplicated as it sounds and may, in fact, create medical problems for both the mother and the baby. The decision has to be the physician's, not the mother's, so she should be willing to seek and to follow the best medical advice she can get.

Postpartum

One of the things that often happens is that a mother is not able or willing to return to work as soon as she had planned. Childbirth may have taken more out of her than she had anticipated, so she needs a rest from her job for a while. Usually, the mother discovers that one small baby is far more work than she ever dreamed possible. She's exhausted from getting up several times a night and from the work of caring for her baby. At other times, she's afraid to leave the baby so soon, she can't get an adequate sitter, or she decides that she prefers caring for the baby herself. Consequently, her plans to return to work are delayed (Salk, 1975, p. 125).

Actually, this is quite usual. The best solution, I feel, is for her to plan as carefully as she can and then to add a number of extra days or weeks to the total time off, in anticipation that they may be needed.

HEALTH PRECAUTIONS

Fatigue

One of the problems of most expectant mothers, and especially of those who are gainfully employed, is the problem of fatigue. Pregnancy puts a strain upon the mother's body, so that she needs extra rest. Ideally, if she can take a midmorning and midafternoon break to lie down on a cot and rest for a while, it will help her a great deal. Many women can't do this at work, so a thirty minute rest during the lunch hour may have to suffice. In some cases, the mother may have to shorten her work day, if possible; otherwise, the result is a feeling of utter fatigue by the end of the day (Alk, 1969, p. 28). If the woman has the assistance of her husband and/or a housekeeper at home, she will be spared the added burden of all the housework. Some women try to fight fatigue by pushing themselves even harder. This is most unwise. The pregnant woman needs extra rest and sleep, so she ought to do everything possible to get it.

Heavy Exertion

Most doctors advise against heavy physical exertion during pregnancy. Even the mother who is used to heavy physical labor will have to give it up during pregnancy. If she is employed in work that requires much physical exertion, she ought to apply for a transfer or make arrangements to modify her work during her pregnancy.

There are some good reasons for this. The extra secretion of female hormones during pregnancy softens the ligaments in the body so that they are easily strained. A strained back is the most common result. Violent exercise and heavy work stimulates the heart to pump faster and harder. Since the heart is already working harder to pump life-giving blood to the uterus, the heart becomes overstrained by heavy exercise and can't keep up. The result is a reduction in blood to the uterus, which, in turn, prevents the fetus from receiving adequate oxygen and nourishment (Alk, 1969, p. 28).

Exercise

All pregnant women need mild exercise, however. It actually improves circulation, tones up the body, and improves overall health. Some women work at jobs where they remain immobile in one place for long period of time. Cavanagh tells of one of his patients:

> Not long ago, when I examined a twenty-year-old typist, I suggested she stop working immediately. She complained of headaches. She had gained an excessive amount of weight. Her legs, ankles, and feet were swollen to almost double their normal size. Because she was in a sitting position all day, her body had a tendency to accumulate fluids (we call this condition edema) at the extreme points of circulation. I advised her to walk and exercise more and to rest frequently with her feet higher than her heart. I also prescribed a salt-free diet, which she would be unable to follow in the company's cafeteria. Perhaps if this mother-to-be had held a job where she walked frequently and had ample rest periods, she might have been able to continue working another month or two [Alk, 1971, p. 29]

Similarly, women who have to be in one place all day will find it helpful to walk about to stimulate circulation in their legs or feet. A brisk walk out of doors to get fresh air and exercise is a must for all pregnant women in sendentary occupations (Birch, 1969, p. 42).

Travel

One of the problems is the working woman who has to travel a great deal as part of her work. Most doctors advise against travel late in pregnancy; some forbid it during the last six weeks of pregnancy, except within a radius of 50 miles from home (Guttmacher, 1973, p. 115). The woman who has to travel by automobile is advised to break up the trip by getting out of the car every 100 to 150 miles. Guttmacher feels that it is unwise for the pregnant woman to motor more than 300 miles a day (Guttmacher, 1973, p. 115). He also cautions the woman against traveling alone at night or over little-frequented roads during the last trimester of pregnancy, because of the potential problems that might arise from a flat tire or from other auto emergencies. As in other instances, the woman is always advised to follow the advice of her own physician. He may discover conditions that make any form of travel inadvisable and will so instruct his patient.

Pregnant women ought to avoid high altitudes where the air is lean and oxygen deprivation may result. This means no driving up high mountains or flying in nonpressurized aircraft at high altitudes. In the old days, even commercial airplanes did not have pressurized cabins, but today all the large commercial airplanes are properly equipped. Actually, air travel is much preferred over other means of transportation, since it is usually a much smoother ride and produces less strain on the pregnant woman.

Noise

Recent experiments suggest that excessively loud noises may have an adverse effect on fetal development. One report showed that when pregnant rats were exposed to loud noises, smaller offsprings were produced (Janov, 1973, p. 23). The explanation was that noise produced fear and stress, which stimulated a faster heartbeat in both the mother and the fetus.

Humans show a similar reaction to noise: the heart beats more rapidly; the blood vessels constrict; the pupils dilate; and the stomach, esophagus, and intestines tense up. The result is increased stress and fatigue, which has an adverse effect upon the fetus as well as upon the mother. One mother reported that when she went to a rifle range, each time a shot was fired, the baby jumped in her uterus (Janov, 1973, p. 24). Other mothers report that their babies are more active in their uterus when they attend a rock concert (Macfarlane, 1977, p. 8).

Emotional Upset

One of the most harmful influences on the unborn child is repeated emotional upset of the mother. One researcher found that when pregnant mothers were upset emotionally for long periods of time, the activity of their unborn babies increased up to ten times the normal level (Sontag, 1966). This activity is actually caused by the increased secretion of adrenalin in the mother's blood stream when she is upset (Freedman & Kaplan, 1972a, p. 20). The adrenalin passes into the system of the fetus as well. As a result, the baby is overstimulated. After birth, such infants are likely to be hyperactive and irritable and to eat and sleep poorly. In fact, they can be born neurotic (Kennedy, 1971, p. 40). Janov writes: "The seeds of neurosis begin with whatever one experiences in life, and life experience begins in the womb" (Janov, 1973, p. 22).

I have the type of work that is very high pressure. If I'm behind, I get nervous and up tight. What should I do?

There are several possibilities for this woman. One is to talk to her boss to see if she can reduce her total work load so she can keep up with it without undue strain. Another possibility is to check with her doctor to see if she has high blood pressure or other physical conditions that contribute to the hypertension (Seidman & Albert, 1963, p. 150). The third possibility is to take time to relax during the day, to consciously try to reduce internal tension. The woman should lie down or sprawl out in a comfortable chair; breathe deeply and deliberately; and, beginning with the top of the head, work slowly down the body, telling each muscle to relax. By focusing attention first on the scalp, then on the cheek and jaw muscles, then on the neck, then on the shoulders, and so on, the woman can deliberately relax each body part and will soon be able to relieve much of her tension. When she does resume her work, she will find that her relaxed state will carry over for some time afterward. Some people use transcendental meditation or other such techniques. They will all accomplish the same results, if properly applied.

Diet

Another important requirement is for the woman to eat the right diet. A lack of vitamins, minerals, and protein in the diet of expectant mothers can cause damage to the growing baby and has been associated with miscarriages, stillbirths, and major deformities. The extent of the damage depends upon the time, duration, and severity of the nutritional deficiencies. A lack of vitamin A or calcium may result in improperly developed teeth. A serious protein deficiency may cause mental retardation, premature birth, low fetal weight, or low resistance to infection (Rice, 1979a, p. 537). Weight control of the mother is also essential in order to protect both her health and the health of the baby (Birch, 1969, p. 32). The pregnant woman should give strict attention to her doctor's advice about salt intake and about food selection and quantities.

Smoking

More and more attention has been given lately to the adverse effects of smoking during pregnancy. The more an expectant mother smokes, the greater the tendency for the baby to be born small and with a weight deficit, the greater tendency for premature birth, and the greater likelihood of miscarriage and stillbirths ("Smoking and Pregnancy," 1971). The best advice anyone can give to the pregnant woman who smokes is, "Don't."

Drinking

Doctors used to tell women that drinking during pregnancy was not harmful as long as it was done in moderation. The problem with such advice is that mothers interpreted the word "moderation" in different ways. Some mothers drink only spasmodically but ingest a number of drinks at a time on such occasions. Other mothers drink daily but only a drink or two at a time. Both types of social drinking habits have been associated with decreased birthweight and brain abnormalities, as well as with a variety of behavioral deficits (Streissguth, 1977).

The effects of drinking heavily during pregnancy have been well documented. Children of alcoholic mothers may suffer from *fetal alcohol syndrome*. Such children are usually very small in height and weight, and they often suffer some mild abnormalities of the face, nose, external ears, or lips, although they are not grotesque or grossly malformed. However, mental deficiency is the most debilitating result, and the extent may range from mild to severe. Heart malformations occur frequently. The infants show poor responses to stimuli, poor muscle tone, and a lack of motor coordination, and they are often very jittery and nervous (Streissguth, 1977). In fact, infants have been born with *delirium tremens* when their mothers were severely alcoholic. When women are both heavy drinkers and heavy smokers, their infants suffer the most severe effects.

Other Drugs

Most doctors advise pregnant women not to take drugs of any kind, not even *aspirin*, without permission. A woman who takes four or more aspirin a day for at least four or five days may cause a severe cardiovascular malformation that can even result in the death of the newborn ("New Aspirin Pregnancy Warning Issued," 1979). Each year, more is learned about the effects of various drugs on the fetus. If the mother is a *heroin* addict, the baby becomes an addict, too (Zelson et al., 1971). There is some evidence that *LSD* has been associated with chromosomal damage and birth defects (Jacobson & Stubbs, 1968). If *birth control pills* are taken after a mother is already pregnant, they can have a feminizing effect upon male fetuses (Money, 1968). Even the antibiotic, *aureomycin*, may later cause yellow teeth in the offspring (Guttmacher, 1973, p. 79). Altogether, there are now over 1,500 substances that are known to have an adverse effect on the developing fetus (Macfarlane, 1977, p. 6). Obviously, the safest thing is for the pregnant woman to avoid taking all drugs, unless under specific orders from her doctor.

Illness

Some illnesses contracted by the mother affect the baby more than others. If a mother gets *rubella* or German measles in the first three months of pregnancy, 12 to 15 percent of the fetuses will be seriously damaged. If the illness comes when the mother has been pregnant about six weeks, the fetal risk may be as high as 50 percent. Rubella can cause deafness, congenital heart disease, mild cerebral palsy, congenital cataracts, pinhead, miscarriage, mental deficiency, or stillbirth (Hardy, 1969). The working mother who has not had rubella ought to be especially careful to avoid exposure to the disease. If she had the disease while she was growing up, she is protected for life. Women already pregnant cannot be given a vaccine.

Other virus infections, such as *infectious hepatitis* and *herpes virus*, may cause damage ranging from serious to mild. Some doctors hesitate to give *flu* shots to pregnant women, since there is some danger that vaccine containing live virus can harm an unborn child. Women who have not had *polio* vaccine should get it, since pregnant women are especially susceptible to the disease (Guttmacher, 1973). Of course, venereal diseases like *gonorrhea* and *syphilis* can be quite serious if left untreated. If penicillin treatment is begun early enough, damage is prevented and the disease is cured.

17

Husbands and Fathers

HUSBANDS' ATTITUDES TOWARD WORKING WIVES

All working women agree that their husbands' attitudes toward their working is crucial to their being able to combine a job with being a wife and mother. Husbands may be grouped into the following categories, according to their attitudes and feelings about their wives' employment: the *insecure husband*, the *competitive husband*, the *selfish husband*, the *resentful husband*, the *indifferent husband*, the *lazy husband*, the *concerned husband*, the *proud husband*, and the *supportive husband*.

The Insecure Husband

Husbands in this category are unsure of themselves. They have doubts about their own self-worth and individual identities. They lack self-esteem and feelings of adequacy. They are uncertain of their masculinity and of their own vocational abilities. As a result, they view their wives' employment as a sign that they have failed as breadwinners in the family. They have the traditional view that it is up to the husband alone to support the family and that if the wife works, it's a "slap in the face to the husband" because it proves to everyone that he has not provided adequate support.

These husbands are also afraid that, if their wives work, they will become too independent, and the husbands will not be able to keep their wives "under their thumbs," as before. One wife explains:

> In my particular circle most of the husbands don't want their wives to work.... I think some husbands seem to feel that once a wife starts to work she gets a certain amount of independence about her which they usually don't want her to feel [Callahan, 1971, p. 89].

Of course, what the husbands really fear is that, if their wives become too independent, they won't have time for them or, in some cases, that their wives will not want to stay married to them.

The Competitive Husband

These husbands are in competition with their wives to prove who is the most capable, who can get the best job, and who can earn the most income. Such a husband can accept his wife's employment if the wife has a job and income inferior to his, but he becomes very jealous and resentful if his wife gets more recognition and prestige than he does, if she has more friends and seems to be more popular than he, if she is promoted faster than he is, or if she earns a salary which is superior to his.

This problem becomes especially acute if the husband and wife are working for the same company, and, particularly, if they have the same profession or occupation. I know of one couple who are both architects. The husband was very proud of his wife as long as she was a student (he taught part time and she even had to take several of his courses), but when she completed the course and started to become as expert as he, he became more and more jealous and resentful, would put her down with critical remarks, and would make her seem less capable than he in other ways. Her capabilities and success became a real threat to him, a fact that contributed to their marital break-up.

Husband-wife competition, if it becomes too serious and intense, is harmful to marital harmony and to a couple's feelings of love and well-being, but it is also hard on the children. One couple write:

> *In another family we know, the mother and father were highly competitive with each other; this resulted in considerable tension that affected their children negatively. It particularly disturbed a son who experienced his mother's competition with father as a more general negative attitude toward masculinity. When an opportunity arose for her to take outside employment, this was at first viewed by her husband and son as part of an enlarged competitive campaign on her part. However, when she began to work and found satisfaction and self-realization in what she was doing, she became softer in her attitudes at home. There was a dramatic decrease in competitive tension, and her son felt more comfortable psychologically* [Fisher & Fisher, 1976, p. 187].

The Selfish Husband

Some husbands are very selfish and self-centered. They treat their wives as slaves, since they expect every conceivable type of personal service, for which they give no pay and very little appreciation in return. These men not only do not cooperate in doing chores and errands, but they expect, and even demand, to be waited on. They not only want their meals on time; they also want plentiful and appetizing food. They want the house sparkling clean and in order, their clothes taken care of, and the children attended to. They object to their wives working if they don't receive as much of their attention or service as before (Shafner, 1972, p. 62).

The Resentful Husband

These husbands are not quite as selfish as those in the previous category, but they still resent their wives working because of the inconvenience it causes them. They resent anything that interferes with their family life and with their time together; they also resent any sacrifice that they might be expected to make because their wives are employed. These husbands are in favor of their wives working, but they object to the time and energy their wives must expend on the job. They resent delayed meals, filling in as babysitters, or unlaundered shirts. They feel that their own jobs and schedules should take precedence and that their wives should adjust their lives and schedules to fit them.

These husbands are difficult to deal with because they say to their wives, "You can work," but at the same time they are nonsupportive of their wives' efforts or even sabotage them. A typical comment would be: "Dear, I'm glad you found a good job, but be sure dinner is ready by 5:25 tonight because I have a meeting" (Lancaster, 1975, p. 1322). Or, any problem that arises within the household is blamed on the wife's employment: "If you were home all day the house would be clean—but I know how much you like to get out of the house." Thus, resentment and dissatisfaction are expressed through sarcasm or through subtle efforts to make the wife's task more difficult.

The Indifferent Husband

Husbands in this category are completely indifferent to whether their wives work or not. As the saying goes: "They could care less." These husbands go their own ways and expect their wives will do the same. These husbands and wives don't get into one other's hair because they lead separate lives. Each has his or her own work, interests, and circle of friends, and there is a sharp division of responsibility in the household. As a consequence, they have very little involvement with one another and scarcely any companionship as husband and wife; they maintain a marriage of convenience rather than an intimate, loving relationship. If their wives are away on a travel job, these husbands are not at all concerned, unless the necessary arrangements have not been made at home. These husbands and wives usually have separate bank accounts, and each has money for which neither is accountable to the other. They may seek sexual satisfaction outside the marriage bond. Actually, this arrangement is acceptable to them because it permits them a maximum amount of freedom, but often there is very little emotional fulfillment in the marriage itself. Most couples want and need fulfillment from one another.

The Lazy Husband

Husbands in this category are pleased when their wives work. In fact, they insist on it. They are essentially quite lazy themselves and will sit back and let their wives do everything, including providing total support for the family—if they can get by with it. The more the wife does, the more the husband demands. Not only are they inadequate providers, but they will sit home all day and watch television while the kids fight or the house becomes a shambles. They won't lift a finger to help and then will holler at their wives when the latter get home from work. They will even expect that their wives provide them with drinking or gambling money or with money to have a good time, even though the money is needed for food and clothes for the children.

Such husbands marry women that they can bully around. Their wives are usually very insecure women with inadequate self-concepts who suffer martyrdom in order to have a husband and to gain some approval and affection from him. They feel degraded, but they refuse to leave because they are afraid of being alone, because they are afraid no one else wants them, or because of their own emotional need to be used and abused by someone.

The Concerned Husband

Husbands in this category approve of their wives working but are genuinely concerned about it. They worry about the strain their wives are under or about the possible effects on the children. These husbands are best described as conscientious worriers. The following is typical of the attitudes of husbands in this category.

> Philosophically, I am convinced that every woman should have the right to have a career and be a mother, if that's what she chooses. I'm also convinced my wife's work is as important to her as mine is to me [Scott, 1977, p. 14].

Another husband remarked:

> I'm genuinely concerned about Nancy. She tries to do so

much that she's killing herself. She's tired all the time. She's one of those women that can't leave anything go. She has to be the perfect wife, homemaker and mother, and to be the ideal secretary too. I try to help her all I can, and to get her to take it easy, but she won't. She's compulsive, a born workaholic. The only way I can get her to lay off is to take her completely away on a vacation, which I insist on, even if it is only two weeks out of the year.

The Proud Husband

Husbands in this category are secure, adequate persons in their own rights who do not feel the least bit threatened by their wives' successes and accomplishments. They are proud of what their wives are doing and brag about them to their friends. One wife describes her husband, Frank, who was this kind of man.

Frank was in favor of my going back to work, was interested in what I was doing, and was convinced that I would be appointed head of my department in a very short time. He tells the children that I'm brilliant. He sends me roses and congratulations everytime I get a raise or reach another rung on the ladder of success. He gives me moral support to help me over the rough spots, and also makes the children proud and glad that I'm working.

The Supportive Husband

Husbands in this category are enthusiastic about their wives working and show by their attitudes and action that they will give their mates all of the support and active help needed. They feel it would be a great waste for their wives not to use their educations and talents. As a result, they share fully in caring for the children, the house, and the marriage. They will do everything from changing diapers to teaching a wife's Sunday School class, as the need arises. They will fully defend their wives' rights to work, and they will cooperate in every way possible to see that their wives are happy and successful in what they are doing.

Comments

Actually, of course, there are no perfect husbands. The categories as outlined are caricatures of various types of husbands, each representative of a kind that usually does not exist in pure form. Usually, any one husband is a combination of types. Even the best of husbands can be jealous or resentful at times and enthusiastic and supportive at other times. What is needed is not a perfect husband, but an understanding, unselfish one who will let his wife be her own best self and then actively support and encourage whatever it is she feels she wants to do. No wife can do the best job—outside or inside the house—unless she has the full cooperation of her husband.

HUSBANDS AS FATHERS

Are Men Inept?

Some wives feel that men can't be good fathers even if they want to. The typical stereotype is the father who diapers the baby and sticks it with the safety pins, who feels too clumsy and awkward to pick the baby up, who gives the baby the wrong food, and who never knows what to do or say to make the baby stop crying. Such husbands mean well, but they are bungling and inept at child care, so their wives will never leave the children with them.

As a result of such prejudices, some wives actually discourage their husbands from participating in child care. The husband says he's going to stop playing golf every Saturday to spend more time with the children. The wife talks him out of it. The husband says he'd be glad to handle household chores each week. The wife thanks him for the offer and then changes the subject. In some cases, these same wives complain that their husbands never help them, but when the husband offers, the wife declines. The truth of the matter is that she either feels that her husband is inept and that she can do the job much better than he or that she is jealous of her prerogatives as a mother and doesn't want to share her responsibilities with her husband. As a result, the husband isn't permitted to take any real responsibility for the children.

The truth of the matter is that some husbands are at least as capable as their wives, and some are more so. One writer points out that "if the maternal instinct is defined as an innate tendency to want children, and to love, cherish, nurture, and protect children, then history reveals that men have had more of a maternal instinct than women" (Stannard, 1973, p. 183). The fact remains that part of the world's outstanding pediatricians are men, who show just as much tenderness, sympathetic understanding, and aptitude for caring for children as do good mothers.

What about the notion that fathers aren't interested in small babies or that they aren't very good at caring for them? The myth grows out of the fact that most fathers of newborns aren't permitted to handle or care for their babies. All they can do is look at them through the nursery window. If it's true (and it is) that early associations between mother and child are important in developing closeness, then it's equally true for fathers as well. One study of lower-class fathers (who traditionally take no direct responsibility in child care) showed that, when given the opportunity, these fathers were interested and active participants in caring for their infants during the days after delivery. When alone with their infants, the fathers were just as nurturant and stimulating as the mothers. In fact, they were more likely than the mothers to hold the infants and to look at them (Parke & Sawin, 1977, p. 111). Other research studies have shown that, on the average, 1- and two-year-old infants are more closely attached to their fathers than to their mothers (Lamb, 1977b; Lamb, 1977a). One of the reasons may be that some fathers are more attentive and playful with babies than the mothers are. Fathers are more likely to hold babies simply to play with them, whereas mothers are far more likely to hold them to change them, wash them, feed them, or otherwise care for them (Parke & Sawin, 1977, p. 111).

Of course, some mothers are so busy providing physical care that they have little time left over for companionship and play. In one Boston study, nearly half the fathers said that they had *never* changed the baby's diapers, and 75 percent said that they had no regular responsibilities for taking care of the child. In all fairness, this study showed that mothers spend an average of one and one-half hours a day feeding their year-old infants, compared with fifteen minutes for fathers (Parke & Sawin, 1977, p. 111). But the point is that fathers *can* be just as capable as mothers, even though in actuality fewer take responsibility for their children's physical care.

Two Parents

Wives can help by letting their husbands know that they expect that their children will have two parents, not one. Certainly, basic care can be shared if the philosophy of both the husband and wife allows it and, in fact, demands it.

In the days when wives stayed home while husbands went out to work, there might have been some justification for the feeling that the children were the mother's primary responsibility. But today, when wives share in earning the income, there is really no justification at all for the continuation of such attitudes. As one author says: "Equality . . . is a state of mind (Curtis, 1976, p. 212)." And equality requires equal responsibilities as well as equal privileges. Curtis writes:

> *If two parents are to work . . . let's put a higher value on childrearing than we have in the past. Let's stop arguing over who is going to spend time with the children; let's accept the indisputable fact of two parents, as well as the importance of childrearing, and raise them, together, with as much foresight and industry as we can manage* [Curtis, 1976, p. 213].

Such a philosophy is not only a life-saver to an already overburdened mother, but it is a fine solution to a child-care problem, and it is beneficial to the children as well. How much and how well fathers interact with their children has a powerful effect on their children's development. Fathers can contribute significantly to their children's emotional security and social and intellectual growth. Children who don't have a father's care miss out on much (See Chapter 21 on Mothers Alone). It has been suggested that fathers be granted paternity leave at the time a child is born so that the father is free to care for his child along with the mother. Having responsibility for the child and free time to carry out the duties of caring for the child will get the father started off right from the beginning.

18

Two-Career Families

A two-career family is one in which both the husband and the wife pursue careers and maintain a family. The word "career" here implies more than just a job. A career refers to employment that usually requires a high degree of commitment and a fairly continuous developmental life, whereas a job may be part time or full time, for part or all of a year, and is usually interrupted periodically for some reason. Thus, whereas many women have jobs, only a part of them pursue careers. Most work for a period of time before marriage and after marriage before their children are born and then drop out of the labor force while their children are young. They do not pursue careers. In fact, many take jobs beneath their capabilities in order to devote more time to their families (Chipman & Sloane, 1976). In contrast, career women strive for positions of responsibility and authority commensurate with their education and abilities. But the higher the position achieved, the less time a woman has to devote to a mate and children.

The two-career family, then, is actually a minority pattern, in spite of the millions of working wives and mothers. As a minority pattern, it is difficult to achieve from a managerial point of view. It is difficult to rearrange husband-wife and father-mother roles. It is difficult to find adequate child care, and it is hard to maintain a close husband-wife relationship. In spite of the problems, there are those couples who do succeed (Rice, 1979a, p. 259).

SOME REPRESENTATIVE FAMILIES

Two Physicians

Mr. and Mrs. S. are both physicians: She is a pathologist and he is a psychiatrist. They both have salaried positions and teach and practice their specialities in a medical school. They met while still in school and, except for the husband's stint in the armed services, have both worked in the same hospital. The wife has a few fixed obligations, but she can arrange most of her other work according to her own schedule. She often takes several hours off during the day, but she may be called to the hospital at any hour of the day or weekend. She admits that private practice would offer far less flexibility in her schedule. She feels that her husband, children and home should come first and that medicine must accept the time and energy that remain. Both she and her husband are in full agreement about careers for married women.

The S's have two small daughters, aged 6 and $4\frac{1}{2}$, who were born while Mrs. S. was in training. The S's have a full-time maid who comes to their home five and a half days a week.

The children have become used to seeing their mother leave them daily since they were infants. She has never considered taking the children to a nursery or leaving them with a neighbor, since she prefers their being cared for in their own home. The children have never been chronically ill, so the mother has never had to take much time off from work. The maid does most of the housekeeping, including the laundry and cleaning, as well as caring for the children. Generally, the mother gives the children her full love and attention while she is home. The family often has Saturday afternoon and all day Sunday together for leisurely activities. They usually have a relaxed family breakfast together. Usually, Mr. and Mrs. S. eat dinner while the children are upstairs (they have been fed earlier), and then they have time with them before bedtime, although there are many nights when the father doesn't get home until after the children are asleep.

The double demands of career and home are taxing. Mrs. S. is frequently tired, and she is occasionally mad at the world, but she is never bored. Social life is limited, usually as a couple. Both believe that their careers improve their marriage (Callahan, 1971, p. 70-78.)

Researcher and Graduate School Husband

Mrs. B. has always worked full time since her marriage. She has to work, since her husband is still in graduate school, but both she and her husband are in agreement that she do so. One of her chief problems has been to find the right kind of job in her own field wherever she has been located, but she is determined that her work have professional continuity and development. This means that she will not accept positions outside her field. Her work is such, however, that her hours are flexible. She can work in the morning, afternoon, or evening. A large portion of her work can be done at home. Consequently, she does not hire a baby sitter, especially since her two children have been in school and she can work during school hours. However, when the children are home sick or for holidays, she does not get as much of her own work done, so she has to make it up in the evenings or at other times. She feels, however, that the flexibility of her work schedule is one of the most important requirements for being a full-time worker and mother. The fact that her husband is also on a very unconventional work schedule requires that her schedule be even more flexible.

Before the children were in school, the mother had to employ baby sitters, and she found a ready supply on college campuses. She also used nursery schools and was able to go with the children until they had settled into the routine.

The couple live in the city, very close to their work, allowing the mother to go back and forth between home and office two or three times a day. She is able to walk to the library where much of her research is done.

The house is usually not kept as neat as the couple would like. Social life is limited and often revolves around what the husband would like to do. The wife finds little time for personal study or activities that would help her grow in her profession. She is usually involved with things she *must* do. She is usually fatigued and more tired than she would like to be (Callahan, 1971, p. 104-120).

WIVES AND HUSBANDS

Wives

What type of women take on full-time careers in addition to marriage and motherhood? One significant factor is that many of them have mothers who were employed and/or parents who were unusually ambitious on behalf of their daughters (Bebbington, 1973). Curtis writes:

> Highly motivated working mothers seemed to produce daughters with strong career motivations. Or else . . . frustrated women encouraged their daughters to seek careers—producing similar results [Curtis, 1976, p. 94].

Occasionally, career women had mothers who were just the opposite: women who had no skills or opportunities for making a living themselves and who were subsequently stuck in an unhappy marriage with dependent children to take care of. As one woman remarked: "I saw what happened to my mother and I decided then and there that the same thing would not happen to me."

Career women more often come from high social class backgrounds than do their conventional counterparts (Rapoport & Rapoport, 1971). Many are only children or are separated from siblings by a wide age gap. Others have had prolonged separation from parents because of attending boarding school or because their mothers worked. There is often tension in their relationships with their parents.

One gets a picture of an "only-lonely" child who is insecure in parental relationships while growing up and who strives for security and self-realization through career achievement. Thus, the desire for a career can be an outgrowth of either positive or negative parental relationships. It is evident that family background and socialization are major factors in influencing young women to pursue careers (Rapoport & Rapoport, 1971).

Husbands

There doesn't seem to be too much difference between the early experiences of husbands in two-career marriages and those of husbands in traditional marriages (Holmstrom,

1973). However, all career wives agree that the most important requirement is that their husbands be supportive of them and their work. One researcher found that:

> Husbands took their wives work seriously, often showing deep admiration and respect for their wives' accomplishments.
> Husbands wanted their wives "to be happy" or "to be the kind of person she was."
> Husbands not only showed positive attitudes toward their wives' careers, but they translated this into concrete, practical acts of support [Holmstrom, 1973, p. 135].

These husbands were willing to accomodate themselves to their wives' careers, to consider their wives' schedules, and to help with domestic and child-rearing duties. One wife remarked:

> ... My present husband had the best attitude toward working that a husband possibly could.... When you're up against it and you need help and support, then you've got to have this from a husband who wants you to do what you're doing, rather than putting up with it [Holmstrom, 1973 p. 137].

Obviously, this means that two-career husbands have to be secure, well-adjusted men whose identities are not threatened by their working or by a nontraditional division of household and child-rearing responsibilities (Rice, 1979a, p. 263). Insecure, immature men who are threatened by their wives' employment may try to sabotage their efforts to establish careers.

BENEFITS

Financial

The financial rewards in a two-career marriage are significant, especially if both persons earn top salaries as professional persons. I know one couple who have just completed their college degrees: he as a mechanical engineer, and she as a school guidance counselor (she just completed her Master's degree). Their combined salaries, to start, are around $30,000 per year. Couples whose careers are well established may earn fabulous amounts of money. One wife, a child psychologist married to a business man, is able to hire both a full-time governess for her children and a part-time housekeeper and cook. She loves having the house clean, the children fed, and her own dinner ready for her when she gets home from work. Dual-career couples are often able to accumulate savings, to provide financial security for the future, and to afford expensive leisure-time activities and holidays. Because they work hard, they often feel that they can pamper themselves with expensive clothes, with eating out a lot, or with rewarding vacations (Rapoport & Rapoport, 1971).

Self-expression

The most frequently mentioned reason why highly qualified women want careers is because of a need for creativity, self-expression, and recognition. Women who are trained for a profession want the challenge of a career in which they can use their talents and feel good about themselves. Many are happier, more satisfied persons because they work and are better wives and mothers because of it. Of course, if they dislike working and if they come home too tired, strained, and anxious, this is detrimental to satisfying marriage and to the welfare of children. A lot depends upon the woman's feelings about her job and what it does for her or to her.

MOVING AND TRAVEL

Moving

The pressure to move about frequently while one's career is becoming established presents some difficulty for the two-career family. Traditionally, employees have to move when the company says move or stay put in places they don't like when the company wants them there. Although some employees are able to resist pressures to relocate successfully, most still have to go where their jobs take them.

This is not as difficult for the family in which only the husband is employed, but it becomes a real problem when both the husband and wife have a career. If one is required to move, whose career is given preference? Traditionally, and even by law, it has been expected that the wife would follow the husband. But under such circumstances, it becomes very difficult for the wife to pursue an uninterrupted career (Heckman, 1977). One can sympathize with this wife's dilemma:

> In six years, with no college education, Mary worked her way up from a file clerk position to a management job with a national insurance company.
>
> Then, a year ago, she was selected to participate in an upper echelon management training program that would have assured her a top position in the company's personnel department in eighteen months.
>
> Last month her husband told her he had been transferred to another city by his company where there were no branch offices of her insurance company.
>
> "It was what we'd waited for, for nine years. It was the dream come true—Ken finally getting into management," she said.
>
> "I love him. I know I do. But I've worked so hard to get where I am, and just because I'm a woman, that's not supposed to matter. I'm angry—I never thought I could be this angry, way down inside."
>
> It did not help one bit that her husband understood [Scott, 1977, p. 56].

In actual practice, the husband and wife have to consider one another's career needs in making decisions about moving.

If a move occurs, most couples try to negotiate simultaneously for a set of positions. If both cannot find positions, either the couple have to postpone the move, if possible; the wife has to follow the husband; or the husband has to follow the wife. Sometimes one remains behind to finish up work or to wait for the children to complete school. At other times, couples commute long distances by plane when their careers are in different locations. Although such arrangements are not common, they are used (Holmstrom, 1973).

It is not always easy for both partners to find suitable employment in one area, especially in less populated sections. Also, some firms have rules against *nepotism:* hiring two persons from the same family. The rule falls hardest on the husband and wife in the same field. If the rule is enforced, it is usually enforced against the wife, since she is the one who is denied employment or permitted to work only part time to circumvent the rule (Rosen et al., 1975). Sometimes, she is forced to work outside her field (Rice, 1979a, p. 266).

Travel

Professional jobs usually require attending out of town conferences or meetings with others. Professional wives are expected to travel on business trips, usually lasting from several days to ten days or so. A few wives have to make extended trips abroad. In such circumstances, the husband usually takes care of the children while their mother is gone, assisted by the baby sitter or by whatever regular help they have. Parents have to be cautioned about leaving young children who have not developed emotional attachments to substitute care-givers (See Chapters 2 and 3).

CHILD CARE

Individual Solutions

Each couple has to solve their child-care problem themselves, since each case is different. The following alternatives are only suggestive of some of the possibilities.

The husband and wife work alternate schedules so one cares for the children while the other is at work. This is a happy solution for the children if both parents are competent, but it is difficult to arrange if jobs are on fixed schedules, and it is hard on husband-wife companionship.

The *husband and wife leave their younger children in the care of older siblings.* This can be done sometimes, but if siblings are in school themselves, they will not be available during school hours. See Chapter 1 about some cautions to observe.

Either the husband or the wife works only while the children are in school, with one home at other times. A good arrangement, if it can be accomplished.

The couple hire *part-time baby sitters* to come to their home during those hours when they are at work and when their children are not in school. This arrangement is all right if competent, regular help can be obtained. The biggest handicap is the rapid turnover of personnel. This necessitates lining up a number of sitters whom the children know and like so that at least one will always be available.

The couple hire a *full-time baby sitter* for young children during those hours when the parents are working. This is a fine arrangement if competent, regular help can be obtained, but it is expensive. Sometimes the baby sitter is also assigned housekeeping duties, but many couples prefer to split the responsibility between two persons.

The couple hire *a full-time, live-in governess* for the children, who may or may not also be the housekeeper, maid, and cook. This is the solution the wealthy choose, but it is also the most expensive and requires the couple to supply living quarters, at some sacrifice to family privacy.

Group Arrangements

The couple arrange to place their child in a *group home-care* arrangement in another person's home. If the person in charge is competent, if the space is adequate, if the adult-child ratio is low enough for the age of the children cared for, and if the children become attached to the person in charge, this can work well. It is inconvenient if parents have to provide transportation to and from the home, which they are usually required to do. It is unacceptable as a total solution if the parents have to work long or irregular hours during periods when their children cannot be cared for in the group. In such cases, they may have to add baby sitters to the group home-care arrangement.

The couple place their child in a *day-care center.* This is a good group solution if the center is well organized and managed, with adequate, stable personnel on the job. It's most appropriate for couples with 9:00 to 5:00 jobs with regular hours, so that they can leave their children during the same hours each day. Children become upset if schedules change frequently. And I do object to leaving children from 7:00 or 8:00 in the morning to 5:00 or 6:00 in the evening as some parents have to do because of their long working days. Such hours are too long, in my opinion.

The couple send their child to *nursery school* or *kindergarten.* This is a fine arrangement if the schools are superior, but most operate on a half-day schedule, so the arrangement is possible only if couples have to have child care for half the day and can be with their own children during the other half, or if they can make some other arrangements for the rest of the time.

See chapters 13 and 14 for a complete discussion of obtaining baby sitters and group care for children.

STRAINS

The strains of a two-career marriage are considerable. The demands of marriage, career, home, and children often leave couples tense and exhausted. Even though many husbands try to help their wives with domestic chores and with the children, the burden of responsibility, fairly or not, seems to fall most heavily on the wife. She is the psychological parent, which means that it is she who feels primarily responsible. As a result, the wife is overworked, and she feels guilty because she can't do everything as well as she would like to (Johnson & Johnson, 1977). Some wives are able to hire adequate help, streamline the work, and arrange schedules so that the strain is not too great. But certainly this takes a lot of money; readily available domestic help; superior management; a cooperative, helpful husband; and an extremely competent, energetic wife and mother. Some couples become so discouraged at getting competent help that they just decide to split the work between them. Couples with older children are able to enlist their aid with the total tasks. Even with adequate help two careers are a real strain on companionate marriage. One woman explains:

> We have twenty minutes at breakfast when neither of us is coherent. . . . We don't see each other again until seven that night. Then it's hurry to make dinner, rush to get some laundry washed, rush to get to sleep so we won't be exhausted in the morning. If this keeps up, we just won't know each other any more [Lasswell & Lobsenz, 1978, p. 78].

For those couples who are able to manage and to work out the problems, two-career marriages can be very satisfying (Rice, 1979a, p. 271).

19

Work Schedules and Home Management

SCHEDULING

Mrs. C., a full-time law student and a mother, describes a typical day one month after her son was born.

> Six A.M. feeding for Jonathan (he was breast fed) . . . a minimum of 45 minutes was required. At the end of an hour and a half, I fixed his 10 o'clock bottle. . . . Breakfast for Edgar and myself. Make beds, stack dishes, fold diapers, somehow catch the bus at 10 minutes to 9 for my first class at 9:10. Class until 12. We paid a neighbor to come in to help three days a week. On the other days, I rushed home, gave Jonathan his 2'clock feeding, and went back to school for an afternoon seminar. Sometimes Jonathan came back with me to sleep in the registrar's office or to crawl around in the library.
>
> The evening found me scurrying to fix dinner, nursing Jonathan while I attempted to eat and, finally, rocking the carriage

with one foot, standing on the other, one hand in the dishpan, and the other turning the pages of the constitutional law casebook [Callahan, 1971, p. 122].

Things are better today for Mr. and Mrs. C. They both finished law school and moved to Washington, D.C. They have a live-in male foreign student who takes care of the children. He gets up when they do and supervises their dressing. The children cook their own breakfast and get ready for school. Mr. C. often has to leave the house early to catch an 8:00 plane. Mrs. C. goes to the office, reads the mail, reviews her cases, sets up priorities with her research assistant, and gets down to serious work. If things are calm, the husband and wife get home by 6:45. The children have already been fed, and their parents can review their homework, discuss problems, cut hair, and listen to violin lessons. The children are off to bed by 8:30. That, from Mrs. C.'s point of view, is an ideal day (Callahan, 1971, p. 124).

It is quite apparent that life has become easier, more predictable, and less hectic for Mr. and Mrs. C. There were two things that made a difference. First, Mrs. C. had finally been able to find and to afford competent help. And second, the family had settled into a daily schedule and routine that allowed them to get most things done.

It has been estimated that a full-time job plus the family's domestic needs require 105 hours a week (Howell, 1973). This means that, if a woman tries to work full time and take care of her family herself, without paid help or help from her husband or children, she will be working fifteen hours a day, seven days a week: more than the equivalent of two full-time jobs. So the basic question must be asked: Why should one member of the family have two jobs when no one else does? (Lancaster, 1975). The first requirement in effective scheduling, therefore, is to realize that the family's domestic chores have to be shared with others.

Task Scheduling

There are two basic approaches to scheduling. One approach is to divide up household tasks. The second approach is to divide up family time. Let's look first at the division of tasks. Broad categories include:
- Housekeeping, house cleaning: This includes everything from vacuuming and dusting to washing floors, making beds, washing windows, cleaning kitchen and bathrooms, tidying up, emptying trash, and the dozens of other chores involved in maintaining a household.
- Food shopping, cooking, serving, dish washing, cleaning up, putting away after meals.
- Laundry, clothes maintenance, ironing, putting away.
- Major house repairs, painting, decorating.
- Landscaping, yard and garden work.
- Snow shoveling.

Most families will want to make up a more detailed list of tasks, so that the work under some of the broad categories may be shared with several family members. Some women also make up a maintenance schedule of daily, biweekly, weekly, monthly, and periodical tasks. This way, each person knows how often a task is to be performed.

Most busy women learn how to save time and effort in repetitive tasks, such as shopping and meal preparation. Here are some suggestions other women have given for saving time on these chores.

1. Buy in large quantities for two weeks or a month, except for those perishables that have to be obtained more often. This eliminates the necessity of having to spend so much time in daily or weekly shopping.
2. Do as much shopping by telephone as possible,

avoiding having to drive around looking for things. In some cases, orders can be all prepared, ready to be picked up.
3. Try to have perishables, such as dairy products, bakery goods, or fresh vegetables and fruits, delivered to one's door, eliminating the need to shop for these every few days.
4. Combine grocery shopping trips with other trips in order to eliminate having to make so many journeys to stores during a short period of time. Some mothers are able to do most of their shopping on the way to and from work.
5. Prepare enough food for several meals at once, so that it can be refrigerated, frozen, thawed, and eaten at a later date.
6. Make extensive use of convenient foods rather than cooking everything from scratch.
7. Buy take-out foods that can be carried home and served.
8. Enlist the aid of other family members so that the responsibility for shopping and meal preparation and clean-up is shared among different family members.
9. Hire a baby sitter and/or housekeeper who can also cook.

One of the basic decisions to be made is how much help to hire and how much family members can assume themselves. This will depend on how much money the family can afford to spend on help, on how capable they are of doing the work themselves, and on how much time they have available. Some wives or husbands are talented at doing carpentry work, painting, gardening, cooking, electrical repairs, and other things. Others are virtually helpless and have to hire assistance for practically everything.

Basic child care, which takes so much work and time, has to be planned for, in addition to household tasks. How much and what will the wife, the husband, or the hired help do? No matter how much hired help the family can afford, children benefit from the loving care and attention of other adults and siblings as well, so it is hoped that the responsibility for younger children will be shared among all capable family members (Blood, 1973).

Time Scheduling

The other basic approach to scheduling is to divide up time. Basic categories might include:
- Employment time—employment outside the home.
- Commuting time—time required to get back and forth to work.
- Household work time—basic tasks in the house and property and family maintenance, as already outlined under task scheduling.
- Children's time—child care, companionship, play, talking.
- Family time—for the whole family to have fun together.
- Couple time—reserved for the husbnand and wife.
- Personal time—for individuals to have to themselves.

One way of assuming that they get to do all the things they want to do is for couples to schedule their time. They might start by keeping track of how much time they spend doing the things under each category. Most couples will discover significant omissions: things they would like to do, but aren't doing. Usually, it's family time, couple time, or personal time that is omitted because of the press of employment, household work, or child-care responsibilities. Couples may find that they need to employ more help to do household work or to assume basic child-care responsibilities, so that they can have more time just talking and playing with the children and with one another.

EMPLOYMENT TIME

How Much Time?

Each husband and wife has to ask: How much time am I willing to devote to employment outside the home? Of course, this may depend partially on how much time a particular job requires. Some types of work require a fixed number of hours; others are virtually unending, so that the person could devote every waking hour to the job, and it still wouldn't be done. The time required for other work is variable, depending upon the season of the year, the state of the economy, and other factors. Basically, therefore, the question is, How much time is needed, and how much time do I want to spend?

Only the other day I heard a wife tell her husband: "I'd rather have you home some than for you to try to work so much to earn extra money. I need you more than the money." One of the chief complaints of middle-class or upper-middle-class wives is that their husbands work so hard that they never have time to see them and that the husbands have no time at all with their families. But each person has the same amount of time: twenty-four hours a day. The real question is: How will that person use the time that is available?

Part-time Work

Some mothers find that part-time work is their answer to child-care and family responsibilities (Angrist, 1976). Scheduling working hours when children are in school or when other responsible family members are home to care for the children enables them to avoid having to hire outside help. Shorter working hours help them to avoid strain and overload and to have more time and energy available for other things. Yet they are also able to work enough to satisfy their personal needs to get out of the house and away from the children, to do something productive, and to earn some extra money.

However, some women find part-time work to be very frustrating. Some find that they are expected to do the equivalent of full-time work on part-time pay. They do not receive the health, retirement, vacation, and other benefits that full-time workers receive. Or they are never able to achieve the responsible, well-paying positions that are filled by career women working full time. Actually, a greater percentage of women working part time indicate dissatisfaction with their work than do those who are working full time (Darian, 1975).

Part of the Year

Another arrangement is for women to work during the school year when the children are in school and then not to work during the summer. This is common practice among school teachers who can afford to take summers off. They also have the added advantage of having more free time during major holidays.

Flexi-Time

One of the biggest helps to the working mother is to be able to set her own hours and to vary her hours from time to time, according to the needs of her children and family. Unfortunately, much of commerce and business activity is based upon an eight-hour day on a rigid schedule, so that a mother who works full-time has to do so from 9:00 to 5:00 or during other times dictated by her employer. There have been a few businesses and industries, however, who have experimented with "flexi-time" and have found it quite successful. A major branch of the Union Mutual Life Insurance Company is located near where we live. The company offices are open from 7:00 to 7:00. Many employees are able to select which of the eight of these twelve hours they wish to work. They can even split their time. For example, a mother can elect to work from 8:00 to 2:00, when her children are in school, and return to work for two hours after 5:00 P.M., when her husband is at home. Or she can work ten hours one day and six of another if she desires. Because the company offers working people a choice of hours, they can combine work with family life in the way that is most convenient for them.

Work at Home

Some types of work can be done at home or in a special office at home. This can include professional work, such as law, medicine, veterinary medicine, dentistry, writing, printing, sculpting, counseling and testing, music lessons, tutoring, accounting, speech therapy, or other fields. If a special room is set aside for work, that portion of total household expenses is also deductible on one's income tax.

Work at home may also include various types of crafts and creative activities: baking, leatherwork, wood carving, pottery, making jewelry, knitting, dressmaking, or tailoring. It may include business activities: typing, addressing envelopes, mimeographing or photocopying, making telephone calls, selling, or bookkeeping. One woman I know organized and operates a baby-sitting service entirely from her home. She enlists the help of high school girls and arranges all appointments for them from her telephone at home.

COMMUTING TIME

Where to Live in Relation to Work

Where a couple decide to live is an important consideration, especially for the working woman with children. Couples who live near their work are able to go home for lunch, if necessary, and sometimes during the day, as needs arise. If a child is sick, and if the illness is not too serious, mothers who live near their work don't have to take off from work to stay home. Also, couples who work near home may be able to save on transportation costs and time if they are within walking distance. Those who are able to walk back and forth to work spend the shortest time commuting, those who drive automobiles spend longer, and those who must use public transportation spend the longest time of all (Erickson, 1977). People who have to commute one or more hours each way to and from work have very little time left to be together as a family. If they live close to work, they have this time available to spend in other ways (Darian, 1975). The greater a mother's responsibility, the more she ought to consider getting a job close to home or moving her residence to be as close to her job as possible (Erickson, 1977). Of course, the location of the husband's job has to be considered, too. The trick is to try to find a place to live that is close to the husband's job and the wife's job. This is not easy to do.

WHERE TO LIVE IN RELATION TO SCHOOLS AND OTHER NECESSITIES

Working mothers with foresight also try to select their place of residence in relation to the location of schools, churches, doctor's and dentist's offices, banks, public transportation, and stores and shops of various kinds. One woman switched pediatricians, dentists, and banks in order to have neighborhood services available. Her children could walk to the doctor and the dentist. She used a local bank's night drop or Saturday morning hours. A local supermarket delivered their groceries, and a family shoe store was only three minutes away (Curtis, 1976). It sounds romantic to be able to live in the country, away from the noise, pollution, and hustle and bustle of the city, but it may not be at all practical if family members have to travel long distances to shop or to go to a doctor or a church, or if the children have to be driven to other children's homes to have someone to play with. Some couples learn to choose a neighborhood before they choose a house or apartment. They look for other children on the street to be certain that their children will have someone to play with. One mother commented: "If your kids have a busy neighborhood, a suitable baby sitter will be easier to find. After all, you don't need wonder woman there, if the kids are outside playing with friends" (Curtis, 1976, p. 128).

One professional couple bought a house with a barn out in the country. The husband commutes one hour and fifteen minutes each way (in good traffic), and the wife is about 40 minutes from her campus office where she teaches. The wife comments:

> We love our house, but as the children get older I'm beginning to see that maybe we've got ourselves a problem. My children, for example, are old enough now to want an independent social life, yet they live too far from most families to get there on their own. I don't mind the commute in good weather, but in the winter I am fearful of driving in snow and ice so a lot of the time I'm nervous, dreading, every morning, the weather and the drive. My husband, who loves the farm the most, is on it the least. His hours are longer than mine and his commute means he gets home that much later than I do. . . .

> I miss out on a lot of social life at the university—I don't mean parties, but concerts, lectures, family gatherings. I've felt for some time that we ought to move closer to the university but we're married to the house, it seems, as much as we're married to each other. If we lived near campus, for example, my youngest could go to the university nursery school, one of the best around, but I have no way of getting her home at noon so she doesn't get nursery school [Curtis, 1976, p. 126].

Where the couple live will also affect the availability of baby sitters, nursery schools, day-care centers, and other sources of child-care help. Who wants to have to spend two hours a day driving a baby sitter back and forth to her home?

CHILDREN'S TIME AND FAMILY TIME

Children's Time

The more time parents have to spend away from their children, the more important it is that they schedule time to be with them whenever they can. But the only persons who can really plan this time with the children are the parents themselves. No matter how competent the substitute care, children want and need their parents—usually during some portion of every day.

Young children, who often get up early anyhow, love to talk and play and visit with parents before the parents go to work. How about getting up an hour early some mornings to spend the time with the children? Of course, this won't work with older children and teen-agers, because they have trouble getting up early enough anyhow. Most love to visit late evenings after supper. Most preschool and young school-age children demand their parents' attention immediately after work. I've mentioned elsewhere the importance of trying to have hired help cook dinner so parents can have time with the children after work and during and after dinner. Each family will have to work out its own schedule, but it's important that the time set aside for the children be all theirs and that it not be spent trying to do a million other things at the same time.

My wife and I work sixteen hours a day, six days a week. When are we supposed to have time for the children?

This couple will never have sufficient time for the children on this schedule, except, perhaps, for some time on the one day a week that is left over. And one day a week is not sufficient to meet children's needs. No one can work from 8 A.M. to midnight, six days a week, and have any time left over for anything else. I would strongly urge such couples to re-evaluate their priorities. Is it fair to have brought children into the world and never to take time to give them of oneself after they are born?

Family Time

I've made a distinction here between children's time and family time. What's the difference? Family time is that spent with the whole family together, doing what they enjoy doing. Going on a family picnic or taking a weekend trip to the seashore or to a ski resort would be examples. Children's time may be spent with individual children. In fact, most children want their parents to themselves part of the time, especially if they feel that they are in competition with siblings for their parent's attention. Susie may want to talk to her mother in private about trouble with her boyfriend. Chuck may want his mother to play a game—just with him. Devoting time exclusively to individual children helps them to feel important and gives them opportunities to talk about things in which they are interested.

COUPLE TIME AND PERSONAL TIME

All married couples need to reserve time for themselves, alone—as a couple—time when they aren't working, involved with household projects, or with children. And each husband and wife needs personal time to be alone. See Chapter 20 for a more complete discussion.

20

Your Marriage

PRIORITIES

Marriage First

The working mother has so many demands placed upon her that she has to establish some order of priorities. Which will come first: her children, her job, or her marriage?

Obviously, each woman has to decide this for herself. As a family-life educator, my order of priorities would be marriage first, children second, and job last. In fact, most working wives and mothers do put home and family before their work, but many put children before their marriage.

Benefits to Children

There are some important reasons why I feel marriage should come first, even before children. The most important contribution that parents can make to their children is to bring them up in a happy home. This means a satisfying, fulfilling, harmonious marriage for the couple. The kind of relationship the couple establish between them, the emotional climate that exists in their home, is the most important factor in determining whether or not their children will grow into secure, loving persons. We have ample evidence to show that an unhappy but unbroken home is just as detrimental to the welfare of children as is a broken home (Landis, 1970). In fact, children may be better off in a broken home if it is a happy one.

In a recent investigation of the mothers of "failure-to-thrive" children, ages 3 to 24 months, it was discovered that these mothers exhibited feelings of inadequacy, high anxiety, depression, alcoholism, passivity, suicidal tendencies, and mental retardation (Pollitt et al., 1975). As a group, the mothers were neither able to assess the needs of their children, particularly hunger needs, nor to show real concern for them. They rarely held, cuddled, played, or communicated with their children, and they generally lacked positive feelings for their children.

Most of the mothers were single, separated, or divorced at the time of their children's births and had made frequent changes of marital status since then. Most mothers were in conflict with their present boyfriends or husbands, and most expressed dissatisfaction with their current marital arrangement.

When the family backgrounds of these mothers were investigated, it was discovered that the same conditions existed in their homes when they were growing up as those they were creating for their children. Many of the mothers had been physically abused or neglected in childhood, had been sexually traumatized as children, and had been brought up in unstable environments by parents who were frequently in conflict with one another in unhappy marriages (Pollitt et al., 1975).

What I'm saying is that it's very difficult to bring up well-adjusted children if the home in which they live is a very disturbed one. Parents can have the best of intentions for their children and can try to do everything to raise them properly, but if the husband and wife are in conflict and if they are upset frequently and feel anger, hostility, and frustration in their relationship, this will have an adverse effect upon their children. In a sense, then, putting marriage first is not neglecting the children, it is doing the thing that will help them the most.

Benefits to the Couple

There is another reason why marriage should come first, and it is because of the positive contribution that a good marriage can make to the lives of the couple. Most couples put a happy marriage high on the list as one of their most important goals in life. When asked to indicate their most important personal values, over 3,500 youths in a nationwide survey listed love as their most important value. Personal fulfillment was second, friendship third, and family was fourth (Yankelovich, 1974). Although wanting to have children can also be an important personal value (it was twelfth on the list in the above study), the fact remains that couples who are married for a lifetime will have dependent children with them at home for only a part of the time. In fact, the number of years that couples have to live together after the last child leaves home is as great as the total number of years of marriage that have gone before (Rice, 1979a, p. 282). If a woman pours her life into her children at the expense of her marriage, she finds it very hard to readjust after her children have gone. For her own sake, therefore, as well as for the sake of her children and her husband, I feel that marriage ought to come first.

Career First?

What about putting a career first?

For the married woman, I feel that it's unwise and unfair to her husband and children to put her career first if, in so doing, she is neglectful of them. (I also feel it's unwise and unfair if the husband puts his career first and neglects his wife and children.) I have no quarrel at all with the single woman who prefers a career to marriage *or* to having children. But these women are in the minority. A nationwide survey (Roper Organization, 1974) among women of all ages showed the following:

> *52 percent wanted marriage, children, and a career.*
> *38 percent wanted marriage and children without a career.*
> *4 percent wanted marriage and a career without children.*
> *2 percent wanted a career only.*
> *1 percent wanted marriage only.*
> *3 percent couldn't decide.*

These results and comparable findings from other surveys show that the majority of women in the United States want the best of all possible worlds: marriage, children, and a career.

The best information we have available shows that there is essentially nothing conflicting about having a career *and* a happy marriage. In fact, there is evidence to support the idea that working outside the home strengthens the marriage relationship (Orden & Bradburn, 1973). But this is true only for wives who work out of choice, because they want to. Wives who are forced to work because of financial necessity, when they prefer not to, are less happily married because of it. Two researchers conclude:

> *Both partners in a marriage are lower in marriage happiness when the wife is denied a choice and is in the labor market only because she needs the money than when the wife partici-*

pates in the labor market by choice. When a married woman is in the labor market only out of economic necessity, there is a significant reduction in her happiness, measured both in terms of her perception of the balance of recent positive and negative experiences and in terms of her long-range evaluation of her marriage. The husband is also lower on both indicators of over-all happiness [Orden & Bradburn, 1973, p. 389].

The important factor here is that the woman have a choice. If the woman is able to make a free choice and to do as she chooses, she, her marriage, her husband, and her children will be better off because of it (Orden & Bradburn, 1973, p. 390).

TIME FOR EACH OTHER

Growing Apart

One problem that all working couples face is that of having time left over just to spend with each other. The demands of a job, the children, and a house leave little time and energy for the couple to spend just relaxing together. One result is that the husband and wife grow apart. They begin to lose some of the warmth of feeling between them, the tender emotions that have meant so much in the past. They omit the little remembrances, the extra niceties that show they care about one another. They remain friends but feel less and less like lovers. This kind of devitalized relationship is actually quite common. It is aptly described by a wife in her late forties:

> *I know I'm fighting it. I ought to accept that it has to be like this, but I don't like it, and I'd do almost anything to bring back the exciting way of living we had at first. Most of my friends think I'm some kind of a sentimental romantic or something—they tell me to act my age—but I do know some people—not very darn many—who are our age and even older,*

> who still have the same kind of excitement about them and each other that we had when we were all in college. I've seen some of them at parties and other places—the way they look at each other, the little touches as they go by. One couple has grandchildren and you'd think they were honeymooners. I don't think it's just sex either—I think they are just part of each other's lives—and then when I think of us and the numb way we sort of stagger through the weekly routine, I could scream [Cuber & Harroff, 1965, p. 48].

Conflict

Another frequent result is increased conflict. Couples spend less and less time actually talking to one another, so problems remain unsolved, differences are never ironed out, and irritations and frustrations increase. As a result, the relationship becomes more and more stormy and less and less satisfying. Couples drift into a pattern of picking at one another and of arguing about every little thing, but they never really communicate. What happens is that the pressures upon them increase, they become more tired and irritable, and they take out their frustrations on one another. Instead of their marital relationship soothing hurt feelings and tired minds, it actually stimulates them. Some couples get divorced because they can't stand the bickering. Others stay married but don't really like it.

Scheduling Time

What's the answer? The only answer I've ever found is for couples to actually schedule time to be alone together—without friends around, without the children—doing little except talking with one another. Some of the talk sessions are pretty stormy in the beginning, but many couples are gradually able to work things out and to feel kind and even loving toward one another again. If they can't do this by themselves, they should get counseling help.

I'm a firm believer in couples reserving time for themselves, even if it's only several hours a week. If they know that Saturday afternoon from 1:00 to 5:00 is *their* time, they will begin to think about the things they want to talk about. They begin to feel closer and more loving once more after they begin to communicate and understand one another again. After a while, they may be able to use their free time in recreational activities, but, in the beginning, I suggest that they spend a lot of time—alone—just talking.

Social Life

Busy couples get so involved just in working that they also forget to set aside time just to have fun. It's important to their mental health that couples pursue some recreational activities in which they can both engage and which help them to forget about work and children and to release the pressures that build up inside them each week. I do feel that whatever offers a change is helpful. The couple who work in offices all week need physical exercise and outdoor recreation. Those whose jobs are physical need quieter, more sedentary types of recreation or those involving mental stimulation. Certainly, the wife who is on her feet all week may want to be able just to sit and enjoy an evening watching a movie or visiting with another couple.

Working couples learn to simplify their social life. Instead of inviting couples over to dinner, which requires much time and effort to prepare, they have others over for before dinner cocktails or after dinner desert and coffee, or they make arrangements to go out together.

Maintaining a social life can be a problem when two people work. What used to be normal entertaining may seem too exhausting to be worthwhile. One secret is keeping entertainment small and simple. Entertaining informally is better than not entertaining at all.

SOLITUDE

Time Alone

Another of the needs of busy people is time to be alone to think their own thoughts and to do what they want to do. The need to be alone is especially acute for those who are always doing things with and for others. One wife remarked:

> *There's absolutely nothing wrong with me . . . I just feel like crawling into a cave . . . quiet and dark and no one around to bug me. . . .*
> *I love working and I love my work. But . . . there never seems to be time left over for me—just me*, [Scott, 1977, p. 166].

Women use different ways of having time to themselves. One woman goes to the hairdresser each week, primarily to have time to relax away from the family. Another enjoys the morning ride on the commuter train. It's her only chance to read her book and to get away from demanding people. A Florida woman retreats to her garden where she can really relax. One California couple worked out a deal whereby the husband can have all Saturday morning—upstairs in bed with a cup of coffee and the newspaper, playing golf, or doing whatever he prefers; and the wife can have Sunday morning to herself—upstairs, writing letters, reading, going for a drive, or doing nothing, if she prefers. During this time, the children have strict orders to leave them alone and not to make any demands upon them (Curtis, 1976, pp. 167, 168).

One doesn't have to travel to an island off the coast of Maine to be alone. It can be a spot in the woods, a chair in the garden, a workshop in the basement, or a room in a nearby hotel. During the summer, one wife gets in the family rowboat and rows along the shore of their lake. This is the time of the week that she enjoys most of all—and she is alone.

SEX

Time for Sex?

I love my life as a working mother, but I have a problem: When do working mothers and their husbands find time for sex? I'm often too tired at night and too rushed in the morning and I'm at my office all afternoon. Life is not much different over the weekend, and once a week, four times a month, is not our idea of a loving marriage [Curtis, 1976, p. 203].

The only real answer I can give is to suggest that couples who really want sex will find time for it: whether in the early morning, the middle of the morning, during lunch, the middle of the afternoon, after supper, late in the evening, or in the middle of the night. The mistake many couples make is getting into the habit of thinking that they can have sex only at certain times of the day or at night. When they get busy and miss out at those times, they miss out entirely. No one is too rushed in the morning if they wake up early enough. In order to get a full night's sleep, they may have had to go to bed early the night before, but it's worth it. It is not necessary to be too tired at night if one plans ahead of time and deliberately schedules a light day so as to still be fresh by bedtime. Many working people, especially those in the professions, are able to take an extended lunch break—at least once in a while. How about a light meal and sex for lunch? It can brighten up an otherwise routine day. Or how about going to work late once in a while in order to have mid-morning intercourse? Actually, research has shown that the level of male hormones in the bloodstream is at a peak in the morning and that sex drive is greatest then. Wives can tell their boss that they have an important ten o'clock engagement and can hop in bed with their husbands. It's a good tonic for the "too tired" husband syndrome.

Husbands or wives can become quite frustrated sexually because of work schedules or because of the pressures of responsibility. One wife complains constantly that her husband, who is a carpenter, comes home so tired at night that he never wants to make love. The husband is a tense, high pressure type of man who has a compulsion to work. He never takes it easy; he says it's the only way he can make any money. One husband remarked:

> *My wife never has any time for me. She works full-time, and she joins so many clubs she's never home. She's an officer in a half dozen organizations, is on a lot of committees, and attends a lot of meetings—especially in the evening. I'm lucky to get to see her, much less have a chance to have intercourse. Last month we had intercourse only once the whole month. As far as I'm concerned, I might as well be living somewhere else. If she doesn't want to be a wife to me, I might as well leave* [Rice, 1978b, p. 117].

Establishing Priorities

In such situations, couples have to examine their lives and think about their priorities. What do they really want out of life? Is work more important than their marriage? If they are busy people, they may have to schedule time together. I recently suggested this to a busy businessman. His wife asked: "You mean schedule sex? Isn't that rather unromantic?" Not necessarily. When two people are courting, they arrange a date and a time to be together. The fact that it is scheduled doesn't detract from the experience. In fact, it gives them something to look forward too. Married people can also arrange dates and times together and can look forward to these appointments as some of the most exciting times of the week. I know husbands and wives who would jump for joy if they had at least one date a week to have sex with their mates.

Couples who never have time for lovemaking are putting other things before their relationship. If that's the way they want it, fine, but if they don't like it and can change their priorities and their schedules and don't, they have only themselves to blame. If they really care, they show their love by trying to fulfill one another's needs (Rice, 1978b, pp. 117, 118).

21

Mothers Alone: Divorced and Widowed

Much of the discussion in this book has implied that there are two parents at home who are able and willing to meet children's needs. In many families, this is not the case. In fact, about 21 percent of all children under the age of 18 are living with one or no parents. Of this total number, 78 percent are living with their mothers, 7 percent are living with their fathers only, and 14 percent are living with neither parent (*Statistical Abstract of the U.S.*, 1978, p. 50). It is only the children who are living with their mothers with whom we are concerned in this chapter.

EFFECTS OF FATHER ABSENCE ON SONS

Effects

One of the questions that mothers without husbands at home face is what effect does the lack of a father have upon their children? Let's look first at the effect upon sons in the family. Certainly, we know that the earlier a boy is separated from his father and the longer the separation is, the more the boy will be affected in his early years. One group of boys who were fatherless before age 2 were found to be less trusting and less industrious and to have more feelings of inferiority than boys with fathers present or those who lost their fathers at a later age (Santrock, 1970a).

Masculinity

But the most important effect of an absent father is on the development of a boy's masculinity. Father-absent boys are more likely to be less masculine; to have unmasculine self-concepts and sex-role orientations; and to be more submissive and dependent, less forceful and aggressive, and less competent in peer relationships than their father-present counterparts (Santrock, 1970b). The reason is that they have no masculine image at home whom they can imitate. They have a blurred picture of what being a man involves (Fisher & Fisher, 1976, p. 191).

Need for Male Models

Mothers can feel somewhat encouraged, however, by the fact that the early effects of father absence usually decrease as boys get older, depending upon whether the mother provides substitute male models (Thomes, 1968). Boys with a father substitute, such as an older male sibling or an older male friend, are less affected than those without a father substitute. Young father-absent boys seek the attention of older males and are motivated strongly to imitate and please potential father figures (Biller, 1971, p. 19). Mothers can help their sons by bringing them into contact with other men. The kindly neighborhood grocery man or milk man. Grandfathers, uncles, cousins, scoutmasters, teachers, and family friends can serve as substitute father images if a boy sees them regularly. Sons can be encouraged to go to summer boys' camps, to join boys' clubs and organizations in town, and to participate in a variety of activities where there are men leaders (Spock, 1977, p. 611). Furthermore, boys need other boys of their own age to play with, which makes nursery school and kindergarten important, and also makes it necessary for the mother to seek out male friends and playmates in the neighborhood.

EFFECTS OF FATHER ABSENCE ON DAUGHTERS

Emotional and Social Problems

Father-absent girls may have trouble dealing with their aggressive impulses; they are more likely to have emotional problems and a high degree of anxiety and to evidence delinquent behavior than are father-present girls. They frequently show school maladjustments, low peer status, and social acting-out behavior (Heckel, 1963). They are often overly dependent on their mothers (Biller, 1971, p. 111).

Sex-Role Difficulties

Girls without fathers also run into sex-role difficulties. There seems to be a tendency for the fatherless girl to be less feminine and to have fewer feminine interests, traits, and self-concepts than her counterpart who grows up with a father in the home. Such girls are likely to feel shy and uncomfortable around men and are slow to develop love relationships with them (Hetherington, 1973). Some girls have difficulty in being sexually responsive in marriage, since they have more difficulty in trusting men and thus in giving themselves to their husbands (Jacobson & Ryder, 1969). Girls who do relate to men during adolescence may pursue them in inept and inappropriate ways. They often begin dating early, are inappropriately assertive and seductive, and are likely to engage in sexual intercourse at an early age and to be sexually promiscuous (Hetherington, 1973).

Fathers appear to play a significant role, therefore, in encouraging their daughters' feminine development. The father's acceptance and re-enforcement of his daughter's efforts to be feminine greatly facilitate the development of her self-concept as a woman. Interaction with a competent father also provides the girl with experiences that help her to feel comfortable around other males and to know how to relate to them in mature ways.

The Mother's Role

The mother can help to alleviate the negative effects on daughters by giving them opportunities to be with men: uncles, grandfathers, cousins, older brothers, and boys and men outside the family. Daughters should be encouraged to make friends with children of both sexes from the time they are little girls. The girl who counts some boys among her friends is certainly going to be more likely to know how to relate and get along with them as she grows up.

EFFECTS OF FATHER ABSENCE ON MOTHER

Mother's Reactions

How father absence affects the children will depend a great deal on how it affects the mother. For example, children whose fathers are dead or whose parents are divorced and who live with their mother are not only affected by their father's absence but are influenced by the mother's reactions, her changed position and status, her adjustments, and her new relationships following the death or divorce. If the mother is quite upset, if her income is severely limited, if her authority and status in the eyes of the children are significantly reduced, if she must absent herself frequently from the home because she has to work, and if she has inadequate care for her children when she is gone, the children are going to be affected, not because of their father's absence, as such, but because of the subsequent effect on the mother. The children may be affected by their mother's upset and/or absence, not by their father's absence as such (Rice, 1979a, p. 574).

Overload

The mother alone is faced with a number of significant problems. One is that she is so overloaded with work trying to manage everything that she and her husband took care of together, as well as working herself, that it is very difficult to have as much time to do everything as she would like to have. If she tries to have any social life of her own, she doesn't have time for the children. If she gives them the attention they need, there's no time left over for her.

Loneliness

Then, too, there is the problem of loneliness, the lack of companionship and friends who can fill her emotional needs. Certainly, all adults need love and security themselves in order to maintain emotional stability, to feel contented, and thereby to meet the needs of their children. But women alone often feel isolated from the mainstream of social life, which is organized for couples. One widow remarked: "I still haven't got used to it. You can be alone in a big crowd" (Schlesinger, 1972). As a result, some solitary parents are so unhappy, discontented, and upset that they have a very upsetting, negative effect upon their children. When children detect their mother's insecurity, they become more uncertain themselves and huddle closer to her for increased affection and support. This may increase the mother's burden and intensify her feeling that she cannot cope alone (Fisher & Fisher, 1976, p. 194).

Another reaction is for the mother to turn to her children for emotional gratification: "I need you. Keep close to me. Don't leave me alone." She tries to possess them, to overprotect them, with the result that the children become overdependent. Lack of independence, autonomy, and delayed marriage may be the result (Biller, 1971, p. 86).

In such a situation, if the mother does find another boyfriend or if she eventually marries him, he may be deeply resented by the children, especially in the beginning, since he is an intruder who is taking their place and stealing their mother's affection. Nevertheless, the only real solution is for the mother to have friends of her own, of both sexes, and to find need fulfillment for herself, just as her children need their own friends. If she does this and is happier and more satisfied because of it, she can also be a better mother to her children.

DIVORCED MOTHERS

Incidence

It is now estimated that over 33 percent of all marriages in the United States end in divorce. Since half of all divorces occur in the first seven or eight years of marriage, it is inevitable that large numbers of children—especially young children—are involved. Nearly two out of three divorces involve couples with children. The average number of children involved per divorce is now 1.2, which means that over 1 million children are involved in divorces that take place in the United States each year (Glick, 1975). In addition, a large number of children are living in families where the parents are separated. Such situations are no longer unique and promise to become even more commonplace in the next few years.

Reactions of Children

Divorce represents a great loss to children. They may go through a period of mourning and grief, and their mood and feeling may be one of sadness and dejection. Sometimes the parent's departure is interpreted as a departure from them, personally. The following account is of a boy's visit to his therapist:

> *Roger, age seven, started the first hour by asking if the therapist had heard the "bad news" of the divorce. He felt "very, very sad about the split" but maintained he couldn't cry. "I have to hold it in, 'cause I'd be crying all the time." Roger observed it would be very embarrassing to cry at school. He mournfully related how he gets his own breakfast and lunch because his mother didn't get up in the morning like she used to. "She must be sick." Roger knew there was trouble from the beginning: "They only knew each other two days and they should have known each other at least nine days before getting*

married!" He sadly recounted to the therapist his unsuccessful efforts to break up his parents' fights [Kelly & Wallerstein, 1976, p. 23].

This same feeling is described by 7-year-old Mary, who sadly describes her vision of divorce as: "It's when people go away" (Kelly & Wallerstein, 1976, p. 24). Mothers need to be aware of what their children are experiencing, to empathize with them, and to offer friendship and companionship (Rice, 1979b).

One reaction to the sense of loss is for children to try to get their parents back together. They "wish that everyone could live together and be happy." The longing for a reunited family may go on for a long time, until children fully understand the realities of the situation and the reason for the separation (Rice, 1979a, p. 467).

Other common reactions are a heightened sense of insecurity and feelings of inferiority. Children feel that "if you really loved me, you wouldn't go away and leave me." Some become very afraid that their other parent will also leave, and the child may become very possessive with that parent. One mother remarked: "Since the divorce, Tommy has been very upset when I go to work or when he goes to school. I think he's afraid that he'll come home and not find me there." Certainly, this feeling is understandable. The child has already lost one parent; he doesn't want to risk losing another one. Some mothers make the mistake of trying to help children overcome their dependency by trying to "push the children away," by shaming them, telling them "not to act like babies" or not to be "mama's boys." This usually makes matters worse. The best solution is to give children so much love, approval, and attention that they know, because of her actions, that their mother does love and care for them. The more insecure children are, the more demanding they become, and the more love and attention they need.

After children get over the initial upset of divorce, one

common reaction is anger and resentment, especially against the parent they hold at fault for the divorce. Sometimes this is directed against the father—especially if he has deserted the family. Even if he hasn't deserted but has moved out and away as required by law, the children may resent the fact of his leaving very much. The child feels: "I hate you, because you have gone off and left me." When the father comes to visit, he may be surprised to find that his children remain cold and aloof. The reason is that they have been hurt, so they have erected defenses, have shut off their emotions, and have tried to remain unfeeling. They don't dare feel again or love or care again for fear of being hurt. They may treat their father very shabbily as an expression of their resentment against him. Usually, these feelings will pass in time if the father doesn't become too angry and strike back in resentment against his children.

Of course, the resentment or hostility may also be directed at the mother, especially if the children blame her for the divorce. Five-year-old Susie blamed her mother for her father's absence: "I hate you, because you sent my daddy away." (Actually, the mother hadn't wanted the divorce.) An older girl, age 12, asked her mother: "Why did you leave my father all alone?" Up to that point, it was obvious that the girl did not understand the reason for the divorce (Rice, 1979b).

Sometimes children develop a terrible feeling of guilt because they blame themselves for the divorce. A child may feel that the parent is leaving because he or she hasn't been a good boy or a good girl. One boy told his therapist that his father left him "because I'm dumb" (Kelly & Wallerstein, 1976, p. 26). Children may also feel ashamed because of the divorce and feel that it somehow reflects on them. "How can I face my friends? What will the other kids think?" Some children withdraw and build a psychological wall around themselves. Parents need to remember that divorce is as hard on children's self-esteem and ego as it is on their's, so that children need a lot of ego-building in the early years of the divorce. Also, parents have to help children understand that the divorce was not the children's fault and that it had nothing to do with them. Then perhaps children won't blame themselves.

What the Mother Can Do

Children's reactions to divorce depend a great deal on the mother's reactions as custodial parent. If she is terribly upset, they will be upset. Often, of course, divorce comes as a welcome relief after months or years of tension and conflict. In this case, the children are much better off afterward, at least in the long run, than they were before. One mother explained:

> I don't know why everyone says that divorce is so horrible. It's the best thing that ever happened to me. I only wish I had done it years before. The children and I have never been so happy.

Research does tend to bear this out: that children are usually better off in a broken, happy home than they are in an unbroken but unhappy home (Landis, 1970). Of course, they are best off in a happy, unbroken home, but divorce may be the next best thing. If the mother can achieve a happy atmosphere in her home, she will help the children a great deal. "The best anecdote to sadness, grief, and depression is a cheerful, happy, loving atmosphere" (Rice, 1979b).

It is also very important that children understand the reasons for the divorce. Parents should explain to the children *why* they can't get along together and why divorce is necessary. "Your father and I never really loved one another, and we shouldn't have married." "We can't agree on anything. We fight all the time, and that's bad for us and for you children." "Your father drinks too much, and he comes home drunk all the time and hits me. I can't take it anymore." If explanations are given, but without any intent to be malicious, children are more likely to be able to accept what has happened. If such explanations are not given, children may feel that it was unfair for one person to have left the other. The upset of children is also minimized if the divorce is uncontested, if parents don't fight bitterly to gain advantage over one another, and if parents don't continue to fight after the divorce is over. Some parents are still so bitter that they continue to try to hurt one another years after the divorce was granted. They continually criticize one another, try to belittle each other in the eyes of the children, and try to get the children to take sides in the battle. This makes things much worse for the children. They love both parents. Whose side are they going to choose? The worst thing any one parent can do is to try to turn the children against the other parent. As a general rule, parents should try not to criticize one another in front of the children.

Unfortunately, vindictive parents use custodial rights or visitation privileges as weapons to get back at the other parent: They refuse to allow the children to phone or write, or they are away when visitation time comes. Quite typically, the spouse with custody complains that, during visitation, the children were allowed to eat too many hot dogs and to stay up too late at night, that they became sick, or that they came home upset because of things that happened or that were said. Sometimes, the spouse with custody goes back to court to try to place further limitations on the visits or to try to curtail the negative behavior of the other parent. Needless to say, the more such fights continue and the more upset the parents are after the divorce, the more the children will be affected negatively (Rice, 1979b). When asked how he felt about his parent's divorce, one 8-year-old replied:

They said it was going to be better, but it isn't! It's worse. . . . It's made, and I just want it to be final! . . . They fight every day. It makes me mad that they fight [Kelly & Wallerstein, 1976, p. 30].

Instead of discouraging visitation, thoughtful mothers (if they are the ones with custody) should actually encourage visitation and other contacts with the noncustodial parent. Children miss their parent. Frequent visits make them feel that they're not deserted, that they are still loved. Older children who are within walking or bicycling distance of their other parent feel good about being able to go over and see the parent as often as they desire (Rice, 1979b).

WIDOWED MOTHERS

Widowed mothers experience all of the same problems of other mothers who are left alone: heavy responsibilities, financial worries, lack of time and energy for everything, the total burden of child rearing, loneliness. But they have the additional problem of dealing with grief: their own and that of their children. I would like, therefore, to focus attention here on this one problem of grief—not because it is the only one widows face, but because it is an extremely important one for them to understand and to deal with if they are going to be of maximum help to themselves and to their children.

Mother's Reactions

No matter how long the death of a spouse has been anticipated, it comes as a shock. There are usually three stages of grief. The first stage is one of shock, during which the surviving spouse is stunned and immobilized with grief and disbelief. The second stage is a period of intense suffering during which the individual shows both physical and emotional symptoms of great disturbance. The third stage is a gradual reawakening to an interest in life. One of the common reactions to bereavement is to purify the memory of the deceased by mentally blocking out all the negative characteristics of the person. One woman who hated her husband remarked: "My husband was a good man." Idealization can prevent the formation of new intimate friendships. Extended bereavement can result in a sentimentalized, nostalgic, morose style of life. The negative impact of bereavement is very real. Widowed women evidence a high rate of suicide and mental illness. The feelings of unhappiness, low morale, and personal isolation can be very hard on the children (Rice, 1979a, p. 301).

Children's Reactions

How children react will depend on their age. Young children—preschoolers and those of early elementary school age—are able to adjust most quickly. The reason is that they deny the finality of death, since they don't completely understand it. Death is like going to sleep and then waking up or like taking a long trip and then coming home. The children can continue to fantasize that mommy or daddy will be coming back. In fact, they will ask when she or he is returning.

Teen-agers are quite upset by the death of a parent. They usually go through the stages of grief which adults experience. But most teen-agers are able to recover more rapidly than are adults. Teen-agers can find relief through emotional outbursts or through sublimated activities, such as dating, hobbies, or social events.

Grade-school children suffer the most. They are old enough to realize what has happened but not independent enough to enter into other relationships or activities to ease their suffering. If the surviving parent is so preoccupied with his or her own grief or anxieties about the future that he or she does not have time to think about the children's feelings, the latter may go through a period of intense sorrow (Rice, 1979b).

What Mother Can Do

Children who are still in a period of mourning may exhibit very silent, sullen, listless, indifferent behavior. They seem to lose interest in everything. One of the hardest tasks is to get these children to talk, to tell how they feel, and to get them to begin expressing feelings again. If, in trying to keep her feelings under control, the mother won't talk about the deceased spouse or let the children do so, the children have no way of working through their grief or of releasing their suffering. It is important, therefore, for the mother to encourage conversation about the children's father, even though it is painful at first to recall.

Children also often want to talk about death itself, in order to understand what has happened and what death really means. They often ask many gruesome questions about dead bodies, cemetaries, caskets, and funerals, but the mother should try to help them to understand. Children aren't frightened by death, unless the parents make them afraid. They find special comfort in understanding that daddy had to leave his hurt or sick body and go "live with God" but that "he still loves us." The particular explanation the mother gives will depend on her religious beliefs, but the mother's goal should be to share her faith and comfort her children by the knowledge that their father will live on in their memories.

The mother can respect her children's mementos of the absent parent, and share with her children in recalling things that daddy did or daddy said. But these times of recall should be kept as cheerful and as happy as possible. The best anecdote to sadness, grief, and depression is a cheerful, happy, loving atmosphere. If the mother can create this climate in her home, her children will recover from the loss of their father more quickly.

References

A Child's Second Birth. *Time*, June 19, 1978, pp. 61.
AINSWORTH, M.D.S. *Infancy in Uganda: Infant Care and the Growth of Love*. Baltimore: The Johns Hopkins Press, 1967.
AMES, L. B. *Child Care and Development*. Philadelphia: Lippincott, 1970.
ANGRIST, S. S. et al. How Working Mothers Manage: Socioeconomic Differences in Work, Child Care and Household Tasks. *Social Science Quarterly* 56 (March 1976): 631-637.
ALK, M., ed. *The Expectant Mother*. New York: Pocket Books, 1971.
BALSWICK, J. O. and PEEK, C. W. "The Inexpressive Male: A Tragedy of American Society." *The Family Coordinator* 20 (1971): 363-368.
BANDURA, A., and WALTERS, R. H. *Adolescent Aggression*. New York: The Ronald Press Co., 1959.
BARMAN, A. "Your First Months With Your Baby." Public Affairs

Pamphlet No. 478. New York: Public Affairs Committee, 1972.

BARTON, K. et al. "Child-Rearing Practices Related to Child Personality." *The Journal of Social Psychology* 101 (Feb. 1977): 75-85.

BAUMRIND, D. "Current Patterns of Parental Authority." *Developmental Psychology Monographs* 4 (1971): No. 1, Part 2.

BEBBINGTON, A. C. "The Function of Stress in the Establishment of the Dual-Career Family." *Journal of Marriage and the Family* 35 (August 1973): 530-537.

BELKIN, E. P. and ROUTH, D. K. "Effects of Presence of Mother versus Stranger on Behavior of 3-Year-Old Children in a Novel Situation." *Developmental Psychology* 11 (May 1975): 400.

BETTELHEIM, B. *The Children of the Dream.* New York: The Macmillan Co., 1969.

BETTELHEIM, B. "Why Working Mothers Have Happier Children." In *Marriage Means Encounter*, edited by G. Roleder. Dubuque, Iowa: Wm. C. Brown Co., 1973, pp. 108-112.

BILLER, H. B. *Father, Child, and Sex Role.* Lexington, Mass.: D. C. Heath, 1971.

BINTER, A. R. and FREY, S. H. *The Psychology of the Elementary School Child.* Chicago: Rand McNally & Co., 1972.

BIRCH, W. G. *A Doctor Discusses Pregnancy.* Chicago, Illinois: Budlong Press Co., 1969.

BLEHAR, M. C. "Anxious Attachments and Defensive Reactions Associated with Day Care." *Child Development* 45 (1974): 683-692.

BLEHAR, M. C. et al. "Early Face-to-Face Interaction and Its Relation to Later Infant-Mother Attachment." *Child Development* 48 (March 1977): 182-194.

BLOOD, R. J. "Division of Labor in Two-Income Families." In *Marriage Means Encounter*, edited by G. Roleder. Dubuque, Iowa: Wm. C Brown Co., 1973, pp. 93-98.

BOWLBY, J. *Attachment and Loss. Vol. I. Attachment.* New York: Basic Books, Inc., 1969.

BOWLBY, J. *Attachment and Loss. Vol. II. Separation Anxiety and Anger.* New York: Basic Books, Inc., 1973.

BOWLBY, J. *Child Care and the Growth of Love.* Baltimore, Md.: Pelican Books, 1971.

BROMWICH, R. M. "Focus on Maternal Behavior in Infant Intervention." *American Journal of Orthopsychiatry* 46 (July 1976): 439-446.

BRONFENBRENNER, U. "Liberated Women: How They're Changing American Life." Interview conducted for *U.S. News and World Report*, June 7, 1975, p. 49.

BRONFENBRENNER, U. *Two Worlds of Childhood: U.S. and U.S.S.R.* New York: Russell Sage Foundation, 1970.

BROOKS, J. and LEWIS, M. "Infants' Responses to Strangers: Midget, Adult, and Child." *Child Development* 47 (June 1976): 323-332.

CALDWELL, B. et al. "Infant Day Care and Attachment." *American Journal of Orthopsychiatry* 40 (1970): 397-412.

CALLAHAN, S. C. *The Working Mother.* New York: The Macmillan Co., 1971.

CHANDLER, C. A. et al. *Early Child Care: The New Perspectives*, edited by L. L. Dittman. New York: Atherton Press, 1968.

CHERRY, F. F. and EATON, E. A. "Physical and Cognitive Development in Children of Low Income Mothers Working in the Child's Early Years." *Child Development* 48 (March 1977): 158-166.

CHESS, S. et al. *Your Child is a Person.* New York: The Viking Press, 1972.

CHIPLIN, B. and SLOANE, P. J. "Personal Characteristics and Sex Differentials in Professional Employment." *The Economic Journal* 86 (Dec. 1976): 729-745.

CLIFFORD, W. B. and TOBIN, P. L. "Labor Force Participation of Working Mothers and Family Formation: Some Further Evidence." *Demography* 14 (August 1977): 273-284.

COHEN, D. J. and ZIGLER, E. "Federal Day Care Standards: Rationale and Recommendations." *American Journal of Orthopsychiatry* 47 (June 1977): 456-465.

COHEN, L. B. et al. "An Examination of Interference Effects in Infants' Memory for Faces. *Child Development* 48 (March 1977): 88-96.

COHEN, S. E. and BECKWITH, L. "Caregiving Behaviors and Early

Cognitive Development as Related to Ordinal Position in Preterm Infants." *Child Development* 48 (March 1977): 152-157.

COLLINS, A. H. and WATSON, E. L. *Family Day Care.* Boston: Beacon Press, 1977.

CORENELIUS, S. W. and DENNEY, N. W. "Dependency in Day-Care and Home-Care Children." *Developmental Psychology* 11 (Sept. 1975): 575-582.

CORTER, C. M. "The Nature of the Mother's Absence and the Infant's Response to Brief Separations." *Developmental Psychology* 12 (Sept. 1976): 428-434.

CROW, L. D. and CROW, A. *Child Development and Adjustment.* New York: The Macmillan Company, 1968.

CUBER, J. F. and HARROFF, P. B. *The Significant Americans.* New York: Appleton-Century, 1965.

CURTIS, J. *A Guide for Working Mothers.* New York: Simon and Schuster, 1976.

DALY, S. J. *Questions Teen-Agers Ask.* New York: Dodd, Mead and Co., 1963.

DARIAN, J. C. "Convenience of Work and the Job Constraint of Children." *Demography* 12 (May 1975): 245-258.

DENNIS, W. *Children of the Creche.* New York: Appleton-Century Crofts, 1973.

Developmental Psychology Today. Del Mar, California: CRM Books, 1971.

DOYLE, ANNA-BETH. "Infant Development in Day Care." *Developmental Psychology* 11 (Sept. 1975): 655-656.

DREIKURS, R. *Children: The Challenge.* New York: Hawthorn Books, Inc., 1964.

DUNN, J. *Distress and Comfort.* Cambridge, Massachusetts: Harvard University Press, 1977.

ELARDO, R. et al. "A Longitudinal Study of the Relation of Infants' Home Environments to Language Development at Age Three." *Child Development* 48 (June 1977): 595-603.

ELARDO, R. et al. "The Relation of Infants' Home Environments to Mental Test Performance from 6 to 36 Months: A Longitudinal Analysis." *Child Development* 46 (March 1975): 71-76.

ENGLISH, O. S. and PEARSON, G. H. J. *Emotional Problems of Living.* New York: W. W. Norton and Co., Inc., 1945.

ERICKSON, J. A. "An Analysis of the Journey to Work for Women." *Social Problems* 24 (April 1977): 428-535.
ETAUGH, C. "Effects of Maternal Employment on Children: A Review of Recent Research." *Merrill-Palmer Quarterly of Behavior and Development* 20 (1974): 71-98.
FAGAN, J. F. III. "Infant Recognition Memory: Studies in Forgetting." *Child Development* 48 (March 1977): 68-78.
FARRAN, D. C. and RAMEY, C. T. "Infant Day Care and Attachment Behaviors toward Mothers and Teachers." *Child Development* 48 (Sept. 1977): 1112-1116.
FEIN, G. G. "Children's Sensitivity to Social Contacts at 18 Months of Age." *Developmental Psychology* 11 (Nov. 1975): 853-854.
FELDMAN, S. S. and INGHAM, M. E. "Attachment Behavior: A Validation Study in Two Age Groups." *Child Development* 46 (June 1975): 319-330.
FIELD, T. M. "Effects of Early Separation, Interactive Deficits, and Experimental Manipulations on Infant-Mother Face-to-Face Interaction." *Child Development* 48 (Sept. 1977): 763-771.
FISHER, S. and FISHER, R. L. *What We Really Know About Child Rearing.* New York: Basic Books, Inc., 1976.
FLEISHER, B. M. "Mother's Home Time and the Production of Child Quality." *Demography* 14 (May 1977): 197-212.
FLERX, V. C. et al. "Sex Role Stereotypes: Developmental Aspects and Early Intervention." *Child Development* 47 (December 1976): 998-1007.
FRAENKEL, J. R. *How To Teach About Values: An Analytic Approach.* Englewood Cliffs, N.J.: Prentice-Hall, Inc., 1977.
FRANCKE, L. B. "Anxiety and the Working Mother." *Harper's Bazaar*, May 1978, 54 plus.
FREEDMAN, A. M. Kaplan, H. I., eds. *The Child: His Psychological and Cultural Development. Vol. 1: Normal Development and Psychological Assessment.* New York: Atheneum, 1972a.
FREEDMAN, A. M., Kaplan, H. I., eds. *The Child: His Psychological and Cultural Development. Vol. 2. The Major Psychological Disorders and Their Treatment.* New York: Atheneum, 1972b.
FROMME, A. *The ABCs of Child Care.* New York: Pocket Books, 1977.

GALINSKY, E. and HOOKS, W. H. *The New Extended Family.* Boston: Houghton Mifflin Co., 1977.
GARRISON, K. C. et al. *The Psychology of Childhood.* New York: Charles Scribner's Sons, 1967.
GIBBONS, P. A. and KOPELMAN, R. E. "Maternal Employment as a Determinant of Fear of Success in Females." *Psychological Reports* 40 (June 1977): 1200-1206.
GINOTT, H. G. *Between Parent and Child.* New York: Avon Books, 1969.
GLICK, P. C. "A Demographer Looks at American Families." *Journal of Marriage and the Family* 37 (February 1975): 15-26.
GLICK, P. C. "Updating the Life Cycle of the Family." *Journal of Marriage and the Family* 39 (Feb. 1977): 5-13.
GORDON, M. "Infant Care Revisited." *Journal of Marriage and the Family* 30 (Nov. 1968): 578-583.
GORDON, T. *P.E.T. Parent Effectiveness Training.* New York: New American Library, 1975.
GROAT, H. T. et al. "Labor Force Participation and Family Formation: A Study of Working Mothers." *Demography* 13 (Feb. 1976): 115-125.
GROTBERG, E. H., ed. Day Care and Child Development Council of America, Inc. Reprint. *Day Care: Resources for Decisions.* Washington, D.C.: Office of Economic Opportunity, 1971.
GUTELIUS, M. F. and KIRSCH, A. D. "Factors Promoting Success in Infant Education." *American Journal of Public Health* 65 (April 1975): 384-387.
GUTTMACHER, A. F. *Pregnancy, Birth and Family Planning.* New York: New American Library, 1973.
HARDY, J. B. "Rubella and Its Aftermath." *Children* 16 (May-June 1969): 91-96.
HARRELL, J. E. and RIDLEY, C. A. "Substitute Care, Maternal Employment and the Quality of Mother-Child Interaction." *Journal of Marriage and the Family* 37 (August 1975): 556-564.
HECKEL, R. V. "The Effects of Fatherlessness on the Preadolescent Female." *Mental Hygiene* 47 (1963): 69-73.
HECKMAN, N. A. et al. "Problems of Professional Couples: A Content

Analysis." *Journal of Marriage and the Family* 39 (May 1977): 323-330.
HETHERINGTON, E. M. "Girls Without Fathers." *Psychology Today* (February 1973): 47-52.
HOFFMAN, L. W. "Effects of Maternal Employment on the Child: A Review of Research." *Developmental Psychology* 10 (1974): 204-228.
HOFFMAN, L. W. and NYE, F. I. *Working Mothers*. San Francisco, California: Jossey-Bass, 1978.
HOLMSTROM, L. L. *The Two-Career Family*. Cambridge, Mass.: Schenkman Publishing Co., 1973.
HOMAN, W. E. *Child Sense*. New York: Bantam Books, 1970.
HOST, M. S. and HELLER, P. B. *Day Care. 7. Administration*. U.S. Dept. of Health, Education, and Welfare. Office of Child Development. Washington, D.C.: U.S. Government Printing Office, 1971.
"How Much Does He Do Around the House?" *Changing Times* 25 (April 1971): 41.
HOWE, V. "Sexual Stereotypes Start Early." *Saturday Review*, October 16, 1971.
HOWELL, M. "Employed Mothers and their Families: Part I." *Pediatrics* 52 (Aug. 1973): 256.
HUNTINGTON, D. S. et al. *Day Care. 2. Serving Infants*. U.S. Dept. of Health, Education, and Welfare Office of Child Development. Washington, D.C.: U.S. Government Printing Office, 1971.
INOFF, G. E. and HALVERSON, C. F., Jr. "Behavioral Disposition of Child and Caretaker-Child Interaction." *Developmental Psychology* 13 (May 1977): 274-281.
JACOBSON, C. B. and STUBBS, M. V. L. "Clinical and Reproductive Dangers Inherent in Use of Hallucinogenic Agents." *Proceedings of the American Association of Clinical Scientists*, Washington, D.C., 1968.
JACOBSON, G. and RYDER, R. G. "Parental Loss and Some Characteristics of the Early Marriage Relationship." *American Journal of Orthopsychiatry* 39 (1969): 779-787.
JANOV, A. *The Feeling Child*. New York: Simon and Schuster, 1973.

JOHNSON, C. L. and JOHNSON, F. A. "Attitudes toward Parenting in Dual-Career Families." *American Journal of Psychiatry* 134 (April 1977): 391-395.

KAGAN, J. *Personality Development*. New York: Harcourt Brace Jovanovich, Inc., 1971.

KAGAN, J. and KLEIN, R. E. "Cross-Cultural Perspectives on Early Development." *American Psychologist* 28 (1973): 947-961.

KELLY, J. B. and WALLERSTEIN, J. S. "The Effects of Parental Divorce: Experiences of the Child in Early Latency." *American Journal of Orthopsychiatry* 46 (January 1976): 20-32.

KENNEDY, W. A. *Child Psychology*. Englewood Cliffs, N.J.: Prentice-Hall, Inc., 1971.

KENNELL, H. J. et al. "Maternal Behavior One Year After Early and Extended Post-Partum Contact." *Developmental Medicine and Child Neurology* 16 (1974): 172-179.

KEYSERLING, M. D. *Windows on Day Care*. New York: National Council of Jewish Women, 1972.

KLEIN, R. P. and DURFEE, J. T. "Infants' Reactions to Unfamiliar Adults versus Mothers." *Child Development* 47 (Dec. 1976): 194-196.

KOHLBERG, L. "Stage and Sequence: The Cognitive-Developmental Approach to Socialization." In Goslin, D., ed. *Handbook of Socialization Theory and Research*. Chicago: Rand McNally, 1969.

KORNER, A. F. "Neonatal Startles, Smiles, Erections and Reflex Sucks as Related to State, Sex and Individuality." *Child Development* 40 (1969): 1039-1053.

LAMB, M. E. "Development of Mother-Infant and Father-Infant Attachments in the Second Year of Life." *Developmental Psychology* 13 (Nov. 1977a): 637-648.

LAMB, M. E. "Father-Infant and Mother-Infant Interaction in the First Year of Life." *Child Development* 48 (March 1977a): 167-181.

LANCASTER, J. "Coping Mechanisms of the Working Mother." *American Journal of Nursing* 75 (Aug. 1975): 1322-1323.

LANDIS, J. T. "A Comparison of Children from Divorced and Nondivorced Unhappy Marriages." *Family Life Coordinator* 11 (1970): 61-65.

LARSON, L. E. "The Relative Influence of Parent-Adolescent Affect in Predicting the Salience Hierarchy among Youth." *The Pacific Sociological Review* 15 (1972): 83-102.

LASSEIGNE, M. W. "A Study of Peer and Adult Influence on Moral Beliefs of Adolescents." *Adolescence* 10 (1975): 227-230.

LASSWELL, M. and LOBSENZ, N. "How Working Couples Make Marriage Work." *McCall's*, July 1978, p. 78 plus.

MACFARLANE, A. *The Psychology of Childbirth*. Cambridge, Mass.: Harvard University Press, 1977.

MACRAE, J. W. and JACKSON, E. H. "Are Behavioral Effects of Infant Day Care Program Specific?" *Developmental Psychology* 12 (May 1976): 269-270.

MARANTZ, S. A. and MANSFIELD, A. F. "Maternal Employment and the Development of Sex-Role Stereotyping in Five- to Eleven-Year-Old Girls." *Child Development* 48 (June 1977): 668-673.

MASTERS, W. H. and JOHNSON, V. E. *Human Sexual Response*. Boston: Little, Brown and Co., 1966.

MCCANDLESS, B. R. *Children. Behavior and Development*. Second Edition. New York: Holt Rinehart and Winston, Inc., 1967.

MCCLELLAND, D. C. et al. "Making It to Maturity." *Psychology Today* 12 (June 1978): 42-53, 114.

MCCORD, J. and MCCORD, W. "The Effects of Parental Role Model on Criminality." In Corvin, R., ed. *Readings in Juvenile Delinquency*. Philadelphia: J. B. Lippincott, 1964.

MEDINNUS, G. R. and JOHNSON, R. C., eds. *Child and Adolescent Psychology. A Book of Readings*. New York: Jonn Wiley and Sons, Inc., 1970.

MEERS, D. R. and MARANS, A. E. "Group Care of Infants in Other Countries." In *Early Child Care*, edited by C. A. Chandler et al. New York: Atherton Press, 1968, pp. 237-282.

MILLER, S. M. "Effects of Maternal Employment on Sex Role Perception, Interests, and Self-Esteem in Kindergarten Girls." *Developmental Psychology* 11 (May 1975): 405-406.

MILLER, T. W. "Effects of Maternal Age, Education and Employment Status on the Self-Esteem of the Child." *Journal of Social Psychology* 95 (February 1975): 141, 142.

MONEY, J. "Influence of Hormones on Psychosexual Differentiation." *Medical Aspects of Human Sexuality*, Nov. 1968, pp. 32-42.

MOORE, T. "Children of Working Mothers." In *Working Mothers and Their Children*, edited by S. Yudkin and W. Holme. London: Sphere Books, 1969.

MURRAY, A. D. "Maternal Employment Reconsidered: Effects on Infants." *American Journal of Orthopsychiatry* 45 (Oct. 1975): 773-790.

NEVILL, D. and DAMICO, S. "Developmental Components of Role Conflict in Women." *The Journal of Psychology* 95 (March 1977): 195-198.

"New Aspirin Pregnancy Warning Issued." *Portland Press Herald*, January 18, 1979.

NORTH, A. F., M.D. *Day Care 6. Health Services*. U.S. Dept. of Health, Education, and Welfare. Office of Child Development. Washington, D.C.: U.S. Government Printing Office, 1971.

NORTHWAY, M. L. *What is Popularity?* Better Living Booklet, No. 530. Chicago, Illinois: Science Research Associates, Inc., 1961.

NORTON, G. R. *Parenting*. Englewood Cliffs, N.J.: Prentice-Hall, Inc., 1977.

NUTTALL, E. V. and NUTTALL, R. L. "Parent-Child Relationships and Effective Academic Motivation." *Journal of Psychology* 94 (Sept. 1976): 127-133.

NYE, F. I. and BERARDO, F. M. *The Family*. New York: Macmillan Publishing Co., Inc., 1973.

ORDEN, S. R. and BRADBURN, N. M. "Working Wives and Marriage Happiness." In *Love Marriage Family*, edited by M. E. Lasswell and T. E. Lasswell. Glenview, Illinois: Scott, Foresman and Co., 1973, pp. 384-395.

OSOFSKY, J. D. "Neonatal Characteristics and Mother-Infant Interaction in Two Observational Situations." *Child Development* 47 (Dec. 1976): 1138-1147.

PARKE, R. D. and SAWIN, D. B. "Fathering: It's a Major Role." *Psychology Today*, Nov. 1977, p. 109 plus.

PIAGET, J. *The Moral Judgment of the Child*. London: Routledge and Kegan Paul, 1932.

POLLITT, E. et al. "Psychosocial Development and Behavior of Mothers of Failure-to-Thrive Children." *American Journal of Orthopsychiatry* 45 (July 1975): 525-537.

POWELL, B. and RESNIKOFF, M. "Role Conflict and Symptoms of Psychological Distress in College-Educated Women." *Journal of Consulting Psychology* 44 (June 1976): 473-479.

QUERY, J. M. N. and KURUVILLA, T. C. "Male and Female Adolescent Achievement and Maternal Employment." *Adolescence* 10 (Fall 1975): 353-355.

RABIN, A. I. *Growing Up in the Kibbutz.* New York: Springer Publishing Co., Inc., 1965.

RABKIN, L. Y. and RABKIN, K. "Children of the Kibbutz." *Psychology Today* 3 (Sept. 1969): 46.

RAPOPORT, R. and RAPOPORT, R. *Dual-Career Families.* Baltimore, Maryland. Penguin Books, 1971.

RICE, F. P. *The Adolescent: Development, Relationships and Culture.* Second Edition. Boston: Allyn and Bacon, Inc., 1978a.

RICE, F. P. *Marriage and Parenthood.* Boston: Allyn and Bacon, 1979a.

RICE, F. P. *Sexual Problems in Marriage.* Philadelphia: The Westminster Press, 1978b.

RICE, F. P. *Stepparenting.* Westport, Conn.: Condor Publishing Co., 1979b.

ROBBINS, L. N. *Deviant Children Grown Up.* Baltimore: Williams and Wilkins, 1966.

ROBSON, K. and MOSS, H. "Patterns and Determinants of Maternal Attachment." *Journal of Pediatrics* 77 (1970): 976-985.

Roper Organization. "Sex . . . Marriage . . . Divorce-What Women Think Today." *U.S. News and World Report* 77 (Oct. 21, 1974): 107.

ROSEN, B. et al. "Dual-Career Marital Adjustment: Potential Effects of Discriminatory Managerial Attitudes." *Journal of Marriage and the Family* 37 (Aug. 1975): 565-572.

Ross, G. et al. "Separation Protest in Infants in Home and Laboratory." *Developmental Psychology* 11 (March 1975): 256-257.

Ross, H. *The Shy Child.* Public Affairs Pamphlet No. 239. New York: Public Affairs Committee, 1965.

Ross, H. S. and GOLDMAN, B. D. "Infants' Sociability Toward Strangers." *Child Development* 48 (June 1977): 638-642.

RUBENSTEIN, J. L. et al. "What Happens When Mother Is Away:

A Comparison of Mothers and Substitute Caregivers." *Developmental Psychology* 13 (Sept. 1977): 529-530.

SALK, L. "Can You Work and Be a Good Mother?" *Harper's Bazaar*, Aug. 1977, p. 88. plus.

SALK, L. *Preparing for Parenthood*, New York: Bantam Books, 1975.

SANTROCK, J. W. "Influence of Onset and Type of Parental Absence on the First Four Eriksonian Developmental Crises." *Developmental Psychology* 3 (1970a): 273-274.

SANTROCK, J. W. "Paternal Absence, Sex-typing and Identification." *Developmental Psychology* 2 (1970b): 264-272.

SCHAFFER, H. R. and EMERSON, P. E. The Development of Social Attachments in Infancy." *Monographs of Social Research in Child Development* 29 (1964): No. 94.

SCHAFFER, R. *Mothering.* Cambridge, Mass.: Harvard University Press, 1977.

SCHLESINGER, B. "The One-Parent Family, An Overview." In *Encounter: Love, Marriage, and Family*, edited by R. E. Albrecht and E. W. Bock. Boston: Holbrook, 1972, pp. 361-373.

SCOTT, N. *The Working Woman: A Handbook.* Kansas City, Mo.: Universal Press Syndicate, 1977.

SEIDMAN, T. R. and ALBERT, M. H. *Becoming a Mother.* New York: Fawcett, 1963.

SHAFNER, E. *When Mothers Work.* Santa Barbara, California: Pacific Press, 1972.

SIPILA, H. L. "Employment-Fertility Relationships." *American Journal of Economics and Sociology* 34 (Jan. 1975): 14.

SKARIN, D. "Cognitive and Contextual Determinants of Stranger Fear in Six- and Eleven-Month-Old Infants." *Child Development* 48 (June 1977): 537-544.

SMART, M. S. and SMART, R. C. *Children: Development and Relationships.* Second Edition. New York: The Macmillan Co., 1972.

SMITH, R. H. et al. "The Man in the House." *The Family Coordinator* 18 (April 1969): 107-111.

SONTAG, L. W. "Implications of Fetal Behavior and Environment for Adult Personalities." *Annals of the New York Academy of Science* 134 (1966): 782.

SORENSEN, R. C. *Adolescent Sexuality in Contemporary America: Personal Values and Sexual Behavior: Ages 13-19.* New York: World Publishing Co., 1973.
SPOCK, B. *Baby and Child Care.* New York: Pocket Books, 1977.
STANNARD, U. "The Male Maternal Instinct." In *Marriage and Families,* edited by H. Z. Lopata. New York: D. Van Nostrand 1973, pp. 183-193.
STONE, L. J. and CHURCH, J. *Childhood and Adolescence.* Second Edition. New York: Random House, 1968.
STREISSGUTH, A. P. "Maternal Drinking and the Outcome of Pregnancy: Implications for Child Mental Health." *American Journal of Orthopsychiatry* 47 (July 1977): 422-431.
SUGARMAN, M. "Paranatal Influences on Maternal-Infant Attachment." *American Journal of Orthopsychiatry* 47 (June 1977): 407-421.
THOMES, M. M. "Children with Absent Fathers." *Journal of Marriage and the Family* 30 (February 1968): 89-96.
THORNBURG, H. D. *Development in Adolescence.* Monterey, Calif.: Brooks/Cole Publishing Co., 1975.
TIZARD, J. and TIZARD, B. "The Social Development of Two-Year-Old Children in Residential Nurseries." In H. R. Schaffer, ed. *The Origins of Human Social Relations.* London: Academic Press, 1971.
U.S. Dept. of Commerce. Bureau of the Census. *Statistical Abstract of the United States, 1978.* Washington, D.C.: U.S. Government Printing Office, 1978.
U.S. Department of Health, Education, and Welfare. Children's Bureau. *Day Care for Young Children.* Publication No. (OHD) 74-47. Washington, D.C.: U.S. Government Printing Office, 1974.
U.S. Dept. of Health, Education, and Welfare. *Infant Care.* Washington, D.C.: U.S. Government Printing Office, 1977.
U.S. Dept. of Health, Education, and Welfare. "Smoking and Pregnancy." In *The Health Consequences of Smoking: A Report of the Surgeon General.* Washington, D.C.: U.S. Government Printing Office, 1971.
U.S. Dept. of Health, Education, and Welfare. *Your Child From 1 to 6.* Washington, D.C.: U.S. Government Printing Office, 1962.

U.S. Dept. of Health, Education, and Welfare. *Your Child From 6 to 12.* Washington, D.C.: U.S. Government Printing Office, 1966.

VENER, A. M. and STEWART, C. S. "Adolescent Sexual Behavior in Middle America Revisited: 1970-1973." *Journal of Marriage and the Family* 36 (Nov. 1974): 728-735.

WAITE, L. J. and STOLZENBERG, R. M. "Intended Childbearing and Labor Force Participation of Young Women: Insights from Nonrecursive Models." *American Sociological Review* 41 (April 1976): 235-252.

WALLSTON, B. "The Effects of Maternal Employment on Children." *Journal of Child Psychology and Psychiatry* 14 (1973): 81-95.

WATERS, E. et al. "Infants' Reactions to an Approaching Stranger: Description, Validation, and Functional Significance of Wariness." *Child Development* 46 (June 1975): 348-356.

WEAVER, C. N. and HOLMES, S. L. "A Comparative Study of the Work Satisfaction of Females with Full-time Employment and Full-time Housekeeping." *Journal of Applied Psychology* 60 (Feb. 1975): 117, 118.

WEINER, I. B. and ELKIND, D. *Child Development: A Core Approach.* New York: John Wiley and Sons, Inc., 1972a.

WEINER, I. B. and ELKIND, D., eds. *Reading in Child Development.* New York: John Wiley and Sons, Inc., 1972b.

WHYTE, W. *The Organization Man.* New York: Simon and Schuster, Inc., 1956.

WULBERT, M. et al. "Language Delay and Associated Mother-Child Interactions." *Developmental Psychology* 11 (Jan. 1975): 61-70.

YANKELOVICH, D. *The New Morality: A Profile of American Youth in the 70's.* New York: McGraw-Hill, 1974.

ZELNICK, M. and KANTNER, J. F. "The Probability of Premarital Intercourse." *Social Science Research* 1 (Sept. 1972): 335-341.

ZELSON, C. et al. "Neonatal Narcotic Addiction: 10-Year Observation." *Pediatrics* 48 (Aug. 1971): 178-179.

Index

A

Adolescents:
  communication with, 191
  friendships, 181
  heterosexual adjustments of, 181
  relationships with parents, 182
  sex education of, 153
  supervision of, 187—184
  time together with parents, 189
  trust of, 189
Affection (see also Love), 11
  and age of children, 14
  and security, 61
  and sex of child, 15
Ainsworth, M. D. S., 21, 311
Albert, M. H., 240, 245, 322
Ald, M., 242, 243, 311
Ames, L. B., 94, 311
Angrist, S. S., 278, 311

Anxiety, as cause of misbehavior, 126
Attachment:
  to baby sitters or teachers, 28
  of day-care children, 34
  decreases in, 31
  and delinquency, 109
  development of, 26, 29, 30
  during sensitive period, 32
  to fathers, 28
  importance of, 25
  insecure, 36, 126
  meaning of, 24
  multiple, 25
  nonattachment, 36
  and response to crying, 37
  and separation, 31
  and socialization, 108
  specific, 29
  theorists, 37
  and the working mother, 33
Autonomy, 82, 129

B

Baby sitters (see Substitute care)
Balswick, J. O., 164, 165, 311
Bandura, A. 109, 311
Barman, A., 55, 311
Barton, K., 124, 312
Baumrind, D., 123, 124, 312
Bebbington, A. C., 265, 312
Beckwith, L., 13, 313
Belkin, E. P., 52, 312
Berardo, F. M., 229, 320
Bernard, H. W., 6
Bettelheim, B., 82, 229, 312
Biller, H. B., 299, 302, 312
Binter, A. R., 96, 312
Birch, W. G., 243, 246, 312
Blehar, M. C., 32, 35, 53, 312
Blood, R. J., 277, 312
Boredom, 128
Bowlby, J., 25, 41, 43, 51, 63, 312, 313
Bradburn, N. M., 289, 320
Bromwick, R. M., 11, 313
Bronfenbrenner, U., 18, 231, 313
Brooks, J., 54, 313

C

Caldwell, B., 35, 313
Callahan, S. C., 74, 76, 191, 203, 226, 229, 230, 232, 251, 263, 264, 274, 313
Chandler, C. A., 218, 313
Cherry, F. F., 97, 313
Chess, S., 4, 313
Child care (see Substitute care)
Child development:
 parents' role in, 4
 philosophies of, 9, 10
 principles of, 3
Children:
 abuse of, 70
 active, 15
 individual differences of, 13
 lethargic, 15
 nature of, 8
 needs of, 14
Chiplin, B., 261, 313
Church, J., 59, 323
Clifford, W. B., 77, 237, 313
Cohen, D. J., 211, 313
Cohen, L. B., 30, 313
Cohen, S. E., 13, 313
Collins, A. H., 215, 314
Communication, 191
Contraception:
 use by teenagers, 154
 and working mothers, 235—239
Corenelius, S. W., 72, 314
Corter, C. M., 40, 314
Criticism, 17, 66
Crow, A., 168, 179, 314
Crow, L. D., 168, 179, 314
Crying, 37, 39
Cuber, J. F., 291, 314
Curtis, J. A., 82, 192, 197, 199, 260, 265, 282, 283, 293, 294, 314

D

Daly, S. J., 190, 314
Damico, S., 76, 320
Darian, J. C., 279, 281, 314
Day care:
  center, 222—224
  children, attachment of, 34
  family day-care homes, 211—216
  group day-care homes, 216—218
  infant-care centers, 218—222
Delinquency, 22, 179
Denney, N. W., 72, 314
Dennis, W., 21, 314
Dependency, 46
Deprivation, 8
  and insecurity, 62
  intellectual, 21
  and long-term separation, 40
Discipline:
  approaches to, 130—138
  authoritative, 123, 124
  authoritarian, 123, 124
  and causes of misbehavior, 125
  as control, 122
  do's and don'ts of, 135—138
  effects of, 12, 95, 124, 125
  and enforcement, 186
  meaning and purpose, 121
  and overindulgence, 68
  and overprotection, 68
  permissive, 12, 95, 123—125
  through punishment, 116, 122

Discipline (cont.)
  through rewards, 115
  and spoiling, 62
  strict, 12, 95
  and verbal instruction, 114
  and the working mother, 138—141, 186
Divorce:
  and how mothers can help their children, 306—308
  incidence of, 303
  reactions of children, 303—306
Doyle, Anna-Beth, 35, 314
Dreikurs, R., 134, 136, 314
Drugs:
  marijuana, 108
  and pregnancy, 246—248
Dunn, J., 30, 40, 56, 314
Durfee, J. T., 52, 318

E

Early influences:
  effect on children, 20
  overcoming, 21, 22
Eaton, E. A., 97, 313
Elardo, R., 93, 314
Elkind, D., 64, 171, 179, 324
Emerson, P. E., 26, 322
Emotional insecurity, in child, 36
  causes of, 62—71
  and child abuse, 70
  and criticism, 66
  and family tension, 64

Emotional insecurity (*cont.*)
  and frightening experiences, 65
  and maternal deprivation, 41, 62
  and overindulgence, 68
  and overprotection, 68
Emotional insecurity, in husband, 17, 251
Emotional insensitivity, 63
  cruelty and aggression, 180
  in males, 164
  and sensitivity, 15
Emotional needs, 6
Emotional security, in child, 24
  development of, 55—71
  and mother warmth, 61
  and physical contact, 60
  and sucking, 60
Emotional upset during pregnancy, 245
Employment:
  after child birth, 241
  and ages and numbers of children, 76
  beneficial effects of, 82—86
  days and hours of work, 77
  and discipline, 138
  effect on children, 33, 72—86
  and family planning, 235—239
  flexi-time, 279
  at home, 280
  and mental growth, 96
  and mother's personality, 74

Employment (*cont.*)
  mother's reactions and feelings about, 72, 73
  opportunities and sex role stereotypes, 161
  part-time, 45, 278
  and pregnancy, 235—249
  seasonal, 279
  and socialization of children, 80
  and substitute care, 79
  time, 278
English, O. S., 67, 180, 314
Environmental influences, 15
Erickson, J. A., 281, 315
Etaugh, C., 82, 315

F

Fagan, J. F., III., 30, 315
Family:
  communication, 191
  day-care homes, 211—216
  lower-class, 96
  members, influence on child, 17
  middle-class, 96
  relatives, influence on child, 18
  tension, 128
  two-career, 261—272
    benefits of, 266
    and child care, 270
    husbands in, 265
    moving and travel, 267

Family (cont.)
  some representative families, 262
  strains of, 272
  wives in, 264
Farran, D. C., 29, 315
Father:
  absence, 298—302
  effect on daughters, 299
  effect on mother, 301
  effect on sons, 298
  are men inept?, 257—259
  care of infant while in hospital, 28
  need for two parents, 259
Fear, 65
Feeding:
  bottle, 57, 61
  breast, 11, 56—60, 64
  and eating habits, 62
  and security, 55
  and weaning, 9, 10, 62
Fein, G. G., 50, 315
Feldman, S. S., 53, 315
Field, T. M., 90, 315
Fisher, R. L., 83, 100, 252, 298, 302, 315
Fisher, S., 83, 100, 252, 298, 302, 315
Fleisher, B. M., 11, 315
Flerx, V. C., 158, 315
Fraenkel, J. R., 111, 315
Francke, L. B., 73, 315
Freedman, A. M., 100, 245, 315
Frey, S. H., 96, 312
Friendships (see also Peers), 146

Friendships (cont.)
  of elementary age children, 172
  gangs and clubs, 178
  of infants and toddlers, 168
  and popularity, 175
  of teenagers, 181
Fromme, A., 199, 315

G

Galinsky, E., 216, 218, 224, 316
Garrison, K. C., 6, 93, 172, 179, 316
Gibbons, P. A., 84, 316
Ginott, H. G., 134, 316
Glick, P. C., 237, 303, 316
Goldman, B. D., 53, 321
Gordon, M., 10, 316
Gordon, T., 134, 135, 316
Groat, H. T., 237, 316
Grotberg, E. H., 5, 125, 159, 226, 227, 229, 230, 316
Gutelius, M. F., 219, 316
Guttmacher, A. F., 238, 239, 240, 243, 244, 248, 249, 316

H

Halverson, C. F., 201, 317
Hardy, J. B., 248, 316
Harrell, J. E., 73, 316
Harroff, P. B., 291, 314
Heckel, R. V., 299, 316

Heckman, N. A., 268, 316
Heller, P. B., 216, 317
Hetherington, E. M., 300, 317
Hoffman, L. W., 75, 82, 84, 97, 98, 317
Holmes, S. L., 73, 324
Holmstrom, L. L., 78, 86, 239, 265, 266, 269, 317
Homan, W. E., 104, 317
Home management:
  and children's time, 283
  and commuting time, 281
  and couple time and personal time, 285, 290, 293
  and employment time, 278—281
  and family time, 284
  finding time together, 189—191
  scheduling, 273—274
    task, 275—277
    time, 277—278
  sharing the work, 184—186
  in two-career families, 272
  and where to live, 281—283
Hooks, W. H., 216, 218, 224, 316
Hospitalization, 31, 41, 50
Host, M. S., 216, 317
Hostility (*see also* Resentment)
  as cause of misbehavior, 127
  and divorce, 305
Howe, V., 162, 317
Howell, M., 274, 317
Huntington, D. S., 218, 219, 222, 317

Husbands:
  attitudes toward working wives, 250—257
  differences with wife, 10
  as fathers, 257—260
  and household chores, 184, 185
  insecure, 17
  in two-career families, 265

I

Income, 85
Individual differences, 13
  and bestowing affection, 14
  in response to stimuli, 91
  in sensitivity, 15
  and stranger anxiety, 53
Infant-care centers
  and attachment, 29
  in Israel, 225—229
  philosophy of, 218
  quality of, 219
  in Russia, 229—231
  and separation anxiety, 48
Ingham, M. E., 53, 315
Inoff, G. E., 201, 317
Intellectual:
  deprivation, 21
  development, 87—105
    of curiosity and creativity, 94, 129
    and family background, 92
    and homework, 104
    and IQ tests, 99
    of language, 92

Intellectual (cont.)
  and maternal employment, 96
  parental expectations, 98
  stimulating reading, 94
  and underachievement, 103
  needs, 6
  retardation, 21, 63, 89
  stimulation, 7, 88
IQ, 99

J

Jackson, E. H., 219, 319
Jacobson, C. B., 248, 317
Jacobson, G., 300, 317
Janov, A., 64, 244, 245, 317
Johnson, C. L., 272, 318
Johnson, F. A., 272, 318
Johnson, R. C., 124, 169, 319
Johnson, V. E., 59, 319

K

Kagan, J., 83, 89, 90, 106, 107, 114, 116, 176, 318
Kantner, J. F., 154, 324
Kaplan, H. I., 100, 245, 315
Kelly, J. B., 304, 305, 308, 318
Kennedy, W. A., 100, 238, 245, 318
Kennell, H. J., 32, 318
Keyserling, M. D., 212—215, 318

Kibbutzim, 225—229
Kingston, A. J., 6
Kirsch, A. D., 219, 316
Klein, R. E., 89, 90, 318
Klein, R. P., 52, 318
Kohlberg, L., 110, 318
Kopelman, R. E., 84, 316
Korner, A. F., 92, 318
Kuruvilla, T. C., 97, 321

L

Lamb, M. E., 259, 318
Lancaster, J., 11, 84, 253, 274, 318
Landis, J. T., 287, 306, 318
Language development, 92
Larson, L. E., 109, 319
Lasseigne, M. W., 109, 319
Lasswell, M., 272, 319
Lewis, M., 54, 313
Lobsenz, N., 272, 319
Love:
  development of, 55—62
  individual need for, 14
  toward the child conceived out of wedlock, 16

M

Macfarlane, A., 33, 245, 248, 319
Macrae, J. W., 219, 319
Mansfield, A. F., 84, 319
Marans, A. E., 231, 319

Marantz, S. A., 84, 319
Marriage:
  education for, 148
  effect of mother working on, 85
  forced, 16
  priorities, 286—290, 295
  and the problem of time, 290—292
  and sex, 294
  and social life, 292
  and solitude, 293
  versus career, 289, 290
Mass media and sex roles, 162
Masters, W. H., 59, 319
Masturbation, 9, 10
McCandless, B. R., 156, 319
McClelland, D. C., 11, 13, 57, 319
McCord, J., 125, 319
McCord, W., 125, 319
Medinnus, G. R., 124, 169, 319
Meers, D. R., 231, 319
Mental development (see Intellectual development)
Miller, S. M., 84, 319
Miller, T. W., 82, 319
Model:
  modeling and moral development, 118
  sex role, 83
  sex role and father absence, 298—300
Money, J., 248, 319
Moore, T., 75, 320

Moral:
  behavior, development of, 113—120
  behavior, teaching, 114—120
  influences, 19
  judgment, development of, 110—113
  needs, 8
Moss, H., 236, 321
Mother:
  alone, 297—310
  child relationship, quality of, 33
  divorced, 303
  personality and effect on children, 74
  self knowledge, 16
  widowed, 308
Murray, A. D., 11, 73, 81, 119, 202, 227, 320

N

Nevill, D., 76, 320
North, A. F., 220, 320
Northway, M. L., 176—178, 320
Norton, G. R., 119, 123, 124, 132, 320
Nursery school and separation anxiety, 49
Nutrition:
  of child, 5
  during pregnancy, 246
Nuttall, E. V., 95, 124, 320

Nuttall, R. L., 95, 124, 320
Nye, F. I., 84, 97, 98, 229, 317, 320

O

Orden, S. R., 289, 290, 320
Osofsky, J. D., 93, 320

P

Parent:
  adolescent relationships, 182
  child relationships, 11, 13
  and individual differences, 13
  communication, 191
Parke, R. D., 259, 320
Pearson, G. H. J., 67, 180, 314
Peek, C. W., 164, 165, 311
Peers:
  influences on children, 19
  in Kibbutzim, 228
  and sex education, 143
Physical:
  care during pregnancy, 241—245
  changes at puberty, 145
  fatigue, 129, 241
  growth, 4
  needs, 5
Piaget, J., 113, 320
Planned parenthood, 235—239
Pollitt, E., 109, 287, 320
Powell, B., 74, 321

Pregnancy:
  calculating birth date, 239
  diet during, 246
  and drinking, 247
  and drugs, 247
  and emotional upset, 245
  and exercise, 243
  and fatigue, 241
  and heavy exertion, 242
  and illness, 248
  and induced labor, 240
  and maternal age, 237
  and noise, 244
  out of wedlock, 154
  and prenatal care, 241—249
  reproduction and sex education, 147
  and smoking, 246
  timing of, 237—241
  and travel, 243
  and V.D., 249
Premature infants:
  and attachment development, 33
  and child abuse, 70

Q

Query, J. M. M., 97, 321

R

Rabin, A. I., 228, 321
Rabkin, K., 228, 321
Rabkin, L. Y., 228, 321

Ramey, C. T., 29, 315
Rapoport, R., 77, 265, 267, 321
Relatives:
  as baby sitters, 48
  influence on children, 18
Resentment, of child conceived
  out of wedlock (see also
  Hostility), 16
Resnikoff, M., 74, 321
Responsibility of child for self, 20
Reunion behavior, 51
Rice, F. P., 6, 7, 66, 99, 108, 112, 121, 125, 149, 154, 159, 161, 163, 164, 181, 189, 192, 238, 246, 262, 266, 269, 272, 288, 295, 296, 301, 304—309, 321
Ridley, C. A., 73, 316
Robbins, L. N., 118, 321
Robson, K., 236, 321
Roper organization, 162, 289, 321
Rosen, B., 269, 321
Ross, G., 39, 321
Ross, H. S., 53, 174, 175, 321
Routh, D. K., 52, 312
Rubenstein, J. L., 203, 321
Russia, day-care programs in, 229—232
Ryder, R. G., 300, 317

S

Salk, L., 64, 121, 205, 208, 209, 241, 322
Santrock, J. W., 298, 322

Sawin, D. B., 259, 320
Schaffer, H. R., 14, 15, 26, 57, 60, 61, 322
Schlesinger, B., 302, 322
School:
  and homework, 104
  and parental concern, 87
  and parental expectations, 98
  and report cards, 101
  and sex education, 143
  and underachievement, 103
Scott, N., 74, 86, 209, 255, 268, 293, 322
Seidman, T. R., 240, 245, 322
Self-esteem, 84, 173, 182
Separation anxiety, 31, 39—52
  and age of child, 41
  and dependency, 46
  factors that affect, 43
  and hospitalization, 50
  long-term, 40
  of newborn children, 47
  and part-time work, 45
  symptoms of, 39
  and vacation, 46
Sex education:
  and friendships, 146
  goals of, 143—149
  and marriage, 148
  methods of, 149—155
  and physical development, 145
  and reproductive information, 147
  and sex attitudes, 143
  and sex behavior, 148
  and sex roles, 147
  sources of information, 142

Sex roles:
 and assignment of gender, 157
 development of, 156—167
 and father absence, 298—300
 female, 159
 male, 163
 meaning, 156
 and sex education, 147
 and social learning, 157
 stereotypes of, 158—160, 163, 164
 working mother as model, 83
Sexual behavior, premarital, 148, 154
Shafner, E., 253, 322
Siblings, influence on younger children, 17
Sipila, H. L., 237, 322
Skarin, D., 52, 322
Sloane, P. J., 261, 313
Smart, M. S., 71, 93, 96, 156, 168—170, 322
Smart, R. C., 71, 93, 96, 156, 168—170, 322
Smith, R. H., 185, 322
Social:
 learning and play, 168—172
 learning and response to crying, 37
 needs, 6
Socialization, 80
 agents of, 107
 cultural variations, 106
 and family factors, 108
 meaning, 106

Socialization (cont.)
 and sex roles, 157, 162, 166
Sontag, L. W., 245, 322
Sorensen, R. C., 154, 323
Spock, B., 56, 169, 178, 299, 323
Stranger anxiety:
 and age of child, 52
 and individual differences, 53
 of men, 54
 overcoming, 53
Stannard, U., 258, 323
Stewart, C. S., 154, 324
Stolzenberg, R. M., 236, 237, 324
Stone, L. J., 59, 323
Streissguth, A. P., 247, 323
Stubbs, M. V. L., 248, 317
Sugarman, M., 241, 323
Substitute care:
 age of, 199
 day-care centers, 222—224, 227, 231, 271
 disadvantages of, 81
 and emergencies, 208
 family day-care homes, 211—216, 271
 finding a sitter, 195—199
 group day-care homes, 216—218
 health certificate, 202
 and illness, 209
 infant-care centers, 218—222, 226, 230
 in other countries, 225—232
 interviewing, 204
 as model, 119

Substitute care (cont.)
  by neighbors, 49
  for the newborn, 47
  nursery school, 49, 271
  personality qualifications, 200
  professional qualifications, 202
  relatives, 199
  selecting a sitter, 199—207
  and separation anxiety, 44
  and socialization of children, 80
  supervising, 207—210
  tenure of, 202
  transportation of, 204

T

Thomes, M. M., 298, 323
Thornburg, H. D., 142, 143, 323
Thumbsucking, 9, 10
Tizard, B., 53, 323
Tizard, J., 53, 323
Tobin, P. L., 77, 237, 313
Toilet training, 9, 10

U

Unisex (see also Sex roles), 166

V

Values:
  of peers, 19

Values (cont.)
  in Russia, 231
Vener, A. M., 154, 324

W

Waite, L. J., 236, 237, 324
Wallerstein, J. S., 304, 305, 308, 318
Wallston, B., 84, 324
Walters, R. H., 109, 311
Waters, E., 52, 324
Watson, E. L., 215, 314
Weaver, C. N., 73, 324
Weiner, I. B., 64, 171, 179, 324
Whyte, W., 164, 324
Widowed mothers, 308—310
  children's reactions to death, 309
  mother's reactions to death, 308
  what the mother can do, 310
Wives in two-career families, 264
Wulbert, M., 92, 324

Y

Yankelovich, D., 108, 288, 324

Z

Zelnik, M., 154, 324
Zelson, C., 248, 324
Zigler, E., 211, 313